Health Professions
ADMISSIONS GUIDE
Strategies for Success

CO-EDITORS

Carol Baffi-Dugan
Robert E. Cannon

CONTRIBUTORS

Robby Bowen
Jane Cary
Paul Crosby
Glenn N. Cummings

Consuelo López Springfield
Karen de Olivares
Chere Pereira
Ann Trail

SPECIAL RECOGNITION

Brice Corder
Editor of the first four editions

NAAHP

National Association Of Advisors For The Health Professions, Inc.

108 Hessel Blvd. Suite 101 | Champaign, IL 61820
Phone: 217/355-0063
Fax: 217/355-1287
Email: tsands@naahp.org
www.NAAHP.org

Health Professions Admissions Guide: Strategies for Success

Tenth Edition

Special discounts on bulk quantities of NAAHP books are available to NAAHP members, professional associations, and other organizations. For details, contact NAAHP, Inc., 108 Hessel Blvd. Suite 101, Champaign, IL 61820. Tel: (217) 355-0063 Fax: (217) 355-1287 www.NAAHP.org

Printed in the United States of America

Published by the National Association of Advisors for the Health Professions, Inc.

Library of Congress Cataloging-in-Publication Data

Health Professions Admissions Guide: Strategy for Success / editors, Carol Baffi-Dugan and Robert Cannon, contributors, Ruth Bingham. . . (et al.).

Includes bibliographic references.

ISBN 978-0-911899-18-4

1. Medicine - Vocational guidance — United States — Handbooks, manuals, etc.
2. Allied health personnel — Vocational guidance — United States Handbooks, manuals, etc.
3. Medical education United States Handbooks, manuals, etc.

   I.   Baffi-Dugan, Carol.
  II.   National Association of Advisors for the Health Professions.

Production Editor: NAAHP, Inc.
Cover Design: Missy Larson, NAAHP, Inc.
Printing and Binding: Premier Print Group

TABLE OF CONTENTS

PREFACE

The National Association of Advisors for the Health Professions, Inc. (NAAHP) is an organization of approximately one thousand health professions advisors at colleges and universities throughout the United States as well as a few hundred health professions schools and associations. The strength and success of NAAHP is derived from its four regional associations, Central (CAAHP), Northeast (NEAAHP), Southeastern (SAAHP), and Western (WAAHP). Established in 1974, NAAHP is the only national organization concerned exclusively with the needs of health professions advisors and their students. The organization serves as a resource for the professional development of health professions advisors, health professions schools, and professional school associations. It is a representative voice with health professions schools and their professional associations, undergraduate institutions and other health professions organizations. The Association promotes high standards for health professions advising at universities and colleges. The Association assists advisors in fostering the intellectual, personal, and humanistic development of students who are preparing for careers in the health professions. In addition, NAAHP has become an important liaison with health professions institutions, many of whom are patron members of the Association. In its continuing enterprise to serve advisors and prehealth professions students, NAAHP is pleased to offer the tenth edition of this guide.

Whether you are firmly committed to a career in one of the recognized health professions, or simply wish to know more about what is required for pursuing various health care careers, this guide is for you. Further, while this publication is intended primarily for students enrolled in two-year and four-year colleges and universities, the importance of the high school years is also recognized.

As you contemplate a career in one of the health professions, be mindful that many factors will contribute to your success, but none will be more important than obtaining accurate health career and health professions school information. Take advantage of the advising services available at your institution. Most colleges and universities have an office or individual who specializes in providing health professions advice and information. This person is commonly known as the "health professions advisor" or "premedical advisor" even though s/he may be a career advisor for all of the health professions. It is to your benefit to seek out this office and become acquainted with the person to whom you can go for information and advice. As you read through this guide you will notice it is frequently suggested that you speak with your health professions advisor about matters beyond the scope of this publication. This recommendation is probably the best advice we can give. The editors view this publication as a supplement; it cannot replace an experienced advisor.

This book became a reality through the efforts of a writing team of experienced advisors. For the first edition, two advisors from each of the four regional Associations were appointed as contributing editors and worked both collectively and independently for eight months to complete the project. The advisors and their respective institutions were:

Jane Diehl Crawford	Cornell University	NEAAHP
William Hussey	Brooklyn College	NEAAHP
Zelda Lipman	University of Miami	SAAHP
Norman Sansing	University of Georgia	SAAHP
Julian Frankenberg	University of Illinois	CAAHP
James Nielsen	Western Illinois University	CAAHP
Cynthia Lewis	San Diego State University	WAAHP
Ronald McCune	Idaho State University	WAAHP

For the third edition, the following advisors were added as contributors:

Carol Baffi-Dugan	Tufts University	NEAAHP
Debra Kirchhof-Glazier	Juniata College	NEAAHP
Sally Olexia	Kalamazoo College	CAAHP
Anthony Smulders	Loyola Marymount University	WAAHP

Peter Van Houten, Health Professions Advisor at the University of California, Berkeley and member of the Editorial Review Board to the NAAHP, contributed the chapter on "The Minority Group Student" for the fourth edition. In previous editions, this chapter was written by Harold Bardo, Southern Illinois University College of Medicine. Subsequently, Cecilia Fox, Occidental College, added much to update the chapter, and most recently Glenn Cummings, Princeton University, and Consuelo Lopez Springfield, University of Wisconsin at Madison, have expanded it further.

Each contributing editor brought valuable experience, abilities and insights to the publication. The editors and NAAHP are indebted to them.

National Association of Advisors for the Health Professions, Inc.

For the fourth edition, members of the Editorial Review Board to the NAAHP were asked to review and suggest changes where needed. John Klein, chair of the ERB, coordinated this effort. Members contributing were:

Robert Cannon	University of North Carolina-Greensboro	SAAHP
John Friede	Villanova University	NEAAHP
John Klein (chair)	John Carroll University	CAAHP
Lee Ann Michelson	Harvard University	NEAAHP
Alice Sima	Benedictine University	CAAHP
Marliss Strange	University of Oregon	WAAHP
Peter Van Houten	University of California, Berkeley	WAAHP

For the fifth:

Paul Crosby	University of Kansas	CAAHP
Cecilia Fox	Occidental College	WAAHP
Helen Pigage	United States Air Force Academy	WAAHP
Edward Trachtenberg	Clark University	NEAAHP

For the sixth:

Laurence Savett	Macalaster College	CAAHP

For the seventh:

Glenn Cummings	Princeton University	NEAAHP
Karen deOlivares	Southern Methodist University	SAAHP

For the eighth:

Kirsten Peterson	Allegheny College	NEAAHP
Consuelo Lopez Springfield	University of Wisconsin, Madison	CAAHP

For the ninth:

Ruth Bingham	University of Hawaii	WAAHP
Paula Goldsmid	Pomona College	WAAHP

Finally, for this edition:

Robby Bowen	Louisiana State	CAAHP
Jane Cary	Williams College	NEAAHP
Chere Pereira	Oregon State	WAAHP
Ann Trail	University of Washington	WAAHP

We also must acknowledge the assistance of the staff from the national office of NAAHP. Thanks go to Theron Sands, Office Manager, and Missy Larson, Media Specialist, for their invaluable work on this project. Appreciation is extended to the NAAHP Advisory Council members — those individuals affiliated with the respective professional school associations who reviewed and updated the entries on their professions in Chapter 5. The associations are:

American Academy of Audiology
American Association of Colleges of Nursing
American Association of Colleges of Osteopathic Medicine
American Association of Colleges of Pharmacy
American Association of Colleges of Podiatric Medicine
American Dental Education Association
American Occupational Therapy Association
American Physical Therapy Association
Association of Accredited Naturopathic Medical Colleges

Association of American Medical Colleges
Association of American Veterinary Medical Colleges
Association of Chiropractic Colleges
Association of Schools and Colleges of Optometry
Association of Schools of Public Health
Association of University Programs in Health Administration
Council of Colleges of Acupuncture and Oriental Medicine
Physician Assistant Education Association

Finally, a very special note of thanks to Brice Corder, who brought the original project to fruition and shepherded it through its first four editions.

Carol Baffi-Dugan and Rob Cannon, Editors

Planning for Your Career

INTRODUCTION TO CAREERS IN HEALTH CARE

Health care is a rapidly expanding career field, both in terms of numbers of individuals needed and entering the field, and in the variety of opportunities. Some people aspiring to a health care career choose it because of altruism, the wish to serve others; others are drawn to the fulfillment, intellectual stimulation and economic security it provides. Finding a career that provides a balance between one's personal and professional life, is compatible with one's life-style aspirations, and allows one to practice with people who share one's commitment, are all very important considerations.

There is no typical story, or stories, for those who choose health care careers, but there are general themes. Some people are attracted to health careers because of interest and aptitude in science, some because of the relationships with patients, some for both of these reasons. Some have been influenced by the personal qualities of role models: a family physician, parent or teacher. Other people choose health care because of a personal experience, positive or negative. An especially moving book – fiction or non-fiction – portraying the life of a health care professional, can also be a catalyst. Some people have dreamed about becoming a nurse, veterinarian, physician since they were young; some come to that decision later in life, during college, or many years later, perhaps after experience in another career.

What is common to all health careers is a desire to help others. While some health care careers require an ability to understand and apply biological and physical sciences, there are some that do not. There are also other helping professions such as social work, clinical psychology and other counseling professions. Some choose these latter professions as a first choice; others make these choices when they discover their predominant academic strengths and intellectual interests lie outside the natural sciences. Openly and honestly taking all of these considerations into account can help you identify careers that fit your interests and values. If you have the opportunity, work with your health professions advisor. In the process of assessing your academic strengths and personal motivation, you and your advisor should share a common goal: to help you find a fulfilling career.

A commitment to life-long learning is required to be successful in any health career. Doctoral fields can take seven or more years of professional school and post-professional school training. Virtually all health professions require continual learning to keep up with advancements in technology and the information that is always being added to the knowledge base. Think for a minute about what your physician, dentist, podiatrist or physical therapist had to learn since graduating. Think about all the research and advancements in sciences and health care that have occurred just in the last decade. The excitement of being involved in a dynamic area like health care also attracts people. You and your colleagues will be part of a health care team shaping the future of how that health care is delivered. To do so, you must be willing to learn and keep on learning.

Health career opportunities are diverse. In medicine, for example, there is a major effort underway to encourage students to consider careers as primary care physicians and as nurse practitioners or physician assistants. Professionals in the latter two careers have varying degrees of autonomy and independence, depending on the relationship with a physician-partner and the community in which they practice.

The United States health care system, however, still accords more autonomy and authority to physicians and others with doctoral degrees. Health professionals in areas that do not require these advanced degrees are important providers and members of the health care team, however, in many cases they ultimately defer to physicians. Even those with advanced degrees may have limitations, which vary from state to state. As an example, a physician assistant may have a docket of patients, but must technically rely on the supervision of a physician. These circumstances do not diminish the importance of any profession; there is definitely increasing recognition of the importance of optometrists, nurse practitioners, physician assistants, occupational therapists and other health care providers. Furthermore, a nurse practitioner or physician assistant often spends more time with patients than a physician does. This kind of lifestyle is appealing for many who value the professional relationship between a patient and health care provider. Think about what you want to do on a daily basis.

CHOOSING A HEALTH CAREER

When choosing a career within the field of health care, or deciding whether a health career is appropriate for you, consider asking yourself the following questions:

1. How much time do I wish to spend with patients and colleagues? Great variety in skills, interests and personal characteristics are needed for various health professions.
2. How much time do I wish to spend studying science? Some programs demand much more science study than others, but preparation for health care careers usually involves some laboratory science study.
3. Am I prepared to enter a career in which I will have to spend time and effort keeping up with developments in the field? All health professions require continual learning.
4. Do I like being in health care settings? Do I have a spirit of altruism, of service to others? Am I emotionally able to deal with a wide variety of people? Not all of health care is as glamorous as people imagine. You should explore your future career and gain a better understanding of the profession by spending time with practitioners ("shadowing"), and by involving yourself in relevant extracurricular activities, such as volunteering in a hospital, nursing home, hospice, or other clinical setting. In these ways you will gain insights that will help you to make a more informed decision about the health career you wish to enter.
5. Do I like working as part of a team of professionals, or do I prefer to work on my own, taking responsibility for my own work? Health care is increasingly a team activity where a successful outcome depends upon each member of a health care team being able to work with others on the team. Communicating, not only with colleagues, but also with the patient and the patient's family, is essential.
6. What lifestyle do I envision? Some health care careers include many emergencies and long hours. Different specialties have varying levels of responsibility. Do I wish to deal with life-and-death situations? A career that involves long hours or high stress leaves you less time and energy for family life and leisure activities.

Before committing yourself to a health career, take the time to get a clear picture of the realities of your chosen profession and of your own abilities, needs and aspirations. You can use the chapters of this book that describe various health professions, as well as the appendices, to begin a thorough investigation of various health professions.

PLANNING A PROGRAM OF STUDY

Some students find their interest and passion in health care at a later time than high school or college. Postbaccalaureate study, taking undergraduate college courses after completing a bachelor's degree, provides another opportunity to meet health profession requirements (see the section at the end of this chapter). There are many different pathways to a career in health care. The traditional route is described first, but this does not imply that it is the best route.

CHOOSING AN UNDERGRADUATE INSTITUTION

High school students who are considering a doctoral health professions career often wonder what college or university would be best for their undergraduate preparation. Any university or college with science departments can offer you preparation for almost any health profession program, although most undergraduate institutions do not offer a specific major in these areas. Most health professions schools require a specific set of college courses for admission. For medical schools, these frequently include: a year each of general chemistry, general biology, organic chemistry, general physics, calculus and/or statistics, English and sometimes other courses in humanities and/or social sciences. Some schools require a semester of biochemistry, psychology and/or sociology. Each health professions school has its own requirements and recommendations, and professional education associations often provide databases or guidebooks that list admissions requirements for many programs.(1)

Sometimes high school students are under the impression it will be helpful to attend an undergraduate institution that is associated with a medical school. While greater ease of establishing contact with medical school faculty through research or volunteering, and/or some preference given to undergraduates by the medical school, there are no data that show this makes a significant difference in a student's chances for admission. It is still most important for an applicant to do well academically and build a strong resume. Most professional schools like to have a diverse student body, which represents a variety of colleges, majors, ethnic groups, socioeconomic classes, etc. Optimally, they want excellent students of fine character regardless of the institution they attended as undergraduates.

Some institutions offer "combined degree" programs in which those initially accepted are offered conditional admission to a professional school directly from high school. Those admitted must still meet course and performance requirements to be continued in these programs.

The most important factor in selecting an undergraduate institution for pre-professional studies is how comfortable you feel in the environment of that school. You may also want to research the health professions advising program at the institution to learn how much information and support you are likely to receive.

Choice of Major

No particular undergraduate major is required for admission to most health professions schools. In general, your chances of admission will not be affected by your choice of major. The abilities to read, write, and think critically and to perform well in sciences are vitally important for successful admission to health professions schools. Again, check with a health professions advisor. Minimums listed for prerequisite coursework may not reflect the academic record of a truly competitive applicant.

Because you have a wide choice of subjects in which to major, your decision should be based on an honest assessment of your interests and talents. You should view your undergraduate years as a time for intellectual growth, not solely as a means to a job. Professional schools want students who have proven themselves not only in required science courses, but also in the humanities and social sciences. They will be looking to see if you allowed yourself sufficient depth and breadth in your studies. The ideal candidate shows not only academic competence, but also evidence of strong, independent judgment and motivation for lifelong learning.

Getting Started

Professional school admissions committees seek students who have attained educational breadth along with meaningful service to others.

Connect with the health professions advisor at your undergraduate institution early and often. Institutions offer different models of advising. Most have specific people, whether faculty or professional staff, designated as health professions advisors.

Make sure you are thoroughly familiar with the information provided by your health professions advisor. You should obtain whatever written material is produced by the health advisor, visit the website, and/or attend information sessions arranged for health professions students.

Your first year in college may be spent taking general college education requirements, as well as starting to take required science courses. Your first goal should be to set up a course schedule that meets these requirements, and with which you are comfortable. Ideally, there should be balance between the laboratory sciences and the non-sciences, although the timing of courses depends on the structure of your undergraduate institution. The major you choose will also be a factor in course selection; some majors have sequenced courses that must be taken prior to moving to advanced courses in that discipline. Make sure you speak with your advisor when making up your class schedule. Be honest about your strengths, weaknesses and goals.

The Middle Years

The bulk of the first three years of college will be spent taking general college requirements, getting started on your major, and completing those courses required for professional school. A significant goal during this period is to maintain a good academic record.

An academically poor semester or year does not necessarily mean the end of aspirations for admission to a health professions program. At some time during your college years, personal, family, financial or health problems may affect your studies. These problems are not insurmountable, if you prove you can handle them and if your subsequent academic record is good. One strong semester, of course, is not enough to counteract several years of mediocre work. Professional school admissions committees will, however, respond positively to a steady upward trend in your academic record.

You are also encouraged to get involved in some extracurricular activities to increase your enjoyment of college and to become a well-rounded individual. Community service, especially in a health care setting, helps you validate for yourself — and for professional school admissions committees — that a career in health care is a wise, informed choice for you. Sustained involvement in a few activities that are meaningful to you may be more valuable that dabbling in many different extracurricular and volunteer opportunities, each for a short period of time. It is important to choose activities because they are important to you, rather than because you think they will look good on an application to a professional school.

Your health professions advisor can assist you in creating your schedule, offering advice if you get into academic difficulty, helping you find research, summer program and "shadowing" opportunities, and generally serving as a sounding board for your ideas, thoughts, feelings and plans.

Two-Year and Four-Year Institutions

Whether you begin your education at a two or four-year college or university may be dependent on financial considerations as well as the health profession you choose. Some two-year schools offer degrees or certification for a variety of health professions. Many health professions schools require advanced level study at a four-year college or university. Admissions visit days at two-year and four-year institutions, as well as health professions schools' open houses and

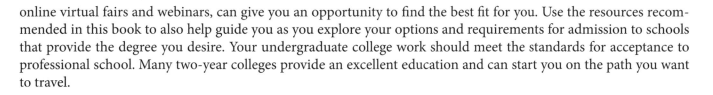

online virtual fairs and webinars, can give you an opportunity to find the best fit for you. Use the resources recommended in this book to also help guide you as you explore your options and requirements for admission to schools that provide the degree you desire. Your undergraduate college work should meet the standards for acceptance to professional school. Many two-year colleges provide an excellent education and can start you on the path you want to travel.

There are, however, some problems to avoid if you attend a two-year college. First, as you would at a four-year institution, make sure you obtain proper advice. If there is no knowledgeable health professions advisor on campus, visit a nearby four-year institution that does have one, ideally at the college to which you plan to transfer. Most likely, the health professions advisor will be helpful. If there is not a nearby health professions advisor available, the National Association of Advisors for the Health Professions (NAAHP) has a volunteer advisor service you can access on-line at www.naahp.org.

Second, there may be problems associated with transfer to a four-year college. Be certain your courses transfer between institutions and avoid trying to transfer a partially completed sequence (e.g., physics or general chemistry), especially if it is taken in a different kind of term (semester vs. quarter or vice versa) from that in the four-year school. A few professional schools require that you take some or all of your sciences at a four-year institution.

Finally, evaluation letters may be difficult to obtain without proper planning. Work closely with faculty at the two-year college, so they can remember you well-enough to write an informed letter. Because letters may be needed after just one year at the four-year college or university, you should also contact faculty and the health professions advisor immediately upon entering. Check to see if they use a "committee letter" format and how one pursues this recommendation process. Be aware, however, that the health professions advising office preparing a "committee letter" may not accept letters given to a student by the letter writer. Know their procedures before asking for evaluation letters.

Postbaccalaureate Education

Many people who change careers decide to pursue health care professions. They often do so after earning their bachelor's degree, and after being out in the workforce for several years. To prepare for careers in dentistry, medicine, optometry, or other health fields, it is necessary to complete prerequisite courses, take admissions tests, and acquire health-related experiences. The required courses may be taken individually in colleges or universities, or may be taken in formal postbaccalaureate ("postbac") programs, designed to meet the needs of a variety of non-traditional students who may be interested in a health career.

Some postbac programs are designed to provide only the basic prerequisite courses. Others allow students to take upper-level courses to improve their GPAs. In some programs, students take courses alongside traditional undergraduate students, while in others, students take courses designed solely for postbac students. Most postbac programs can be completed in two years or less.

Admissions requirements and costs for postbac programs vary considerably, and completion of a postbac program in no way guarantees admission into dental, medical, or other health profession schools. Information about postbac programs can be obtained from the colleges and universities that offer them, on the NAAHP website (www.naahp.org, under Resources), and on the Association of American Medical Colleges database at https://services.aamc.org/postbac.

References

1. Admissions Requirements Guides. These are books and databases that are revised annually, and include

information about each professional school, including course requirements, selection factors and tuition costs.

For example:

- *Medical School Admission Requirements (MSAR) Database.* Published by the Association of American Medical Colleges, and can purchase access through www.aamc.org/students/applying.
- *Online Physician Assistant Programs Directory.* Published by the Physician Assistant Education Association, and can purchase access through www.paeaonline.org.
- *Osteopathic Medical College Information Book.* Published by American Association of Colleges of Osteopathic Medicine, and download available for free through www.aacom.org.
- *Official Guide to Dental Schools.* Published by the American Dental Education Association, and can be purchased through www.adea.org.

See the Appendices of this publication for a more comprehensive list, or an individual profession's entry in Chapter 5 for its own publication.

CHAPTER

2

Applying to Professional School

In the preceding chapter, you were encouraged to think about your people skills, desire to study science, and the importance of staying informed. As you prepare your application to professional school, choose the schools to apply to, and present yourself in interviews, consider developing thoughtful answers to the following basic questions:

What draws me to my chosen career in health care?

Am I making an informed career choice?
- How much do I know about what it is like to be a patient?
- How much do I know about what it's really like to practice the health profession I have chosen?

Do I have a good head on my shoulders?
- Do I have the intellectual capacity to do the work required by the professional school?
- Do I have the ability to perform the work required of the professional?
- Am I open to new ideas? Creative? Have I developed the ability to look at a problem in more than one way?

Do I have a good heart?
- Do I understand the meaning of empathy? Altruism?
- Do I appreciate the importance of the relationship between the professional and the patient ("the professional-patient relationship")?
- Am I comfortable with diversity; i.e. with people who are different from me?

Am I prepared to make a serious time commitment to reach my goals?
- Am I willing to spend the time required to prepare for the practice of the profession and for the practice itself?
- Am I willing to spend sufficient time with each of my patients to meet his or her needs?

Considering these questions helps you to validate for yourself and for the professional school admissions committee that your career choice is a thoughtful one. (1) You have a number of opportunities to address these questions in the application process: personal essays, supplemental question forms from individual schools, and your interview.

The purpose of the application process is to go beyond a list to reveal in depth the qualities these accomplishments may foreshadow, such as: intelligence, creativity, initiative, resilience & adaptability, communication skills, ability to work as part of a team, ethical responsibility, leadership, compassion, knowledge of the profession, professionalism and motivation. Thus, the different components of the application process show the professional school admissions committee more of who you really are than can be obtained by simply recounting what you have done. Beyond your grades, scores and activities, the committee looks for evidence of intellectual depth and personal reflection. You demonstrate the ability to engage your intellect and reflect when you thoughtfully describe what you have learned

from each of your important experiences. Specific examples can help illustrate the points you wish to make.

Considering the questions outlined above will also help you determine when to apply. Recognize also that:
The best year to apply is when your application is the strongest. If there are major gaps in your knowledge and/or preparation, you should consider delaying your application until those gaps are filled. Your advisor can help you identify those gaps.

- Health professions schools often issue acceptances on a rolling basis; applying and completing your application early in the application cycle is better than late.
- While they are important, it's not all about grades and test scores. Professional schools are looking for human qualities – service to individuals and to the community, for example, and some sort of leadership experience. A good predictor of future altruism is past altruism.
- Professional schools want applicants to have a sampling of the professional experience, so that they are familiar with the career. Your advisor may be able to help you make those connections. You demonstrate initiative, however, by looking in your community for opportunities. Check out volunteer programs at your local hospital. Volunteer at a nursing home. The American Association of Colleges of Podiatric Medicine (AACPM) has a service, "Contact a Mentor," that allows you to locate a podiatrist in your area who is willing to allow shadowing. In making connections you can also learn more about your community. Become involved in activities that improve others' lives.
- Professional schools look for excellence in any major, not just a major in a science. Choose a subject you want to study, and then reflect on your reasons. For example, a predental student explained in her interviews that she chose to major in psychology because she wanted to learn how to better set up her practice to accommodate patients with disabilities. Other students have chosen majors in philosophy in order to study ethics; while still others choose anthropology or sociology to better understand culture and society. Remember, though, whatever major you choose, you will still need a solid foundation in physical and life sciences. Choose a major that allows you to go beyond the minimum in these areas.
- Professional schools often look for scholarship beyond the classroom: research in, or in-depth study of, any subject or other activities that show intellectual inquisitiveness. Research, however, should not be viewed as a "box" to check off. It should be an activity generated by a desire to explore a question or understand the process of generating knowledge.
- Professional schools are looking for cultural competence – a sensitivity and awareness of diversity. You can develop this through volunteer activities, outside reading, and/or classes that help you increase your awareness of the people you will care for in your profession.

The most important first question is not, "How do I get in?" but rather, "What's the right career for me?" That means making an informed choice. In the pages that follow the questions raised above are expanded, and other issues related to becoming a successful candidate to a health professions school are discussed.

What draws me to my chosen career in health care?

Nearly every serious candidate for admission has the desire to help and to serve. Yet each person has made a unique personal journey. Every story is influenced by different experiences, role models and the communities to which a person belongs. Think about your goals in the context of the variety of health careers (and careers in the other helping professions). Doing so can help you answer whether the career you intend is right for you.

Am I making an informed career decision?

A career in medicine, for example, requires at least 7 years after college (four years of medical school and three or more years of residency), a large financial outlay, and commitment to life-long learning. Unless you have some awareness of what being a physician is like, then you are making an uninformed choice. One can gain knowledge about health care professions and the patients professionals serve from:

- Personal or family experience with illness;
- Paid or volunteer activity serving others in a clinical setting;

(Find opportunities to interact with patients and their families and to observe the interactions (a) between professionals and patients, and (b) among professionals. These opportunities exist in hospitals, nursing homes, hospices and other settings. Be observant and sensitive to others around you. Ask questions of the professionals with whom you are working. Once staff in a clinical setting see you are responsible, reliable and have a genuine interest, you may have the opportunity to observe in other areas or see procedures that a volunteer might not normally observe); or

- Reflecting on your experience

(A favorite question in counseling and teaching, and in interviewing students for professional school, is: "What did you learn from this?" Ask yourself this question often. Ask also, "What did this experience mean to me?" It helps to keep a journal to record your reflections. A journal also helps you see how you have grown in understanding yourself and the world around you. That is part of the purpose of reflection; understanding your strengths and limitations can help you better serve your patients. And the record of those reflections can be a valuable resource when you write a personal statement for your application to professional school).

Do I have a good head on my shoulders?

- If all that professional schools required was a good academic record, then they could fill their classes with students who have 4.0 grade point averages (GPAs) and perfect (or nearly perfect) admission exam scores. But schools look for more. Consider GPAs and test scores as only a threshold, and an early way to screen for intellectual capacity. One advisor put it this way: "Your 'numbers' may get you into the game. Everything else keeps you in the game."
- The intellectual capacity to do the work of the professional does not require genius, but you should have some aptitude for science, an open mind and intellectual curiosity. These latter qualities enable an individual to explore alternatives in order to look at complex and difficult problems in new and creative ways. The good professional examines all the information, draws a conclusion, then takes a step back to ask, "Is there yet another way to look at this?"
- A career as a health care professional requires a commitment to life-long learning — from teachers and colleagues; from texts, journals and continuing education courses; and from patients. Begin developing the disposition for learning early. When you take a class, make an effort to extend your reading beyond that required for class. Look for articles in academic journals that build on concepts taught in class. Look up legislation related to health care and find out about what is being proposed in your state. Attend special lectures offered at your university or in your community. Look for presentations on a variety of topics.
- The ability to look at an issue in depth is another important consideration, often illustrated by undergraduate work in some concentrated area or the extended study of an issue or problem. For example, if you are interested in how patients react to physical surroundings, you might take courses in architecture, engineering, psychology and/or anthropology. If you are interested in decisions that are made about when patients are taken off life support, you might take classes in philosophy, religion, public policy and/or political science.
- Being a non-science major is not a disadvantage in the application process. Any major is acceptable, so long as science grades are strong, prerequisites are met, and an applicant has sufficient depth to manage the curriculum s/he will be expected to master.

Do I have a good heart?

- A career in a health care profession requires more than technical skill. Professional schools carefully look for human qualities in their candidates for admission. A career in health care is built on relationships:

between professional and patient, among professionals in the same career, and across professions. Draw upon your experiences and reflections. Reflect especially on the meaning of "the professional-patient relationship," empathy and altruism. Ask yourself how you might demonstrate these qualities, not just through volunteer activities, but also in your daily life.

Am I willing to make a serious commitment in time?

- Be certain that you are aware of all matters related to time, especially the importance of providing adequate time in the individual transaction between the professional and the patient. Commitment is also about the time spent in preparation. Included in this book are references to resources on the web and in print that can help you better understand the type of commitment you will be expected to make to prepare for entering a profession, as well as what you might expect when you do enter that profession. Use the following timetable as a guideline to help you plan that journey.

TIMETABLE FOR DOCTORAL PROGRAM PREPARATION

Many applicants underestimate the time required to complete the application process. You will need to complete primary and often supplementary applications, take admissions tests, submit results of those tests to the professional schools, request evaluation letters, submit those letters to the professional schools and arrange for transcripts to be sent to the schools or centralized service.

An application that arrives just before a deadline may have a lower chance of favorable action. A late application may be viewed as an indication that you may not be committed to the career or the school. An application prepared hurriedly in order to meet a deadline may not present you in the best possible way. Finally, an application submitted at the deadline may arrive after many interviews and acceptances have already been issued. By the time your file is complete and you have been interviewed, only a few positions may be left in the entering class because many schools use rolling admissions; therefore, everything must be done in a logical and timely manner.

Timetables vary. The following timeline applies to those students who plan to matriculate into health professional school directly after earning the bachelor's degree (an increasingly smaller group). Well more than half of the applicants from U.S. colleges and universities are taking a year off before matriculating at health professional school. The timeline below, however, allows you to keep the option open to matriculate directly after graduating from college in case that is what, as an underclassman, you think you would like to do:

Freshman, Sophomore, Junior Years

- Speak with a health professions advisor, preferably in person.
- Take the required courses for admission to a health professions school at a reasonable pace. Expect that you will need to double up on sciences some semesters.
- Get some experience related to your anticipated career. Many schools now want to see evidence that you have had some clinical exposure; some types of schools require a minimum number of supervised hours.

Junior Year (Spring Semester/Quarter)

- Speak with a health professions advisor about your intention to apply that summer.
- Take the standardized admission test.
- Attend the meeting on the application process, if your school has one.
- Access the online application.

- Obtain a transcript at the end of the year for your own use in preparation of the application.
- Request that official transcripts be sent to the individual schools or the application service.
- Arrange for letters of evaluation to be collected and sent.

Summer after Junior Year

- Complete your application ideally before Labor Day.
- If you are applying through an Early Decision Program (less common), check to see that your letters of evaluation have been submitted and prepare for interviews.
- Check deadlines for submission, as they vary for different application services. Always apply several months before the deadline.

Senior Year (Fall Semester/Quarter)

- Complete supplemental (secondary) applications, if you have not already done so. Secondary applications are ideally completed during the summer because interviews are generally not granted until this portion of your application is complete and all fees are paid. Some schools begin arranging interviews in August; thus, having this part complete is as important as completing the primary application. Make sure you know the timeline for the professional schools to which you are applying.
- Arrange for letters of evaluation to be sent before or as your secondaries are complete.
- Interviews are arranged at the discretion of the professional school.
- Send an updated transcript at the end of the fall semester/quarter. Update schools about any new activities of interest, or honors.

Senior Year (Spring Semester/Winter and Spring Quarter)

- Interviewing may continue.
- Submit financial aid applications.
- Decision time:
- Discuss your options with your health professions advisor.
- Choose a school (for MD, before May 15).
- Make alternative plans if not accepted.

Late Summer and Early Fall after Senior Year

- Begin professional school.

You may decide, in consultation with your health professions advisor, that you should delay applying until you are a more viable candidate. Or you may decide that you want time after college to pursue some work, community service, special scholarship, etc. and will apply to attend health professions school later., However if neither of these situations is the case, then you should complete the application process on schedule. Remember, you want to present the best possible application; however, many factors enter the admissions decision process. Your application may be considered even if your test scores and GPA are not at the middle to high end of the range. Your health professions advisor can help you weigh your options. If you decide to repeat the standardized test for professional school (MCAT or other) later on in the summer, check the box on the application indicating that you plan to repeat it. This notifies the professional program to delay final action on your application until receipt of your new scores.

Normally, the centralized application services give you online access to check the progress of your application. Then the individual schools to which you have applied will also do the same. Health professions schools will notify you of your status after the admission committee has acted on your application. You can expect to fall into one of four

categories: acceptance, rejection, placement on an alternate or wait list, or placement on hold. The last category merely means that the committee considered your application but did not make a final decision. You are less likely to be notified of this status than of the other three.

After receiving an acceptance, you may request a deferral for such reasons as study abroad, doing research or other personal reasons. However, applicants are advised not to submit an application with the intent to request a deferral. Some health professions schools will grant a one-year delay in matriculation if it is sufficiently justified. The health professions schools, not the applicant, determine what is considered justified.

INTERNATIONAL STUDENTS

Students who are citizens of other countries (international students) often have a significantly reduced chance of obtaining admission to health professions schools unless they can finance their entire education. Many schools have both citizenship and residency requirements. There are, however, some private schools that will accept non-US citizens. International students should contact their health professions advising office to learn where to find the names of the professional schools that will consider their applications, or if they do not have a health professions advisor available, contact the volunteer advising service through www.naahp.org. Permanent residents, those with a green card, are generally treated as U.S. citizens for admission purposes.

NON-TRADITIONAL STUDENTS

More and more students enter the application cycle later than the above timetable because of a change in majors, a change in interest or a change in careers. Some non-traditional students have a bachelor's degree in a non-science field without the required science and math courses. In fact, there are increasing numbers of people who decide to enter a health professions program later in life (from age 25 to over 40). They have been referred to as non-traditional students, and their numbers are increasing, so much so that this has almost become the more traditional timeline for application.

Many colleges and universities offer post-baccalaureate programs with a compressed schedule of science and math courses (see Chapter 1). Many also offer a complete year of inorganic chemistry, organic chemistry, biology or physics during a summer session. This can allow a student to take the admission test in August and begin the application process at that time, but beware; studying for an admissions test while completing classes is often overwhelming and self-defeating. It is inadvisable to commit yourself to so compact a schedule without consulting with an advisor and determining if you are able to produce a record that will make you viable for favorable consideration.

STANDARDIZED TESTS FOR ADMISSION TO PROFESSIONAL SCHOOL

Essentially all health professions doctoral programs, and some master's level programs, require a standardized, nationally administered test specific to the profession, to support the application for admission. Why is there a reliance on standardized tests when evaluating a student for admission? First, grades alone do not tell the complete story when predicting whether or not an applicant has the aptitude and intellectual capacity to complete a demanding professional program in the health sciences. Second, an applicant may have attended an undergraduate institution whose academic standards are not particularly well known to the admissions committee. The standardized test helps establish the validity of the student's grades.

As an example, the Medical College Admission Test (MCAT) is a computer-based test offered on approximately twenty dates throughout the year (www.aamc.org/mcat). Other tests like the Pharmacy College Admission Test (PCAT) are also offered multiple times annually. Information about which test may be required can be found on the official websites of the professional organizations and the required test is listed in each health profession's entry in Chapter 5. The following provides information applicable to preparing for standardized admissions tests in general:

- Test Format and Content. One of the first things a student anticipating taking such a test should do is to learn as much as possible about the test, both its content and format. Knowing how you will be tested is an important part of preparation. One should plan to utilize the official practice examinations available from publishers of the test as well as their handbooks and web-based materials that provide information about the examination and how it is scored. Practice tests can be important in identifying areas of weakness and strength and in allowing the student to become more familiar with the format of the test and the level of difficulty of questions. Practice tests should be taken under conditions approximating real test conditions, particularly regarding the time available for the test.

- Review. The greatest value of a careful review may be the feeling of confidence you develop as you become increasingly familiar with the material to be tested. An organized, systematic review of the topics to be tested is important. For biology, chemistry, physics and other subject tests, the program of study should include taking the required subjects before these tests are taken. Save your class notes to re-study,

- Some undergraduate colleges and universities offer an in-house review of science topics (general chemistry, organic chemistry, biology, and physics).

- Some students take a commercial test preparation course before taking these admission tests. Commercial test preparation courses are expensive, sometimes costing $2000 or more. Some commercial companies may offer a reduced rate for students on significant financial aid, if they provide documentation from their health professions advisor and/or from the school's financial aid office. For students with poor test-taking skills and those with less self-discipline to review on their own, the cost of a commercial test preparation course may be worth the price. You would gain considerable experience with practice problems and thereby sharpen your test-taking ability. There are no experimental studies to show that students who take a commercial course perform better on standardized tests than do students who organize their own disciplined study. Whether you take a commercial course or not is your decision. Anecdotal evidence shows some students who do not take a commercial course scoring well and some scoring poorly. The same variation applies for those who do take a course. Your decision about how to prepare should be based on an honest assessment of what will work for you. No matter what you decide, there is no substitute for diligent study and the taking of practice tests in the same format as the real thing.

- Study Groups. Some students form study groups to prepare for the exam. Others prefer to review on their own, using commercially available materials to supplement their class notes and textbooks. Again, the method you choose should be based on your resources, study habits and self-discipline.

- Timing. Whatever method is chosen to review the material for the test, it is best to begin well before the test date (usually several months in advance). Professional schools vary regarding the acceptable interval between the time the test was taken, interview, and acceptance. Plan to take the test so that your scores will be valid within the acceptable interval. A specific block of study time should be set aside. This review schedule should then be followed faithfully. Study on a daily basis is better than an attempt to review huge blocks of material during a short time. Your class notes, tests and textbooks are particularly valuable resources. The emphasis ought to be on familiarizing yourself with concepts learned previously rather than on learning new material. There are no tricks or strategies that can substitute for knowledge of subject matter, particularly in the science sections. The questions are often posed so that application of general principles is stressed much more than regurgitation of facts. You must know the facts, but you must also be able to apply these facts in solving problems.

Try to get a good night's sleep before the test and arrive at the test center in plenty of time. If the testing center is near to where you live or are staying, you may even want to take a preliminary trip to the testing site so you know the best route for getting there. Make sure you know the testing center procedures. Many testing centers require specific forms of identification and limit what a person can take to the center. You can find out about these on-line and by carefully reading instructions that accompany your registration or that are accessible when you register. Eat well before and during any breaks. And, easier said than done, try to remain calm before entering the testing room. When you actually sit down to take the test or when taking a practice test under simulated conditions, certain tactics may help avoid errors and improve your score. Part of preparation is learning tactics that work for you:

- Pace yourself. A timer is visible on the testing monitor. Do not spend a great deal of time on a difficult problem or question, only to not answer the easier ones for lack of time. All questions usually count the same.
- Read through the entire question carefully and be certain that you understand the point being tested before responding. A choice among the early answers may appear correct until you read further and find a better answer. There will be sufficient time for most people to read all questions carefully, unless they are slow readers.
- Do not waste time with questions that will require involved calculations or otherwise use a great deal of time, even if you feel that you could eventually get the right answer. Go back to those questions when you have answered the others. As time begins to run out, make sure you leave sufficient time to mark an answer for all questions, even ones you may have skipped earlier in that section.

In order to enable your health professions advisor to better counsel you on where to apply, check the box on the registration or test form that will release your test scores to the advisor. Allowing your advisor access can be important when it is time for her or him to send in your letters of recommendation or Committee packet. Test score information also helps in the preparation of summary reports, but individual scores are never released without written authorization from the student.

If your scores are not as good as you had anticipated, you may need to repeat the test; however, this decision should not be made hastily. Ask yourself the following questions:

- Are my scores consistent with my grades? If not, why not?
- Did I prepare adequately and conscientiously for the test?
- Will I have the time and the motivation to prepare properly for a second test? Merely taking a test over is no guarantee that your scores will improve; scores may go down as well as up.

Your best source of information and advice when considering whether or not to repeat is usually your health professions advisor.

If you believe you are a poor standardized test taker, address the problem early in your undergraduate studies. In some cases uncompetitive test results are due to poor reading skills. Some students score poorly on admission tests because of learning disabilities. If this is the reason for poor scores, federal legislation guarantees you certain rights if you have had a professional evaluation that establishes that you have a learning disability. Depending upon the diagnosis, this may include granting additional time for the test because of reading difficulties, or it may allow a person who is easily distracted by noises or movement to be isolated during the test. If you believe that your low scores on an admission test are caused by a learning disability, discuss this possibility with a knowledgeable advisor. It is expensive to take tests that diagnose the condition and allow it to be certified, but keep in mind that some of our most distinguished health professionals suffered from such problems. If you have the motivation and the academic aptitude to become a health care professional, there is little reason to abandon this dream because of dyslexia or some comparable disability.

APPLYING

Choosing the schools to which you want to apply

As you consider different schools and choosing among those in different locations, ask yourself these questions:

- What sort of city do I want to be in for the next four years, big or small?
- Is it important for me to be near people who are my support system, to be close to family and friends?
- If I have a strong identity, related, for instance, to national or ethnic origin, religion, or sexual orientation, is there a community for me at the school and/or in the city where it is located?
- What is the "culture" of the school? Are the faculty members and my peers committed to my success? Does the school recognize the importance of the human side of medicine? Of community service?
- What about financial considerations? Is there a state institution that provides financial benefits to its resident students?
- Where will my clinical exposure happen? What sorts of facilities, and are they near to, or far from, the home institution?

Your advisor, and friends and alumni who are currently at the schools you are considering, can help you address these questions. You may be tempted to use rankings, often found in commercial publications. Be wary of this approach, for rankings are often based on criteria that do not pertain to your own needs.

Application forms and services

There are two ways to apply to health professional schools: through a centralized application service or through direct application to individual schools. The number of schools using a centralized application service is large and growing so that there are now only a handful that require individual applications. You can find out which schools use a centralized service and which don't by talking with your advisor and by consulting resources listed in the appendices.

As your application process proceeds and time elapses, check frequently with the application service to be certain that material has been received, processed and forwarded to the desired schools. Most application services have a website link that allows you to monitor the receipt of your application materials. If this service is not offered, learn how best you can keep track. Use phone calls and email when appropriate. Check your email frequently for messages from the application service and specific schools. Disable any filters that may interfere with your receiving those messages by categorizing them as "junk".

Centralized Application Services

The centralized application services provide standardized information to each of their participating health professions schools from a single form that you complete. The advantage of applying through a centralized service is that initially only one set of application materials and official transcripts need be submitted, regardless of the number of schools to which you apply. The application services provide detailed admission information to health professional schools and to undergraduate health professions advisors, in addition to processing the primary application.

Appendix B lists the services that oversee the centralized application processes of each professional school association. Most now offer web-based applications. You can access those applications, along with instructions, on the association's website. While advisors no longer receive paper applications from most services, they may have additional material or experience that can aid students when completing the application. Each professional school has its own specific deadline for receipt of the application.

All application services require a basic processing fee, plus a sliding scale fee depending on the number of schools to which you request the application be sent. Certain fee reductions or waivers are available to students with documented financial need. Check online with the respective application service regarding the earliest submission date. Directions about how to complete an application and information on fees are available on the websites for the application services. Read these first rather than calling or emailing with questions for which answers are readily available. Many application service websites also have a "Frequently Asked Questions (FAQ)" section. Go through this section before calling, and ask your advisor. S/he may have answers to your questions. Checking other sources before contacting the application service enables the people at the application services to handle issues that require clarification and/or special problems that may arise.

Direct application: Some professional schools do not participate in these centralized application services. You must either contact these schools individually to request their application materials or access the application at the school's website.

Advanced standing and transfer applicants should also contact all schools directly for application instructions.

Official transcripts are required before or after submission of the application, depending on the health profession. Knowing when transcripts are needed is important, and you should plan accordingly so that your transcript(s) are received in a timely manner. Application services — and often professional schools — will perform an item-by-item check comparing all courses in the academic record section of your application against your official transcript; thus, you should review your transcript(s) prior to submitting it to check for errors. Also, application services may recalculate your GPA in order to standardize across colleges and universities. What they calculate may be lower than that on your transcript because, for example, any grade of A+ is changed to an A. The application is copied after grades are verified and sent to all the schools you designate. If you decide to apply to additional schools before the application deadline, you need to submit an additional designation form with the appropriate fees, and your application will be forwarded to those schools.

Make certain you review all application forms early in the application cycle, so that you understand exactly what is expected of you and so that you give yourself sufficient time to prepare an application that allows you to make the best impression.

Generally, each application requires basic biographical information followed by questions relating to your academic strengths and weaknesses, extracurricular activities, honors, and other matters.

Make certain you carefully read and follow all instructions. See your health professions advisor, or call the application service or schools, to answer any questions you may have. When you have completed the forms and have checked carefully for errors, submit your materials to the application service, which then verifies and reproduces your application and forwards it to each school you have designated. If there is an application service, individual member schools may then send you supplementary application materials ("secondaries") to complete after assessing your initial set of credentials. When you submit a secondary application, schools typically require an additional fee.

Be sure to retain copies of all materials that you submit as part of the application process. It is also a good idea to retain draft material, because information you leave out of your personal statement may be worthy of inclusion in response to questions on the secondary application (see below). Submit your application early, because most schools have a rolling acceptance system; that is, the admissions committee acts on the application once it is complete in all its parts, including secondaries, letters of recommendation, and interview. Even schools without rolling admission have a limited number of interview slots available to candidates, so applying early best enhances your potential to receive an invitation to interview.

Send academic grade reports, as required and as they become available during the year of application, to all schools where an application is pending. Determine if schools require only a copy of these transcripts or an official transcript; the latter may be required only after acceptance but before matriculation.

Personal statement or essay

Most application forms require a an essay. For many students, this is the most difficult and challenging part of the application process. *Your personal statement should be personal.* There is no universal formula. Your essay may explore or describe a variety of topics: your personal journey toward your chosen career; important experiences and what you learned from them; the special strengths you feel you offer the profession; your goals for your education and career; how you will contribute to the diversity of your class.

Anecdotes and stories from your personal experience are often more effective than declarative statements, such as: "I am compassionate" or "I have been a leader." A well-written passage about delivering meals to an elderly home-bound person may communicate more about you as a person than simply listing such qualities as compassion, empathy, understanding, and a sense of humor. Also, it is wise to limit the number of experiences you choose to write about. Trying to cover all of your accomplishments in one short essay usually results in a "resume in prose form," which adds very little to the material about you already submitted.

If you have anything in your background that you feel needs to be explained, include it in your personal statement. If you missed a year because of illness or family problems, or had a difficult semester because your work schedule was too heavy, discuss it here. On the other hand, do not feel compelled to discuss the only "C" you got, as this will just call attention to it. Make any explanation as positive as possible, stressing what you have learned from the experience. Take responsibility for your actions; excuses create a negative impression. Don't exaggerate. Don't compromise your credibility. Could it be that you are a stronger candidate because you have been through this experience? Ask yourself, as many interviewers will ask, "How did it affect me? How did I grow from this experience?" If you are uncertain about the viability of discussing a certain academic or personal issue, speak with your advisor about it; often describing the situation to an advisor helps to clarify whether or not it is a topic worth discussing in the limited, very valuable space of the personal essay.

In general, you should obtain critical feedback about your essay from people whose judgment you trust. Ask a peer and/or an advisor to review your application, particularly those parts that require essays or other extensive text, before you submit it. It never hurts to get another opinion. You may choose to purchase a copy of *Write for Success* from NAAHP, through its website www.naahp.org.

When you are interviewed, the interviewer likely will have read your personal statement and your responses on the supplemental application material. Thus, anything you choose to write about should also be something that you feel comfortable discussing. Make sure you save a copy of your application, including your essay; re-read the essay prior to an interview. You may choose to purchase the brief brochure, *Interviewing for Health Professions Schools,* through the NAAHP website at www.naahp.org.

Supplemental application material ("Secondaries")

Upon receipt of the applicant's materials from the centralized application service, each school will notify the applicant directly regarding the need for any additional material, or you may be able to access secondary applications directly from the school's website once you have submitted the primary application. Check directions and ask your advisor. Generally, on secondary applications you will be asked to answer a variety of essay questions, These question or questions may be specific to that school, call for your opinion, or ask you to deal with a controversial topic. Some supplementary applications also request more information about your personal or academic history. Some also will inquire about why you are interested in that particular school. Each school has its own format.

Motivated students quickly, but carefully, complete and submit the secondary applications.

Letters of evaluation; choosing whom to ask

Whether you have the intellectual capacity to do the work of your profession will become clear to the admissions committee when they receive your undergraduate transcript and the scores from your national standardized test. However, there are other qualities upon which you will be judged, such as motivation, maturity, perseverance, judgment, compassion, integrity, interpersonal and communication skills, cultural sensitivity, resilience and adaptability, ability to be part of a team, and the potential for continuing intellectual and professional growth.

Absence of one or more of these qualities is most often responsible for keeping a student with high grades from being accepted; if these qualities were not important, then the incoming class could be selected entirely by a computer. Although some of these characteristics can be gleaned from your application and your interview, evaluation letters are one of the most important sources for describing and appraising these traits.

You can expect that, after initial screening, admission committees will require letters of evaluation. The more personalized and specific the evaluation is, the more valuable it can be for you. Regardless of the system your school uses for collecting these letters, you should understand that it is to your benefit to get to know well a few faculty members, in order to fulfill this requirement when the time comes to apply to professional schools.

There are alternative methods used in submission of letters of evaluation:

- Individual letters prepared by faculty members and others who know the applicant well, with the letters going directly to each professional school to which the student applies;
- Individual letters sent to a central site overseen by the application service or by the specific professional school association, and then forwarded by the application service to each professional school to which the student applies;
- A composite evaluation prepared completely by your health professions committee;
- A composite evaluation generally prepared in a health professions advising office. This method uses letters of evaluation from faculty members and others chosen by the applicant, with summary comments and ratings prepared by the chief health professions advisor.

If your school has a committee system and you cannot use it — you might have transferred into the school and do not know enough professors to contribute to your file, or are a non-traditional student who took much of your work with faculty who are no longer at the school, or prefer not to use it for some other reason — then you may arrange for individual letters to be sent. In such cases, it is a good idea to let your health professions advising office know about what you are doing, so that the advisor can assure professional schools that you are applying with his/her knowledge and are not trying to circumvent your school's system. On the other hand, if your school has a committee system and denies you a supportive committee letter because you do not meet their criteria, it is still your prerogative and right to arrange for individual letters to be sent to the professional schools of your choice. Professional schools will accept letters and make the definitive decision whether or not you qualify to attend their school.

In gathering your letters of evaluation from faculty and others, the most important factor is that your evaluator knows you well and is not just going to submit a standard letter for all his/her A students, another for B+ students, etc. Here are some guidelines:

- Do not be reluctant to ask those whom you choose, "Can you write a strong letter on my behalf?" If the person can't, find someone else.
- If letter-writers are college professors, be certain that they can go beyond your grade to describe you as a person.
- Stress the importance of a prompt letter. Give your evaluators both a deadline and sufficient lead time. A

tardy letter can hold up an invitation for an interview and/or overall consideration of your application. Keep track of your evaluations; do not assume that they have been sent because the professor said s/he would do so soon.

- Be prepared to furnish your evaluator with additional information about yourself. Let your evaluators know the type of health professional school to which you are applying. Prepare an autobiographical sketch for your letter writers, and make an appointment to discuss your career plans. Tell them why you are motivated to pursue a particular career.
- Professional schools are interested in your science capability and usually require at least two evaluations from science faculty.
- Diversify your evaluations by submitting them from several different disciplines, including humanities and social science faculty.
- If you request an evaluation from a professor with whom you are currently taking a course, suggest that s/he draft the evaluation after the course has been completed. Alternatively, you may want to alert the professor that you will ask for a letter at some future date.
- Faculty with whom you are involved in research or other individual or small-group curricular projects may be in a better position to evaluate you than those who know you as but one face in a large class.
- Letters from physicians, family friends, peers, clergy, etc. come under the category of character references and should not be confused with faculty evaluations. If such references are required, these may be sent directly to those schools by the persons writing them, but check the procedures at your undergraduate institution if you are going through that school's health professions committee process.
- Most schools designate the types of letters they prefer. It is usually best to avoid soliciting a letter from political figures, if it is written simply as a favor to a constituent, rather than as an endorsement based on personal knowledge or interaction. Letters from former employers are often of value since they can address such personality characteristics as maturity, reliability, responsibility, independent judgment, and interpersonal skills. If you have assisted in any research, especially at a health professional school, a letter from that project director can discuss both your cognitive and personal attributes in a way meaningful to an admission committee. If you have done volunteer work with a health practitioner or in a health care facility, a letter from your supervisor might also be appropriate.
- For MD applicants, the Association of American Medical Colleges has developed guidelines for writing letters of evaluation that you may want to give to your evaluators (www.aamc.org/applicants). Other professional schools may have similar guidance available, so it is advisable to check the websites for their centralized application services.

Under the provisions of the Family Educational Rights and Privacy Act of 1974, known as the Buckley Amendment, you have the right of access to all educational records including letters of evaluation sent to health professional schools by your health professions advisor and/or your faculty. You can either waive or retain your right to read these letters. Admission committees often prefer confidential letters because they assume that a more candid and, therefore, a more helpful evaluation will usually be written if the professor knows that the confidentiality of the evaluation is to be respected. Be assured that your letters are confidential and will only be sent to the institutions that you designate. That said, unless you waive your right, it is your civil right to insist on access to your academic records and evaluations.

THE INTERVIEW

When a letter arrives inviting you to an interview, you have every reason to be optimistic since most schools only interview a fraction of their applicants. Your application and transcripts have been carefully scrutinized, and the reviewers have deemed you to be an acceptable candidate for strong consideration. Read the instructions that come with the invitation to the interview very carefully and respond promptly. Delaying your response or unnecessarily

putting off the interview may imply lack of interest in the school. You may choose to use a written resource to help you prepare for your interview (for example *Interviewing for Health Professions Schools* published by NAAHP)

See the interview as reciprocal. The health professions school representative is, of course, interviewing you, but you are also trying to determine if the school would be a good fit for you. The interview is also an opportunity for you to enhance and complete the picture they have of you, to show that you can think and speak clearly, to give an indication of how patients might see you some day when you are in a clinical setting, and to illustrate how you form a relationship. At the same time, the school is trying to recruit really good candidates, and so you want to use the time to address any questions you have about the school. Not only is the interview your single most important opportunity to express or explain yourself to the admission committee, it is also your opportunity to learn something about the institution firsthand. It provides you the opportunity to ask questions about the school's programs and faculty and to tour the facilities. During the interview day, you can gain information that might not be available in the institution's website, literature, and other public documents.

Most health professions schools use an interview to assess a number of personal qualities deemed necessary for successful academic progress and professional practice. Regard the interview as an opportunity to present yourself as a person with realistic goals and aspirations. Deciding in advance what you want your interviewers to know about you and your special strengths helps. Take advantage of these services if your undergraduate institution provides opportunities for mock interviews and/or videotaping for a later debriefing of strengths and weaknesses during the interview.

The interview provides the admission committee, through its representatives, with the opportunity to meet you, verify your credentials and supplement its knowledge of you. The interview is also used to obtain explanations and insight into any problems encountered with your application. For example, you may wish to explain health or family problems that adversely affected your academic performance. Moreover, the interview gives you an opportunity to view the facilities and the area around the school and to interact with students. If you are already traveling to a particular city or region for interviews and have not yet heard from other schools nearby, it is acceptable to contact those schools. If they had planned to grant you an interview, they may be willing to arrange it at that same time.

At the interview, most schools use a one-to-one format with one or more interviewers. A few schools use a committee interview, with three or four persons on the panel, or they may interview several applicants in a group. A relatively small number of health professional schools use the Multiple Mini-Interview (see below). Interviewers are typically clinical faculty, basic science faculty, or students, especially where multiple interviews are the custom. These personal interviews are often relatively unstructured and usually last from thirty minutes to an hour.

Interviewers will likely evaluate you to assess your personal qualities, including:

- Your understanding of the career: Do you know what it is *really* like and what patients need from you as a professional?
- Your motivation: How strong is your desire for your chosen career? The interviewer might want to further test your motivation by posing questions regarding your experiences in the field you have chosen.
- Your level of maturity and judgment: How well and logically do you think on your feet? Are you emotionally stable and mature?
- Your intellectual curiosity: What is the evidence that you recognize the importance of life-long learning? How well do you learn from experience?
- Your interpersonal skills: Do you communicate with the interviewer easily and clearly? How well do you relate to the interviewer? What evidence is there that you can work well with others? Since you will be caring for patients with both physical and psychosocial problems, the interviewer will be interested in assessing your ability to relate to, communicate with, and empathize with people from various cultural and ethnic backgrounds.

The Multiple Mini-Interview (MMI)

Some medical schools (and at least two U.S. dental schools) conduct multiple short interviews, usually 5-10 minutes each, instead of the traditional longer interviews. Candidates at these schools are asked to address a specific ethical dilemma or issue in the profession, provided to them just before they meet their interviewer. Typically they have 7-10 of these brief meetings as well as a longer presentation about the school by an admissions officer.

Interview Tips

- Preparation for your interview involves thinking about your goals, strengths, weaknesses, and the information you most wish to communicate to the admission committee. This preparation is of enormous help if your interviewer begins the session by saying, "Tell me about yourself." Think about the current state of the profession and how you stand on various issues related to the profession. There are no "correct" answers for these questions; the interviewer wants to determine whether you have thought seriously about the profession and can defend your positions in an articulate manner.
- In advance, learn about the school by looking at its website, reading its publications and by talking to students on that campus before your interview session. A common interview question is: "Why are you interested in attending our school?"
- If possible, arrange to arrive at the school early enough to avoid stress and to look around and get a feeling for the campus.
- Spend time with current students and find out more about the school and its atmosphere. Are the faculty and your fellow students committed to your success? Does the school attend as much to the human side of medicine as the technical part? Some schools help you make arrangements to stay overnight with a student or at inexpensive accommodations. Your health professions advising office may be able to give you names, phone numbers and addresses of alumni from your college who are current students there.
- The school will inform you in advance where you are to report for the first interview, general information session, or tour. Often you will be told the names and positions or titles of the interviewer(s). The interview can be "open- or closed-file." For the latter, the interviewer has not been given your letters of evaluation or information about your academic background. But even in closed-file interviews, your personal statement and your answers to questions on the secondary are often available.
- Refrain from anything that might be viewed as objectionable by the interviewer, such as gum-chewing and nervous mannerisms. Maintain good eye contact. Display your best "professional manner." Dress professionally, but comfortably, and remember that this is not the time to make a statement with your clothes, hairstyle, jewelry, piercings, perfume or deodorant. Remember to turn your cell phone off. While it is impossible to eliminate all the stress inherent in the interview process, the most important thing to remember is to conduct yourself naturally and calmly. First impressions are important.
- Try not to appear defensive. If you make an error in one of your statements and realize it, admit it. Never try to bluff a response. Try to be open-minded and willing to learn. Understand the difference between questions requiring factual responses and those asking for opinions. Do not be reluctant to take the time to think before responding, as a complex question requires some thought; the silent interval is usually shorter than you imagine.
- Do not be reluctant to express your feelings appropriately during the interview. Be open about your concerns. Many interviewers ask that you continue if you are too brief; be prepared to give more detailed explanations. They often ask about your family and the kind of relationship you have with family members. The open-ended format gives you an opportunity to describe accomplishments while giving background information. Don't sound boastful, yet take the opportunity to make the committee aware of positive factors about you that would be difficult to present in any other way.
- If you feel that the interview went badly, many admissions officers will respond favorably to a request for second interview with a different interviewer.

Some schools give you a comment sheet after the interview that asks for feedback. It is important and appropriate to express your concerns as soon as possible, especially if the interview went badly. Such comments are normally considered confidential by the administrator in charge of the interview process. Your health professions advisor can usually help you decide how to handle this situation, and you should certainly inform her/him of any problems you encountered, particularly with regard to what you believe to be illegal or improper questions.

Many applicants write or email thank you notes to their interviewer after the interview.

NON-ACCEPTANCE

Some applicants are not accepted on the first try. Here are a few possible reasons:
- There are more qualified candidates than places in the first-year class.
- The application process reveals too many gaps in your preparation for professional school.
- Grades and admission test scores may be inadequate. Ask yourself, have I done my best? Do not make the mistake of interpreting a rejection from the professional school as one based solely on your test scores and/or grades. There may be other reasons. The best way to find out is to ask.
- There is inadequate or unclear evidence of motivation and altruism. The best indicator of future altruism is past altruism. Ask yourself, "What's this all about? Do I *really* want this career?"

For help in addressing the reasons for non-acceptance, get advice about remedies from an admissions officer at two or three of the schools that rejected you and from a health professions advisor.

If you are really motivated, <u>do not give up</u>. Reapply when your application is stronger. Many have been accepted on the second and third try. Many regard the interim time as especially productive and fulfilling.

There is more about non-acceptance in a subsequent section of this book.

AND FINALLY...

Once again, remember that you are more than your resume. You are more than a list of your accomplishments — grades, scores, activities and jobs. The purpose of the application is to tell the professional school admissions committee who you *really* are.

Recognize that applying is a complex process. If you have emotional ups and downs during the process, be assured that others have had the same experiences and have been successful applicants. While more than 42,000 applicants applied for about 19,500 first year places in U.S. allopathic medical schools in a recent cycle, for example, your chances of acceptance are far greater than the 45% implied by that data if you are a strong applicant.

Use your advisors. Whether you are a current student or an alumnus or alumna, if you haven't already done so, make an appointment soon to talk to your advisor in depth about this process, and do not be reluctant to speak with the advisor more than once.

After the Application

Once your application has been submitted, events will dictate the concerns you will have from that time forward. While you will be involved in interviews, you can also turn your attention to what happens after the admissions committees make their decisions. If you are accepted, one of your first concerns will be to develop a plan for meeting the financial demands of attending a health professions school. On the other hand, if you are not accepted by any school, you will need to be concerned with "What happens now?" This chapter seeks to provide you with some guidance for responding to each of these possible outcomes.

FINANCIAL PLANNING & AID

Including tuition and living expenses, the total cost of attending a four-year health profession program can exceed $250,000. Costs of programs vary widely, depending in part on the type of program, its length, and whether or not your tuition is partially subsidized by state taxpayers (in-state vs. out-of state tuition). Some students are fortunate enough to have sizable family assets with which to pay for part or all of their education and training. Most are not so fortunate. As a consequence, beginning financial planning for your health professions education is important, even as early as you begin your undergraduate program.

The Association of American Medical Colleges has developed a program called FIRST (Financial Information, Resources, Services and Tools) for students that offers valuable information for college students planning to become physicians, and much of the information is also helpful for students planning to enter other health professions. It can be found online at www.aamc.org/services/first/first_for_students/.

Minimizing Undergraduate Debt

Minimizing any debt you might assume while completing your undergraduate studies can be beneficial later when you are facing paying for post-graduate education. Interest which compounds over the time necessary to complete the undergraduate degree and the health professions program will add substantially to your overall debt load at the completion of your program. Do not carry a balance on credit cards, and do not tempt yourself with a larger credit line or more credit cards than you can use responsibly. Consider reducing the number of credit cards that you carry. Debts during college can make it more difficult, even impossible, to finance a professional school program. It is also vital that you maintain a clean credit record. This cannot be overemphasized. If you have any reason to believe you have a poor credit history, you should request a copy of your credit report (www.annualcreditreport.com). If there are negatives on the report, you must make every effort to resolve these problems.

There are numerous types of financial support. You should first exhaust all scholarship possibilities at your undergraduate school. This can be handled by a Financial Aid Office, or a Scholarship or Dean's Office. Need-based support is usually handled by a Financial Aid Office. Most financial aid available through that office will be in the form of the

College Work Study Program (CWSP) and a variety of grant and loan programs. The CWSP should be used to the greatest extent possible before tapping into loan programs. Most loan programs have a maximum total amount that can be borrowed, and some of these serve both undergraduate and professional programs, so it is to your advantage to carry as much of this eligibility over to your professional program as possible.

Learn to distinguish between needs and wants. Make a budget and stick with it! You will thank yourself many times over in the future when you begin repaying loans that have been accumulating since your undergraduate years. Strategic planning for your overall financial needs for both undergraduate and professional education, with the help of your undergraduate college or university Financial Aid Office, will pay you many dividends. Working part-time is an option but be careful that it does not interfere with your academic performance. Do not defeat your purpose by working so much that you are not able to achieve the academic success and competitive credentials necessary for admission to health professions schools.

You must also plan for the cost of the application process. For example, the cost of applying to and interviewing at ten professional schools (a reasonable number) might come to $4,000 or more, including the standardized examination fee, a centralized application service fee, supplemental application fees and travel for interviews. Don't let this cost limit your application horizons. Even though this expense may seem formidable, it is actually a small fraction of your total cost of attending a health professions school. You should look upon this cost (as well as the cost of your professional education) as an investment in your future, or an investment in you as a professional. If you amortize this cost over your lifetime, it actually is a small price to pay to achieve the desired goal. If you plan for this cost, you can avoid using credit cards. The AAMC, AACOM and AADSAS offer fee assistance/reduction programs for individual applicants with demonstrated financial need.

Financing a Professional Education

Even though the cost of health professions education continues to rise, financial support is usually available to complete even the most costly program. In general, you will find that major financial aid will have to come from a variety of loan programs. Most students enrolled in graduate health profession programs receive some form of financial aid. There are two main types of funds. The first type comes from a series of different loan programs, including the federal Stafford loans and private loans designed specifically for health profession students. To access these funds, you must be a U.S. citizen or have a Permanent Resident Visa. The second type of funds is usually referred to as institutional or need-based financial aid. These funds include both loans and scholarships. They come from several sources — the professional school, the federal government, and private foundations — and are distributed by the Financial Aid Office at the school you attend. As these funds are limited in amount, most professional schools must ration them and may use an analysis of parental financial resources (potential parental contribution) to determine the student's eligibility.

The financial aid application process begins between January and April prior to the professional school academic year, when you submit detailed information about income and assets on the Free Application for Federal Student Aid (FAFSA) form and indicate all schools to receive your federal financial aid data. From this information will come a determination of financial need, which the Financial Aid Office will use to develop your financial assistance plan. If you apply for need-based aid, your parents' income information is sometimes part of this analysis. It is essential that you and your parents keep good financial records (complete tax returns early during the year you will apply for financial aid) for this process to be completed efficiently.

The health professions school Financial Aid Office is required to calculate a Cost of Attendance figure for each academic year. Under ordinary circumstances, the amount of financial aid you receive from all sources, including merit and service obligation scholarships, cannot exceed this figure. Federal financial aid regulations specify what types of expenses can and cannot be included in the cost of attendance. Among the allowable costs are tuition, fees, books, educational supplies, and living expenses. Costs that are not allowed include car payments, prior consumer debt, and moving expenses. Once again, from a financial perspective, the best way to start professional school is free of consumer debt.

Loans

There are two major types of loans: Subsidized loans (based on financial need) and Unsubsidized loans (not financial need-based). The following is a listing of some of the major and most often used loan programs you may wish to research. These programs are constantly being revised and funding limits change. Seek up-to-date information from each school's Financial Aid Office. Even the availability of some programs may be in doubt in any given year, so ask about any individual program. As mentioned earlier, eligibility for an aggregate total sum of money from several of the programs may extend across undergraduate and professional educational years. That is, borrowing less money as an undergraduate will increase the number of dollars available to borrow when you are in the health professions program. These loans generally offer the lowest interest rates available:

1. Federal Perkins Loan: A subsidized program for students with exceptional financial need.
2. Federal Subsidized Stafford Student Loan: For students with financial need.
3. Federal Unsubsidized Stafford Loan: Not need-based, but interest is not subsidized.
4. Federal Loans for Disadvantaged Students – Health Resources and Services Administration (HRSA): Need-based loans for students from disadvantaged backgrounds.
5. Graduate PLUS Loan: Federally guaranteed, fixed interest loans for graduate and professional students.
6. Private Alternative Loan Programs. Generally, these programs allow students to borrow the difference between their cost of attendance and the other financial aid they have received. These funds are provided by banks, and the loans are not guaranteed by the federal government.

Medical school students may be eligible for the Primary Care Loan (PCL) program. This HRSA loan program provides long-term, low interest loans for those students who commit to going into a primary care residency and practice (primary care includes Family Medicine, General Pediatrics, Internal Medicine and Preventive Medicine). This program is a need-based loan and thus requires the submission of parental information, unless a student has been independent for at least 3 years and is at least 24 years of age

Other special loan programs may be available, depending on the health professions school where you enroll. For example, several loan consolidation, repayment, and forgiveness programs have been developed in recent years.

Loan Consolidation, Repayment, and Forgiveness Programs

To fund your education, you may need to borrow from several different sources, and to simplify repayment, you may want to consider consolidating your student loans. Most federal loans are eligible for consolidation into a Direct Loan program (see www2.ed.gov/offices/OSFAP/DirectLoan/index.html.) Although loan consolidation may simplify repayment, it may not be financially advantageous, and, therefore, must be investigated carefully before being undertaken. Loan repayment assistance for federal student loans may be available through the College Cost Reduction and Access Act of 2007. Loan forgiveness programs can result in cancellation of part of student loan debt when a person is working in an appropriate public service job. These programs include military service, and federal and state programs.

Service Obligation Programs

If you plan to go to medical school (MD or DO), dental or optometry school, or other health professions school, a major source of support can be the United States Armed Forces Health Professions Scholarship Program, which includes separate programs for the Air Force, Army and Navy. These programs pay all tuition and fees, buy required

books, materials and supplies, and pay a taxable stipend for rent and other living expenses. In return, you will be obligated to serve as a health professional on active duty (holding the rank of captain or equivalent) one year for each year of support with a minimum requirement of three years. You may be required to spend 45 days on active duty each summer if your professional school program schedule allows it. When possible, postgraduate medical education (i.e., internship and/or residency) must be done in a military program. Time spent in postgraduate medical education is not considered "payback time." It does, however, count toward military retirement and promotions. These scholarships are competitive and are awarded to the most highly qualified students. Your health professions advisor should be consulted to help you develop the best strategy for consideration for such a program. You need to consider carefully whether you wish to pursue this avenue of financial support. Having your medical education expenses covered could be of great benefit. You need to decide if the limits on where and how you practice, and the required payback time, are acceptable in exchange for their support.

A limited number of National Health Service Corps Scholarships are available for individuals planning primary care careers. Payback occurs in the form of practicing in an underserved location. Details of this program are similar to the Armed Forces Program with a two-year minimum commitment. Selections are made from enrolled first year medical students. The Indian Health Service (IHS) also has loan repayment and scholarship programs. Some states may also have payback programs, such as the Alabama State Loan Repayment Program (ASLRP).

Scholarships

A wide variety of scholarships (awards that do not need to be repaid) are available through federal and state government programs, through private businesses, organizations, and individuals, and through professional schools. For example, some hospitals will offer programs to health professionals who agree to work for them for a specified time. Eligibility criteria also vary widely, but may include academic merit, financial need, underrepresented minority status, intention to serve in an underserved community (The National Health Service Corps Scholarship Program, or in the military (The Armed Forces Health Professionals Scholarship Program).

Working with Financial Aid Offices

The precise details of financial aid programs change from year to year. Help in sorting through these programs is available through the Financial Aid Office at the health professions school. These offices view it as their responsibility to help you meet your financial aid needs with the best possible mix of money from personal sources, scholarships and loan programs.

Finally, everyone involved in this process agrees that financial planning is an absolute necessity. As you move through your undergraduate program and on to a health professions program, you will appreciate that fact many times over. In all cases, you should seek the opportunity to speak with an institution's Financial Aid Office. It is ultimately your responsibility to learn about all of your financial aid options, and successfully manage your debts.

IF YOU ARE NOT ACCEPTED

Your worst fears may be realized when you receive that last thin letter. By now you know the lines all too well. "We are sorry to inform you that we are unable to offer you a place in the class entering in the fall." Although it is true, it does not help much that the letter goes on to state that the school regrets that the large number of highly qualified applicants makes it impossible for all of them to be accepted and they hope that you will have an opportunity at another school. You may know you are qualified, and that you would be successful, if given the chance. The choices admissions committees make between qualified candidates can seem arbitrary, and sometimes unfair. And, you may not receive your last letter until late in the application process.

If you are typical of most applicants who are not accepted, you may feel rejected, angry, embarrassed, sad, or depressed. For some, it is nothing more than a temporary career crisis. Some students have acknowledged the possibility that this could happen and have planned accordingly. They at least have some sense of direction at this point and have considered the options that are open to them. For others, it is not only a career crisis, but also an identity crisis. Although this may not bring much comfort, you should know that many do not succeed on their first try. The question is, "What do I do now?"

Now What?

Just as you sought advice on your initial applications, you now need advice with which to plot your best course of action. Some students will not seek help at this point because their knee-jerk reaction is to reapply; their minds are closed to anything other than immediate reapplication. This may not be realistic, and even counterproductive. Rather, begin to gather facts about what you will need to do. One source is your health professions advisor. While you may be too embarrassed or upset to go to your advisor's office, s/he is more objective than you can be and has experience helping many applicants deal with this situation. Another possibility is an admissions officer at a school to which you applied, although many do not have time to talk individually with applicants.

Unfortunately, students may be less likely to consult these individuals than to talk to family and friends. The advice they give, however, is often less objective than what you will receive elsewhere, and likely focuses on the issue of reapplication to professional schools and may not contain specific information about what you can and should do to achieve your primary goal. They also may not offer alternatives for you to consider. They sympathize with your plight and are concerned for your welfare, but they do not have the up-to-date information, experience, or perspective to advise you best. There is nothing wrong in talking over your situation with family and friends, but you are cautioned not to base your decisions solely upon their advice.

You need to conduct an honest appraisal of yourself as an applicant, and re-evaluate your preparation and credentials. You need to know if your credentials were not competitive enough, and, in order to answer that question, you also need to know the profile of the admitted applicant. It is not at all difficult to find out the accepted applicants' academic profile. Your health professions advisor may have such information readily available. The Medical School Admission Requirements (MSAR) and similar information reference materials for the other professions can also provide this information. One of the professional schools to which you applied may provide information on the schools' website about their average grades and test scores or even give you national averages. Did you apply to enough schools? If yes, did you include schools that afforded the best probability for admission? Did you consider state of residency? Was your application timely? These questions and many more need to be answered.

Reapplication

Now that you have had time to reflect, and have sought preliminary advice about your lack of success, you may decide to pursue reapplying seriously. Persistence can pay off and the statistics for reapplicants are promising enough to justify serious consideration of trying again. If so, it is time to adopt a positive approach. Shift your focus from why you were not accepted to what you can do to become more competitive. Most admissions committees are interested only in candidates who have made a significant improvement in their credentials.

You may be able to enhance your qualifications for admission by performing well in additional courses, or, if necessary, by re-taking some courses. Is it possible to take enough courses in one year to raise your GPA significantly? Hopefully, you did not compound the problem by letting your grades slide during the application year because you anticipated admission on the first try. If you do need to raise your GPA, should you consider pursuing another major field of study, or should you pursue graduate work in biology, or another area? The answer to these questions is, "It depends." If you select either option, you should consider the other prospects that a second degree or graduate

program can lead to, beyond just accumulating hours and getting grades. In other words, your plans should focus on what you will be able to do with that degree if you are once again unsuccessful with your application. Will it lead to an alternative career that, although perhaps at first look may not as satisfying as your first choice, would be a realistic and appealing option for you? Although a graduate degree may enhance your credentials, keep in mind that graduate course grades will not change your undergraduate GPA.

A possibility is that you are a "late bloomer." Perhaps you had a rough start in the early undergraduate years because the adjustment from high school to college was difficult. Or perhaps you had not decided to pursue a health career at that time and lacked the motivation to perform well academically. In any case, you should know that this is not insurmountable. Health professions admissions committees are interested in an accurate assessment of your potential for academic success and will, therefore, consider trends in your grades. Taking additional undergraduate courses or successfully completing a graduate program may help demonstrate a transformation. The idea is to address directly any questions or concerns an admissions committee might have about you as a candidate.

You may be able to develop your qualifications for admission by re-taking the admission test. If you decide to re-take the exam, consult with your health professions advisor and develop a plan for improving your scores. Your strategy should include a thorough review of core science concepts, as additional time will have passed since you took the courses covering this material. Consider taking a speed reading course and working to improve your vocabulary. It is also important to take as many practice tests as possible, especially if you did not do this in your first round of preparation.

Not all applicants with above average grades and test scores are accepted to professional schools; this demonstrates that health professions schools are looking for more than just academic potential. Again, your health professions advisor will be able to give you more information about your credentials in this regard. By reviewing your resume with you, your advisor may help you see areas where you might have acquired more health-related experience, taken on a leadership role, or been involved in community service. Although s/he may not have access to the interview reports from professional schools, your advisor often has established relationships with admission staff members that may allow for some feedback from the school. Your advisor should also have access to the letters of evaluation if they were channeled through his or her office. Even if they were confidential and your advisor is unable to reveal the contents to you, h/she may be able to make suggestions about an additional letter or two. Remember that professional schools are looking for more than numbers (grades and test scores), and although these additional characteristics are more difficult to assess, an objective appraisal of your strengths in these areas is necessary.

You may be able to improve your qualifications for admission through gaining additional health care experience, and engaging in significant scientific research, social service, teaching, and/or leadership activities. If all you need is experience, you may want to consider devoting a year to a health related service program. Your activities will, in turn, help you earn strongly supportive evaluation letters, and give you more to present in your applications and interviews.

Once you identify the qualifications you would most like to develop, it would be wise to consult with your health professions advisor, and decide how to accomplish your goals. You may want to develop and implement your own independent improvement program, perhaps by continuing your education at your undergraduate school. Alternatively, you may want to apply for admission to postbaccalaureate (after bachelor's degree) programs designed to help reapplicants become more competitive.

Postbaccalaureate Programs

According to Baffi-Dugan and Lang (1999), there is a wide variety of postbaccalaureate (postbac) health professions programs. One of the biggest distinctions is between programs designed for students who decide to become health professionals after completing education in other areas, and those designed to enhance reapplicant qualifications. Some are designed to help both career changers and reapplicants. In addition, some programs are specifically intended to develop or enhance the qualifications of disadvantaged or underrepresented minority candidates. The Association of American Medical Colleges maintains a fairly comprehensive list of postbac programs at https://services.aamc.org/postbac/. AspiringDocs.org provides a general description of postbac programs and is a resource for students who want to know more about medical education. Another good source of postbac information may be found at www.naahp.org.

Beyond the populations they are designed to serve, postbac programs differ widely in the focus and range of support they offer, and in the affiliation agreements they have with particular professional schools. These affiliation agreements sometimes involve guaranteed interviews or a number of openings for program participants, accelerated admissions cycles, and/or offering conditional admission to postbac students who meet academic and admission test criteria. Programs that are relatively comprehensive and those offering affiliation advantages are also likely to be competitive for admission. As in applying to professional schools, apply to the postbac programs that can best meet your needs.

In addition to target population, support and affiliation agreements, you may want to consider program length, full-time versus part-time involvement, advisor availability and experience, admission test preparation availability, cost and availability of financial aid, location and potential impact on state residency, and undergraduate versus graduate standing. Some programs help you develop other possibilities by leading to partial or full completion of a master's degree, often in health or biomedical sciences. Review the section above regarding financial aid; exceeding your allocated amount for financial aid can have consequences for the ability to pay for the health professions program to which you may be admitted after completing a postbac program.

Opening Other Doors

If you decide not to reapply, consulting with your health professions advisor is still a wise move. Meeting with a general career counselor for help clarifying your career values and goals might also be helpful. When examining careers, it is important for you to evaluate your earlier motivations and goals for a career in health care. What were the challenges, satisfactions, and rewards you anticipated? Examining your own life goals and talents, and matching these to a career can be hard work, but the effort is worthwhile, especially if it leads you to a fulfilling lifetime career.

Perhaps one of the other health care careers discussed in this book could become a satisfying option. Explorehealthcareers.org can provide information on other health professions careers about which you may not have learned yet and for which you have credentials. See Appendix A for brief descriptions of a number of these health professions.

Some people, who are initially interested in health careers, are also interested in social, helping professions such as teaching, social work, or clinical or counseling psychology. Some are more interested in scientific research, and enter graduate programs in related areas. And, some move on in other directions.

References

1. Baffi-Dugan, C., and Lang, G. (1999). A Postbac Primer. The Advisor, 19(1): 17-21.

2. AAMC FIRST (Financial Information, Resources, Services, and Tools): https://www.aamc.org/services/first/

Diversity in the Health Professions

INTRODUCTION

In our global community, one that is increasingly transnational and mobile, a diverse pool of healthcare professionals is critical in making healthcare available to those needing it most. According to the U.S. Census, nearly half of the U.S. population will consist of racial and ethnic minorities by 2050, about one-fourth of whom will be Latino. Yet, in contrast to the growing diversity of our nation's population, our healthcare industry is not nearly as diverse. While African Americans, Hispanic Americans, and Native Americans represented more than 31 percent of the U.S. population in 2010, less than 9 percent of nurses, 6 percent of physicians, and 5 percent of dentists are from these populations according to the latest figures available, (IOM). Coupled with this problem of under-representation is the fact that minority groups have less access to healthcare and receive poorer quality healthcare than today's population at large. Most minority communities are more likely to have family incomes less than 200% of the federal poverty level than whites and less access to culturally sensitive healthcare. Studies have clearly shown that minority physicians are more likely to treat minority and indigent patients and to practice in underserved communities.

Contributing to our nation's growing health disparities is ineffective cultural competency education within the environments of both medical training and patient care. While racial and ethnic diversity contribute to the educational experiences of all health professional students, broadening perspectives and increasing cognitive outcomes for all groups, challenges to building a critical mass of underrepresented racial and ethnic students remain as Affirmative Action programs are increasingly under assault.

To achieve equity in healthcare, a variety of educational initiatives are nonetheless under way, sponsored by private foundations, professional associations, government, and educational institutions. The Federal Government's Title VII authorizes the health professions education and training programs administered by the Health Resources and Services Administration (HRSA). These programs support the education and training of the full range of all healthcare providers, including physicians, dentists, pharmacists, nurses, psychologists, and public and allied health professionals in education and training through loans, loan guarantees, and scholarships to students, and grants and contracts to academic institutions and nonprofit organizations. Designed to improve the supply, diversity, and distribution of the health care workforce, Title VII diversity programs increase minority representation in the health professions by strengthening the pipeline to a health career. Similarly, the primary care medicine and dentistry programs expand the primary care workforce, while the interdisciplinary, community-based linkage programs facilitate training in rural and urban underserved areas. Together with Title VIII nursing education programs, health professions programs are a critical component of the health care safety net, training a diverse supply of health professionals who are more likely to serve in community health centers and other rural and urban underserved settings.

One of the most visible of the HRSA programs is your state Area Health Education Centers (AHEC). Approximately 120 medical schools and 600 nursing and allied health schools work collaboratively with AHEC's to improve health

for underserved and underrepresented populations. The best way to find out where the closest AHEC office is to your school is to go to the National AHEC Organization website, www.nationalahec.org, and click on the Directories and Maps tab at the top of the page. While not all AHEC's do the same things, they generally support health professions students and health and community development. To implement their goals, they target economically disadvantaged students and those from underrepresented backgrounds for programs such as summer health careers camps, summer institutes, and cultural immersion programs, among many others.

These organizations realize that to reduce healthcare disparities while promoting compassionate and culturally competent care, diverse healthcare professionals are needed in the educational pipeline. LGBT (lesbian, gay, bisexual, transgendered) people represent a minority of the U.S. population who are also underserved. Expanding the ranks of LGBT practitioners is essential, for all too often, identification invokes stigma and prejudice in healthcare settings. More "out" medical professionals are needed to increase visibility of LGBT health issues in an effort to foster more comfortable and effective treatment of LGBT patients as well as increase awareness throughout the medical community. Sexual orientation is virtually overlooked in population-based national health surveys and among those that do, funding requests for federal support have mostly been denied.

RESOURCES

Building a Support System

Those involved in admissions know that having a support system is a key element in ultimate success. Seek advice routinely from your health professions advisor, as well as other advisors and mentors on your campus. These individuals may be located in academic and advising departments, administrative units, scholarship programs, or multicultural affairs offices. While they may not have comprehensive knowledge of the preparation process for entry into a health profession, they can play a vital role by guiding you toward good resources and helping you clarify your goals. Also, be sure to take advantage of academic support personnel offering assistance through tutorials, learning centers, and academic departments. And do not forget to visit members of the faculty during office hours to discuss your choice of courses and other academic projects. Since you will need faculty letters of recommendation, share your perspectives and understanding of course material with them on a one-to-one basis. Faculty may also be instrumental in helping you to find research opportunities and to explore your academic strengths. Student organizations offer outstanding opportunities to glean information on health careers, volunteer opportunities, and campus visits. They can help to connect you with others who share your dreams and can support you with study circles. Some may focus on minority or multicultural issues; others may be of general interest. Do not become disconnected! Make sure that you have a healthy cadre of students among whom you may develop leadership skills while learning more about support services.

Websites and Publications

Publications of interest to minority students are often available in your health professions advisor's office. Sections of publications noted elsewhere in this book, and in publications such as the AAMC's *Medical School Admission Requirements* (MSAR), provide valuable information and resources for minority candidates. Another valuable AAMC resource is www.AspiringDocs.org. AspiringDocs.org is both "a web site and an outreach effort to provide undergraduate minority students with the support, information, and guidance they need to apply to and enroll in medical school." It is a resource designed to connect you with other students and with the resources you need everything from summer program opportunities to the latest information on the medical school application process. The site includes a "tool kit" for doing outreach to minority communities, to "encourage more well-prepared African American, Hispanic/Latino, and Native American students to pursue careers in medicine." It might also be worth your while to see if your advisor has a copy of the AAMC book called *Diversity in the Physician Workforce: Facts & Figures*. This publication provides a complete, quite detailed overview of demographic characteristics of doctors who graduated from allopathic medical schools over a thirty year period, 1978-2008. As for osteopathic medicine, D.O. schools have long been committed to promoting diversity in medical school classes. Look for information about osteopathic medicine and the application process on www.aacom.org.

The American Dental Education Association biennially publishes *Opportunities for Minority Students in United States Dental Schools*. Copies of this book are mailed to health professions advisors at colleges and universities. If your college does not have a copy, you can order one. Visit the ADEA website at www.adea.org or call (202) 289-7201. The cost is $10.00. You will find this book has facts, descriptions of clinical specialties, and a listing of special outreach programs.

Another valuable website is www.ExploreHealthCareers.org, which offers a wealth of information about all health professions, summer internships particularly geared to disadvantaged students, and many other resources. This is a comprehensive and easy-to-use site.

The NAAHP website, at www.naaahp.org, has a section on diversity that offers information on a wide range of health professions and their efforts in this arena. Websites and publications for the different health professional organizations frequently list persons who coordinate minority recruitment programs. These officials are good sources of information and support. They frequently sponsor open houses or advising sessions at their schools or on college campuses that you should attend. Contact them to be placed on mailing lists to receive up-to-date information and guidance, as well as feedback on the progress of your preparation or status of your application.

Check the "Resources" section at the end of this chapter, as well as the Appendices in this book for a more complete list of publications and websites. Many of them have specific sections geared toward minority students.

Resources for Enrichment and Research

A valuable source of guidance and support may be found in a wide variety of enrichment programs located either on your campus or at various health professional schools. At some colleges, there are programs to introduce minority and/or disadvantaged students to recruitment, research and clinical opportunities. Professional schools often have a Diversity or Minority Affairs office which sponsors summer programs, conferences, research opportunities, mentoring etc. They may maintain a mailing list of prospective students and this allows students to "get on their radar" for future opportunities. These programs offer many advantages to those who participate by providing guidance and support plus the important opportunity to test your interests and capabilities for a career in that field. As all health professional schools desire to see evidence of firm and clear motivation to serve in the field, these opportunities to explore your intended field should be pursued eagerly.

A number of summer enhancement programs are offered to minority/disadvantaged students by health professions schools. Visit AspiringDocs.org or ExploreHealthCareers.org for lists of various programs. These summer programs include varying combinations of research, clinical experiences, entrance test preparation, academic review, and study skills development. Since they are held at the health professions schools, participation can provide you with a good understanding of the life of students and practitioners in those health professions. Those who take part often return to their campuses with renewed focus, enhanced skill, and a better understanding of what lies ahead in their pursuit of a career in a health profession. Ask your health professions advisor or minority contact person at health professional schools for details on these programs and for information on applications. Some of the publications and websites mentioned in this book provide listings of such programs. Among them is the Summer Medical and Dental Education Programs (SMDEP), a free six-week academic enrichment program for freshmen and sophomores with activities including science and mathematics, career development, clinical experiences, financial planning and study skills seminars. It is important to remember that applications for some summer programs are due as early as

December, with many other deadlines in January and February. Recommendation letters and essays are often needed for these programs, so plan ahead to meet application requirements.

For pre-dental students, the American Dental Association has a mentoring program called the Student Ambassador Program, through which dental students organize programming and serve as vital contacts for current and potential pre-dental students, hoping to recruit more under-represented students into the dental profession. Details about the Student Ambassador Program can be found at www.ada.org and also on the diversity section of www.naahp.org. The program works closely with the NAAHP, so students will also want to talk to their advisor about this program.

Postbaccalaureate Programs

A number of people decide that they want to enter a health profession late in their college careers, or take a detour in their science coursework. For that reason many schools offer programs that are called "postbaccalaureate" ("postbac" for short), through which students can complete the courses they lack for entrance into a health professions school after they have earned their bachelor's degrees. See more on Chapter 1.

Other postbac programs may offer opportunities for students who have already taken all their pre-health required science courses to improve their academic records by taking additional courses and thus become more academically competitive for admission. A few programs are intended for minority students, but most are open to all students. If a postbac program interests you, discuss your options with an advisor. Most often, those hoping to improve their academic records need to show strength in science courses. Carefully assess your potential and motivation to significantly improve your grades. As with every step in the preparation process, thoughtful self-assessment and appropriate responses will increase the chances for success. Consult with those experienced in minority admissions matters to gain additional insight into ways to enhance your application. Frequently, applicants do not take the appropriate steps to improve their credentials. If the science grade point average needs improvement, only additional course work in the natural sciences is appropriate; more volunteer work or a job will not help when you need to remedy a grade deficiency. You need to take the appropriate action to make yourself more competitive. See more on this in Chapter 3.

A FEW NOTES ON THE APPLICATION PROCESS

Minority Status

Some health professions applications offer candidates opportunities to identify themselves as minorities on the basis of race, ethnicity, and/or disadvantaged status. Moreover, some applications invite applicants to write a short statement on diversity. Make sure you take the time to complete these short essays thoughtfully. Additionally, self-identification may well result in opportunities to provide additional information on your background, including the characteristics of home and community, demonstrated interest in your community, financial status, or other special circumstances. It is important to respond to such questions carefully so that the schools will gain a clear picture of you and any obstacles or special challenges encountered, especially those that you have overcome. This information will provide them with insight on how you will respond to the demands of a health professions school. School officials want to be sure that all accepted applicants have the drive, determination, and support they need to successfully complete their academic program.

Selecting Schools

School selection is important. The admissions process is subjective and somewhat unpredictable. Yet, with good information, careful thought, and informed advice, you can significantly increase your chances for success. By carefully

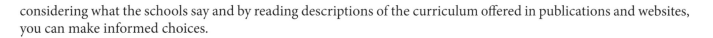

considering what the schools say and by reading descriptions of the curriculum offered in publications and websites, you can make informed choices.

In most cases, public schools give preference to state residents. Yet, public schools will often accept highly qualified out-of-state underrepresented minorities. Private schools normally have no state preferences. If you are applying to medical schools, reading the Medical School Admission Requirements (MSAR) and the College Information Book for osteopathic medical schools, and similar official publications for other health professional schools, you can increase your chances for a successful application.

Information on minority enrollment in each school is often available. For example, see the *MSAR* or the *ADEA Official Guide to Dental Schools.* However, remember that such figures do not reflect how many minority students were accepted--just how many enrolled. Attempt to determine your "fit" at the various schools through pre-application visits, interview trips, and contact with the schools, including members of minority student groups and minority contact officials. Many organizations such as the AAMC, the ADEA and the ASPH (described elsewhere in this book) hold large student fairs in the city where they are holding their annual conference. This can be an excellent opportunity to meet many school representatives in one place.

Your advisor can also help. S/he may be able to provide you with information on the profile of applicants who are from underrepresented groups on your campus who have been accepted at various health professions schools, or a composite sketch of the "successful applicant." Take this advice into consideration but remember that there are few absolutes in the admissions process. Most advisors recommend applying to a range of schools and not just to "places I dream of attending." A realistic variety of choices, again resulting from a careful self-assessment and review of the schools' admission policies, will be helpful in obtaining success.

Financial Aid

The cost of applying to and attending a health professions school is a concern for all applicants. Be sure to review the financial aid section of this book and to consult references to locate sources of financial aid.

If you have extreme financial limitations, you might be able to receive fee reductions or waivers for required admissions tests and the applications themselves. For medical school applications, information and application materials about the Fee Assistance Program (FAP) are available at www.aamc.org/students/amcas/fap.htm. By receiving an AMCAS fee waiver, you not only reduce the cost of the initial application, but also may be able to obtain a waiver of the fee for the secondary application. Be sure to ask for fee waivers early in the process, as time-consuming documentation will likely be required. Also consult minority contact officials at the health professions schools for information on fee waivers, as well as special sources of financial aid for minority students. At some schools it is possible to obtain a fee waiver just by requesting it. Some professional schools also have funds to help competitive applicants defray the costs of traveling to interviews; and some schools have scholarships for minorities, especially highly competitive candidates eager to help underserved populations.

Most schools will automatically consider you for their various scholarships based on your financial aid application. Some schools may require you to send a separate application for each individual scholarship. When applying for the scholarship, check the background of the person whose name the scholarship is set up for and the reason it exists. This will help you with the appropriate tone of your application/essay for the scholarship. Talk with your advisor and/ or the admissions staff at the schools to which you have been invited for interviews for more information.

Since 1946, National Medical Fellowships, Inc. (NMF) has helped to improve the health of low-income and minority communities by increasing the representation of minority physicians, educators, researchers, policymakers, and health care administrators in the U.S. training minority medical students to address the special needs of their communities;

and educating the public and policymakers to health problems and needs of the underserved populations. This non-profit organization has awarded more than $39 million to over 28,000 participants, each demonstrating financial need.

Lastly, scholarships for Disadvantaged Students (SDS) are federal need-based scholarships based on exceptional financial need as determined by parents' income and assets, even if the applicant is an independent student. The applicant must come from a disadvantaged background, based upon family income or environment. The amount and the number of awards are based on the allocation of funds from the federal government. Contact individual schools regarding application process. For more information about the scholarships themselves go to bhpr.hrsa.gov/DSA/sds.htm. The federal government also has a loan program for disadvantaged students (LDS) with information at bhpr.hrsa.gov/dsa/lds.htm.

See Chapter 3, "After the Application," for more complete information on financing your education including information on loan repayment programs.]

Some Final Words of Advice

Society at large will be better served when disadvantaged low-income, minority, LGBT, and non-English speaking populations are fully integrated into a diverse pool of health professionals, helping to make healthcare equally accessible to all. It is important for students to be aware of the people, resources and projects working to diversify the medical community by recruiting, educating, and supporting minorities of various backgrounds. We encourage you to pursue solid information by speaking with advisors, admissions representatives, practitioners, and professional organizations. Research information online and attend meetings of student organizations that will help you on your journey to self-growth. And use every available opportunity to gain biomedical research and clinical experiences, networking skills and, above all, scholarly attainment in all areas of intellectual pursuit.

Selected Web-Based Sources of Information for Minority/Disadvantaged Students

1. www.aspiringdocs.org, a website sponsored by the Association of American Medical Colleges (AAMC).

2. www.aacom.org, the website for the American Association of Colleges of Osteopathic Medicine.

3. www.explorehealthcareers.com, a comprehensive website on the health professions including career descriptions, summer listings and articles of interest.

4. www.nationalahec.org, the website for the national Area Health Education Centers (AHEC).

5. Joint Admission Medical Program (JAMP), www.utsystem.edu/jamp, an initiative by the Texas legislature aimed at providing opportunities for highly qualified, economically disadvantaged undergraduate students who want to pursue medical education.

6. National Network of Latin American Medical Students (NNLAMS),www.nnlsms.com.

7. Latino Medical Student Association (LMSA), www.lmsa.net.

8. National Medical Fellowships, Inc., 5 Hanover Square, 15th Floor, New York, NY 10004; 212/483-8880; 212/483-8897; info@nmfonline.org; www.nmf-online.org.

9. *Opportunities for Minority Students in United States Dental Schools*, published by the American Dental Education Association, 202/289-7201; www.adea.org.

10. The Point Foundation is the nation's largest scholarship-granting organization for Lesbian, Gay, Bisexual, and Transgender (LGBT) students of merit. For medical students, Point Foundation offers the Gay and Lesbian Medical Association (GLMA) Point Scholarship and the Decker Scholarship. www.amsa.org/lgbt/scholarships. cfm. glma.org.

11. American Medical Student Association, www.amsa.org. This site includes, among other things, very helpful information for LGBT students interested in entering the medical field.

12. Student National Medical Association (SNMA), 5113 Georgia Avenue, NW, Washington, D.C., 2011; 202/882-2881; www.snma.org.

13. The Summer Medical and Dental Education Program (SMDEP), www.smdep.org.

Selected Health Professions

ACUPUNCTURE AND ORIENTAL MEDICINE

General Description of the Profession

Acupuncture and Oriental medicine (AOM) is an ancient and empirical system of medicine based on the concept of *qi* (pronounced "chee"), which is usually translated as bio-electric energy, and which travels along designated meridian pathways in the body. AOM treatments identify a pattern of energetic imbalance or blockage within a patient and redress that disharmony in a variety of ways. Any or all of the following methods may be used in AOM practice: acupuncture needling, cupping, acupressure, exercises such as *tai ji quan* and *qi gong*, as well as Chinese herbal preparations and nutritional recommendations. AOM is a medicine that considers the whole person and tailors specific treatment for each person's patterns of disharmony. Patients are viewed from a holistic perspective, taking into account their physical, mental, and emotional health. Thus, practitioners spend time developing a collaborative relationship with their patients, assisting them in maintaining their health and promoting a consciousness of wellness.

Although the history of acupuncture and Oriental medicine (AOM) extends over a period of 3,000 years, its practice in the U.S before the 1970s was first confined within Asian communities associated with work on the transcontinental railroad in the 1840s. A resurgence of interest occurred in the 1970s following the publication of an article by columnist James Reston in the *New York Times* newspaper. Reston extolled the benefits he received from acupuncture anesthesia for an appendectomy in China when President Nixon made his historic visit to that country in 1971. Today the AOM profession boasts numerous national organizations, over 50 colleges and programs offering the highest level of training in the field, some 25,000 practitioners, significant research interest by the conventional western medical community, and increasing integration of AOM practitioners into conventional medical settings.

The AOM profession is highly organized in the U.S. with a national accrediting body recognized by the U.S. Department of Education (Accreditation Commission for Acupuncture & Oriental Medicine — ACAOM), a national certifying body accredited by the Institute for Credentialing Excellence (National Certification Commission for Acupuncture & Oriental Medicine — NCCAOM), a national professional association for practitioners (American Association of Acupuncture & Oriental Medicine — AAAOM), and a national membership association for AOM colleges and programs (Council of Colleges of Acupuncture & Oriental Medicine — CCAOM). Each of the foregoing organizations was established in 1982 when the AOM profession made a concerted effort to build credible organizations for the profession in the U.S. In addition, the profession has other organizations variously dedicated to AOM research (Society for Acupuncture Research — SAR), disaster and emergency relief (Acupuncturists Without Borders — AWB), addictions treatment (National Acupuncture Detoxification Association — NADA), state legislative and regulatory initiatives (Council of State Associations – CSA), Asian bodywork therapies (American Organization for the Bodywork Therapies of Asia — AOBTA), and botanical studies for Oriental medicine (High Falls Foundation — HFF). Beginning in 2005, a number of these national organizations have been meeting annually at the invitation of CCAOM to discuss issues of common interest to the AOM profession and to explore collaborative opportunities. The most recent meeting was held on March 2, 2013, and was attended by AAAOM, ACAOM, AOBTA, CCAOM, CSA, NCCAOM, NFCTCMO (National Federation of Chinese Traditional Chinese Medicine Organizations, and SAR.

AOM Colleges

For AOM practitioners educated in the U.S., the most comprehensive training available is that provided at an institution that has been accredited by ACAOM, the national accrediting agency for the profession. A comprehensively trained acupuncturist receives between 1,500 to 2,600 hours of training specifically in acupuncture as part of an AOM educational curriculum that typically exceeds 3,000 overall hours of training. ACAOM's accreditation standards require a minimum of 450 hours (which range up to 700 hours in some colleges) in biomedical clinical sciences and training, which includes appropriate referral to another medical provider in certain cases. Some state laws address appropriate referral, but in general AOM practitioners determine the appropriateness of medical referral to another provider. Most patients self-refer for acupuncture and a few states require a medical referral for a patient to see an acupuncturist.

There are currently 51 AOM colleges in the Council of Colleges of Acupuncture and Oriental Medicine (CCAOM), which since 1982 has been the national membership association for ACAOM-approved programs in the U.S. These colleges are located in 20 states, with some institutions having branch campuses in the same or other states. The mission of CCAOM is to advance AOM by promoting educational excellence in the field. Membership eligibility in CCAOM requires a college to have obtained either accreditation or accreditation candidacy status with ACAOM. A map showing the location and contact information for all CCAOM member colleges may be viewed at www.ccaom.org. The most recent data indicates that approximately 8000 students are currently enrolled in AOM programs in the U.S.

AOM colleges offer students opportunities to participate in off-site clinics in communities where the colleges are located. Practitioners of AOM in the U.S. are actively involved in bringing services to a broad cross-section of the American public. These services may be provided in multidisciplinary clinical settings that reflect the growing trend toward integrated healthcare delivery involving conventional medical, AOM, and other providers of complementary and alternative medicine (CAM). There are over 100 off-site healthcare clinics in local communities throughout the U.S. in which the Council's member colleges participate, thus reflecting the AOM profession's commitment to public service to diverse patient populations, as well as the extent of public acceptance of and need for acupuncture services. The types of integrated community settings where the Council's member colleges are active include:

- hospitals
- urgent care centers
- multi-specialty centers
- research-based centers
- end-of-life palliative care centers
- long and short-term rehabilitation centers
- family practice clinics
- nursing homes
- out-patient geriatric/assisted living centers for seniors
- drug treatment centers
- HIV/AIDS treatment facilities
- pediatric, cancer, and other specialty care centers
- clinics for specific community groups, e.g. women's health and inner city/low income/multi-racial groups
- sports medicine clinics

State Licensure

Beginning with the enactment of the first acupuncture practice acts in the U.S. in 1973, states have responded to public demand for acupuncture services by adopting statutes and regulations for the profession. Today some 44 states and the District of Columbia have enacted practice act legislation for the AOM profession and legislative efforts to obtain practice rights are underway in the remaining states.

The scope of practice for AOM varies among the states. State practice acts often define acupuncture as the stimulation of certain points on or near the surface of the human body by the insertion of needles to prevent or modify the perception of pain, to normalize physiological functions, or to treat certain diseases or dysfunctions of the body. Some state statutes reference the *energetic* aspect of acupuncture, its usefulness in controlling and regulating the flow and balance of *qi* in the body, and its ability to normalize energetic physiological function. Acupuncture may also be defined in the statutes by reference to traditional or modern Chinese or Oriental medical concepts or to modern techniques of diagnostic evaluation.

Depending on the state law, AOM practitioners may be authorized to employ a wide variety of AOM therapies such as needling, moxibustion, cupping, electroacupuncture, Oriental or therapeutic bodywork, therapeutic exercise and meditation, acupressure, dietary recommendations, herbal therapy, injection and laser therapy, ion cord devices, magnets, *qi gong*, and massage. Within applicable limitations specified by the law, the treatment of animals, the ordering of western diagnostic tests, and the use of homeopathy may also be within the scope of practice for AOM in some states.

Licensure is the most common form of state authorization to practice AOM. In most states, practitioners have independent status. In a few states, practitioners may be subject to some supervision or prior referral by an MD. The most common designation for a comprehensively trained AOM practitioner is "Licensed Acupuncturist (LAc)," with some states conferring the licensing title of "Doctor of Oriental Medicine" or "Acupuncture Physician." Although the nature of the administrative body that oversees the practice of AOM in the states is not uniform, the most common structures are those of an independent board of acupuncture composed of professional acupuncturists, or an acupuncture advisory body under the oversight of a state medical board.

Outlook for the Future

The future of AOM is bright with great opportunity for graduates in this field, particularly with increased recognition by the general public and conventional medical practitioners of dimensions of health care that lie beyond the physical nature of a person and the related focus on well-being through the application of holistic perspectives and therapies. AOM also addresses the energetic causes of disease and imbalance, using natural holistic means and safe and effective therapies to bring about healing. Increasingly, AOM practitioners are making important contributions in integrated health care settings involving physicians and other practitioners of complementary and alternative medicine. With continuing research interest in AOM, coupled with consistent favorable patient outcomes, this ancient form of treatment is well-suited for persons who seek a career in a health profession that embodies a holistic ideal and for patients who seek a safe and effective means of care.

An AOM practitioner can create a financially supportive career that is rewarding and fulfilling, with a flexible work schedule that allows for a balanced life style. The practice settings in which AOM practitioners can work include an independent private practice, a multi-disciplinary clinic with other health care professionals, or a hospital. Other career options include teaching, translating, publishing, research, or working with an herb or acupuncture supply company. AOM practitioners also work in the following settings: cruise line ships; spas and fitness clubs or resorts; substance abuse treatment facilities; hospice, elder care, nursing, and long-term care facilities; oncology centers; community acupuncture clinics, military/veterans facilities, sports teams, and corporate wellness programs.

There are approximately 25,000 AOM licensees throughout the United States. A recent estimate, based on employment listings, reports an annual income range of $30,000-$60,000 and notes that gross annual income can be as much as $115,000. Acupuncturists who work in hospitals reportedly make over $75,000 annually, while those who work for non-profit organizations make under $30,000 annually. *Chronicle Guidance Brief* 249 (2012)[Acupuncturists].

Variables affecting income may include the nature of the acupuncturist's practice, geographic location, and personal factors such as the ability of the practitioner to relate well to patients, professional demeanor, and marketing savvy. California, New York, and Florida have the most AOM practitioners, but there are a significant number of practitioners in other states.

Planning a Program of Study

ACAOM's minimum requirements for admission into an AOM college include satisfactory completion of at least two (2) academic years (60 semester credits/90 quarter credits) of education at the baccalaureate level that is appropriate preparation for graduate level work, or the equivalent (e.g., certification in a medical profession requiring at least the equivalent training of a registered nurse or a physician assistant), from an institution accredited by an agency recognized by the U.S. Department of Education. Many AOM colleges exceed this minimum standard and require a Bachelor's Degree for admission. Prospective students should inquire directly about admissions requirements with an AOM program of interest and may also refer to the full text of Standard 6 in ACAOM's *Accreditation Handbook* at www.acaom.org/documents/accreditation_manual_712.pdf, which contains additional standards concerning assessment of prior learning, transfer credit, advanced standing, and English language competence.

In the U.S., ACAOM-approved AOM colleges offer the highest level of training in this medicine. The length of training at most AOM colleges is approximately three (3) to four (4) years for acupuncture and four (4) years for Oriental medicine programs. The latter type of program includes the study of both acupuncture and Chinese herbal medicine.

Currently the Master's Degree, available in either Acupuncture or in Oriental Medicine, is the entry-level standard for professional AOM practice in the U.S. There is also post-graduate clinical training through the Doctorate of Acupuncture and Oriental Medicine Degree (DAOM) degree. Training at either level is available at colleges that ACAOM has approved to offer these degrees, with a minimum of 1200 hours of advanced AOM training required at the doctoral level. Institutions offering the DAOM degree provide students with an opportunity for specialization within the AOM field. Some of the specialty areas that exist in these doctoral programs include geriatrics and aging disorders, women's health, oncology, pain management, and fertility. A list of ACAOM-approved colleges that offer the DAOM degree may be viewed at www.acaom.org/find-a-school/. Most recently, ACAOM has approved standards for a first-professional doctoral degree in acupuncture and/or Oriental medicine and is currently accepting applications from those AOM programs it has accredited that wish to offer this new degree.

Admissions Process

While each AOM college specifies its own admissions procedure, AOM colleges generally focus more broadly beyond just admitting academically well-qualified students. Equally or more important is finding individuals who possess the capacity for open-mindedness and compassionate care-giving based on the recognition that the relationship between a patient and the health care provider is crucial to the healing process. Thus, most AOM colleges use a holistic admissions process, giving greater weight to the complete picture that a student presents, rather than looking at GPA or standardized test scores alone.

Prospective students may access the websites of AOM colleges from the CCAOM website (www.ccaom.org), view catalogues from colleges of interest, and compare programs at various institutions. It is highly recommended that prospective students personally visit a college to talk to administrators, faculty, current students, and graduates to gain insight into the unique emphasis and general atmosphere of a program. For example, there is significant diversity among AOM schools in the U.S., with representation for the traditional and classical Chinese traditions, Japanese traditions, Five Element traditions including Worsley practice, Korean traditions, and Vietnamese traditions.

ACAOM is the only national organization recognized by the U.S. Department of Education for the accreditation of

AOM schools and programs in the U.S. It is important for students to attend an AOM college that is accredited or has achieved accreditation candidacy status with ACAOM, whose standards the highest level of AOM institutional or programmatic quality assurance available in the U.S. today. Graduation from an ACAOM candidate or accredited school is a pre-requisite for taking the national certification exams in this field offered by the National Certification Commission for Acupuncture and Oriental Medicine (www.nccaom.org). A list of ACAOM's candidate and accredited schools may be viewed at www.acaom.org/find-a-school/.

Resources

1. The Council of Colleges of Acupuncture and Oriental Medicine's website (www.ccaom.org) has specific information for both advisors and students, school locator information, and general information about the AOM profession in the U.S.

2. ACAOM's *Accreditation Manual* may be viewed at www.acaom.org/documents/accreditation_manual_712.pdf and information about specific AOM schools is also available at www.acaom.org/find-a-school/.

3. NCCAOM's website (www.nccaom.org) has information concerning various national certification exams in AOM and other information to assist practitioners in their practices.

4. For information concerning AOM research, see the website of SAR at www.acupunctureresearch.org.

5. The national professional association for AOM is AAAOM, whose website is at www.aaaomonline.org.

6. For information about the role of acupuncture in disaster relief and emergency situations, see the website of Acupuncturists Without Borders at www.acuwithoutborders.org/.

 *Chapter 5*

General Description of Profession

Audiologists evaluate, diagnose, treat, and manage individuals of all ages who have hearing, balance and related ear disorders. Hearing and balance disorders can result from a variety of causes, including problems during pregnancy or birth, trauma, viral infections, genetic disorders, exposure to loud noise, aging, among other a variety of causes. If untreated, a hearing or balance disorder can affect social life, education, and livelihood. People who cannot hear have difficulty in communicating effectively with others and those with balance disorders may have difficulty engaging in everyday activities. Loss of hearing can also negatively affect the development of language, speech and in some instances comprehension. A hearing or balance disorder left uncorrected can seriously impact one's quality of life.

In testing for hearing loss, audiologists use complex and sophisticated electronic equipment. They use audiometers, computers, and other devices that facilitate the measurement of hearing loss.. They use audiometers to measure the softest intensity at which a person hears sounds and a person's ability to distinguish between sounds at those frequencies important for communication, including the recognition of speech sounds, to help determine the nature and extent of a person's hearing loss or other auditory disorders. The audiologic evaluation may include examining and cleaning the ear canal. Audiologists perform advanced evaluations which include measurement brainstem and central auditory function. Some audiologists who work in hospitals and medical centers perform monitoring of nerve functioning in the operating room ("intraoperative monitoring") to help surgeons preserve nerve functioning in patients who are at risk for nerve injury during surgery. For persons with balance problems, audiologists may assess the integrity of the vestibular (balance) mechanism.

Audiologists interpret the test results and coordinate them with medical, educational, and psychological information to make a diagnosis and determine a course of treatment. When hearing loss or balance disorders have a cause (such as infection) requiring medical or surgical management, audiologists refer their patients to an appropriate physician. For this reason, audiologists often work directly with otologists or otolaryngologists.

Audiologists then plan and carry out audiologic treatment programs to help their patients optimize residual hearing and to prevent further hearing loss when possible. They also provide non-medical vestibular treatment services to individuals with dizziness and balance problems.

As part of the treatment plan, audiologists may recommend, fit, and dispense personal amplification devices, such as traditional hearing aids, bone anchored hearing aids and other hearing assistive technology. Audiologists conduct tests to determine whether a hearing aid or other technology will help the individual's communication disorder. Audiologists are also an integral part of the cochlear implant team. They evaluated patient for cochlear implant candidacy and are responsible for programing of the cochlear implant(s) following surgery. Audiologists program the devices (both hearing aids and cochlear implants), teach the patients how to use and maintain the devices, dispense the devices, and provide any needed follow-up to ensure successful use of the devices. Audiologists may also consider large area amplification systems, such as FM and infrared looping systems and alerting devices in the overall audiologic treatment plan for their patients and for the benefit of the community at large. Audiologists also develop audiologic rehabilitative programs to help the patient optimize hearing performance with the hearing aid.

An important part of an audiologist's work in audiologic rehabilitation is counseling individuals on strategies they can use to adjust to and cope with a hearing or balance disorder because of the impact these disorders can have on a person's daily life. Counseling also includes discussion regarding the importance of hearing protection throughout the lifespan.Audiologists teach their patients communication strategies for use in a variety of environments and techniques for coping with the stress and misunderstandings that may arise. Audiologists also engage with family members to help them recognize and change negative behavior patterns that can impede communication with the person.

Audiologists, particularly educational audiologists, also conduct and oversee hearing screenings in public schools to identify children with hearing loss and help manage educational problems that may result from an auditory disorder. Because audiologists are the preferred hearing healthcare providers, teachers, parents, physicians, and nurses refer children to an audiologist to determine if a hearing loss exists and the extent of the loss. Working with speech language pathologists and classroom teachers, audiologists develop individual or group audiologic rehabilitation programs, counsel parents and teachers, and address classroom acoustics to improve the listening and learning environment, and provide instruction in listening and communication strategies for students with hearing loss or auditory processing disorders. In order to meet a child's needs, audiologists often confer with parents, speech-language pathologists, health professionals, teachers, and school administrators. They assist in the development of individualized education and family service plans for these children.

In the United States, most children undergo a newborn hearing screening prior to discharge from the hospital. Audiologists screen and evaluate hearing in these newborns and infants. They may examine all newborns or infants at risk of hearing loss because of different causes, such as a family history of hearing loss, or whose mothers had an infection early in pregnancy or who were born prematurely. If a child is identified with hearing loss, they will recommend and fit appropriate amplification and recommend appropriate services such as speech-language pathology.

Some audiologists measure noise levels in work places and conduct hearing protection programs in factories and other industrial settings and also in schools and community settings. They may serve as consultants and expert witnesses in cases about hearing loss occurring from exposure to noise in the workplace and other matters.

In addition to their clinical work, audiologists maintain records on the evaluation, progress, and discharge of patients. Thorough record keeping is important in evaluating the effectiveness of treatment and hearing stability.

Practice Sites

There are over 16,000 audiologists in practice in the United States. About half are employed in health care facilities, such as in offices of audiologists or physicians, and in hospitals, clinics, and outpatient care centers.

About a third of audiologists, are starting or joining private practices. Those in private practice must manage the business aspects of running an office, such as developing a patient base, hiring employees, ordering equipment and supplies, finances, and bookkeeping in addition to providing clinical audiologic care of their patients. Audiologists in private practice may provide hearing healthcare services in their own offices, work under contract for schools, healthcare facilities, or other establishments, or provide consulting services.

Audiologists also have a role in the advancement and future practice of audiology. They may teach audiology students in didactic and clinical settings as well as medical students, residents and others in colleges and universities. They may conduct basic or applied research on the causes and treatment of hearing, balance, and related disorders. They may work with speech language pathologists, medical specialists, educators, engineers, scientists, and other professionals to design and develop diagnostic, corrective, and assistive devices and techniques for use with persons who have hearing and balance disorders. Some audiologists work with manufacturers on the design, development and research of hearing aids, cochlear implants and diagnostic equipment.

Audiologists also work in the military service branches and others in elementary and secondary schools. Other practice sites include hearing conservation programs and federal, state, and local government agencies.

In audiology clinics, audiologists independently develop and carry out diagnostic and treatment programs. In some settings, audiologists work with other health and education providers as part of a team in planning and implementing services for children and adults. Audiologists who diagnose and treat balance disorders often work in collabora-

tion with physicians, particularly otologists and otolaryngologists, physical therapists, and occupational therapists. Audiologists may work with a variety of other individuals in the care of their patients and in research, including acoustical engineers, educators, industrial hygienists, nurses, psychologists, safety engineers, special educators, and speech-language pathologists, among others.

The Decision to Pursue Audiology

People who choose audiology must be good listeners and good speakers. Audiologists must be able to establish a rapport with patients and their families. They should be able to explain test results, diagnoses, and proposed treatments so that the patients understand them. They must approach problems objectively and provide support to patients and their families. Patience and compassion are also important because the rehabilitative process may be lengthy depending on the severity of a patient's hearing or balance disorder, medical conditions, related health and psychosocial factors, and numerous other factors. The attributes of patience and compassion are also important in meeting the emotional needs of patients, their families and caregivers during the diagnosis, treatment, and rehabilitative processes.

Outlook for the Future

The employment outlook for audiologists is good. The Bureau of Labor Statistics predicts employment for audiologists to grow about as fast as the average for all occupations through the year 2016. The popular press, such as Kiplinger and US News & World Report, has noticed as well, identifying audiology as a top career and a growing profession. Various factors have contributed to this anticipated growth. According to the National Institute of Deafness and Communication Disorders, approximately 17% (36 million) American adults have some degree of hearing loss and 2 to 3 out of every 1,000 children in the United States are born deaf or hard-of-hearing. Hearing loss is strongly associated with aging, with nearly one of every three people over age sixty five having a hearing problem. Many elderly people also have balance problems. The rapid growth of an aging population will notably increase the number of persons with a hearing and balance problems.

Medical advances are increasing the survival rate of accident and stroke victims, and also of premature infants, who then need assessment and possible treatment. Greater awareness of the importance of early identification, diagnosis, and treatment of hearing loss in infants and young children also will increase the need for audiologic services.

Federal laws dictate that children with disabilities receive special education and related services, which will continue to increase the need for audiologic services in the schools. Audiologists are also needed to manage and direct hearing conservation programs.

For audiologists interested in private practice, the outlook is especially promising. The number of audiologists in private practice is predicted to rise due to the increasing demand for direct services to individuals, as well as increasing use of contract services by hospitals, schools, and nursing care facilities.

Compensation varies with education, experience, responsibilities, locale, and hours worked. According to the Bureau of Labor Statistics (May 2010), the median annual wages of audiologists were $66,660. The highest 10 percent earned more than $102,210.

Planning a Program of Study

Students can choose to pursue the clinical Doctor of Audiology (AuD) degree or those interested in research may pursue a Doctor of Philosophy degree (PhD). Requirements for admission to an AuD program typically include undergraduate courses in biology, chemistry, communication, English, mathematics, physics, and psychology among others. In addition, a standardized test, most typically the GRE is required. Doctoral course work in audiology typically includes anatomy and physiology, auditory and vestibular (balance) assessment and treatment, business, diagnostics and rehabilitation, electrophysiology, pediatrics, geriatrics, ethics and other professional issues, genetics, normal and abnormal communication development, pharmacology, practice management, among others.

The AuD degree requires approximately three-four years of graduate university education after the bachelor's degree. The AuD degree program includes numerous clinical practicum experiences throughout the program and a full-time, year-long, supervised professional clinical externship during the final year.

Students who are interested in a career in audiologic research may pursue a Doctor of Philosophy (PhD) degree. Over 50 of the AuD programs also offer the PhD program. Some students enroll in a PhD degree program following completion of their AuD degree program. Some of the PhD programs, however, offer a combination AuD/PhD program so that a student can work towards both degrees jointly.

The Student Academy of Audiology (SAA) is the national student division of the American Academy of Audiology that serves as a collective voice for students and advances the rights, interests, and welfare of students pursuing careers in audiology. The SAA introduces students to lifelong involvement in activities that promotes and advances the profession of audiology and that provide services, information, education, representation and advocacy for the profession and for consumers of audiology services.

The SAA has over 1,500 members, consisting of students enrolled in AuD, PhD, or other accredited audiology doctoral programs for a first professional degree in audiology as well as Undergraduate students. The SAA has 65 registered chapters across the United States.

Admissions Process

There are approximately 74 AuD programs that are are accredited by the Council on Academic Accreditation in Audiology and Speech-Language Pathology (CAA) and/or Accreditation Commission for Audiology Education (ACAI) CSDCAS is a central application service that services 19 AuD and the list of certified programs can be found at: www.csdcas.org/index.html.

Following completion of their doctoral audiology programs, audiologists must continually upgrade and enhance their knowledge and skills through post-graduate professional development (continuing education). They attend seminars and workshops, and read scholarly and practice journals to stay current with new techniques, technologies, and discoveries to incorporate into their practices.

Licensure

Audiologists are regulated by licensure or registration in all 50 states, the District of Columbia, and Puerto Rico. Some states may also require audiologists to have a separate license to dispense hearing aids, although in many states audiologists dispense hearing aids under their audiology license.

Audiologists must have at least a master's degree in audiology to qualify for a state license to practice audiology. Because university audiology programs no longer offer a master's degree in audiology, a professional doctorate degree, typically the Doctor of Audiology (AuD) degree, which is now the standard entry level of education, is required for licensure in some states. . Each state sets its own education and other requirements for licensure. In some states, certifications from professional associations may satisfy some of the requirements for licensure. Many of the states also have professional development (continuing education) requirements for licensure renewal, although the number of required hours varies by state.

For information on individual state licensing requirements, interested persons must contact that state's audiology licensing board.

Professional Certification

Professional certification is optional and can be obtained from two certifying bodies:

- Audiologists, including new graduates who do not yet have a state license, can earn the Certificate of Clinical Competence in Audiology offered by the American Speech-Language-Hearing Association. To qualify, applicants must earn a graduate degree in audiology, complete a specified number of hours of supervised clinical practicum, complete either a year-long externship or other post-graduate experience, and pass a national examination.
- Audiologists who have met similar entry requirements and also have a doctoral degree, a state license to practice, and professional experience may earn board certification through the American Board of Audiology in recognition of their advanced competency.

Both of these certifications require professional development (continuing education) to maintain certification.

Resources

1. For more information about audiology, contact the American Academy of Audiology.

   - Professionals/Members: www.Audiology.org
   - Students: www.StudentAcademyofAudiology.org
   - Consumers/Public: www.HowsYourHearing.org
   - Foundation: www.audiologyfoundation.org

Additional information can also be found by visiting the American Speech-Language Hearing Association at www.asha.org.

CHIROPRACTIC

General Description of Profession

The doctor of chiropractic degree is a four year clinical doctorate. Chiropractic focuses on the relationship between the body's main structures – the skeleton, the muscles and the nerves – and the patient's health. Chiropractors believe that health can be improved and preserved by making adjustments to these structures, particularly to the spinal column. They do not prescribe drugs or perform surgical procedures, although they do refer patients for these services if they are medically indicated.

Chiropractic has become a well-recognized and highly respected health care field. Chiropractic services are covered by health insurance, including Medicare, and chiropractors are bound by the same regulations and ethics as physicians..

Most patients seek chiropractic care for back pain, neck pain and joint problems. However, many patients choose a chiropractor as their primary care doctor, because they prefer treatment plans that do not rely on medication or surgery. Because of the emphasis on holistic health care, chiropractic is associated with the field of complementary and alternative medicine.

State Licensure

All fifty states license doctors of chiropractic. During the course of the chiropractic program students take four national board exams that states use in the licensing process.

Outlook for the Future

The Wall Street Journal in April, 2013 published a story citing the chiropractic profession as the eleventh most promising profession to enter. Last year's study indicated it was the nineteenth most promising career to enter. The story used the U.S. Department of Labor's Occupational Outlook annual study as a resource.

Planning a Program of Study

For 2014 the chiropractic accrediting body, the Council on Chiropractic Education, modified the pre-requisite courses of studies in order to allow more flexibility with entrance requirements. Each program has its own requirements but the previous requirements provide guidance to the courses that should be considered.

Admissions Process

Each program has its own admissions staff and prospective students are urged to contact the colleges in which they have an interest. There is a centralized application service ChiroCAS.

Chiropractic Programs

There are eighteen chiropractic programs in the United States. Accredited chiropractic programs last 4 years and lead to a Doctor of Chiropractic (D.C.) degree. The standard curriculum covers:

- anatomy
- biochemistry
- physiology

- microbiology
- pathology
- public health
- physical, clinical and laboratory diagnosis
- gynecology & obstetrics
- pediatrics
- geriatrics
- dermatology
- otolaryngology
- diagnostic imaging procedures
- psychology
- nutrition/dietetics
- biomechanics
- orthopedics
- neurology
- first aid and emergency procedures
- spinal analysis
- principles and practice of chiropractic
- clinical decision making
- adjustive techniques
- research methods and procedures
- professional practice ethics

Resources

1. Association of Chiropractic Colleges
   4424 Montgomery Avenue, Suite 202
   Bethesda, Maryland 20814
   www.chirocolleges.org

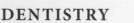

DENTISTRY

General Description of Profession

Dentistry is a profession that combines science and technology with helping people to enhance and maintain their oral health. As health care practitioners, dentists diagnose, treat, and help prevent diseases, injuries and malformations of the teeth and mouth. They improve a patient's appearance by using a variety of cosmetic dental procedures; perform surgical procedures such as implants, tissue grants and extractions; educate patients on how to take better care of their teeth and prevent oral disease; teach future dentists and dental hygienists; and perform research directed to developing new treatment methods and improving oral health.

The majority of the more than 190,000 professionally active dentists are private practitioners. Most dentists practice in an office setting, typically in a solo practice with an average of five employees. The majority enter a practice immediately after receiving a doctoral degree in dentistry, either a Doctor of Dental Surgery (D.D.S) or a Doctor of Dental Medicine (D.M.D) (there is no difference between the two degrees).

About 79% of dentists in the U.S. are general practitioners. The remaining 21% of dentists are involved in one of the nine dental specialties recognized by the American Dental Association, which require additional education after the D.M.D. or D.D.S. The nine specialties are: (1) orthodontics and dentofacial orthopedics — the treatment of problems relating to dental development, missing teeth, and other abnormalities affecting both normal function and appearance; (2) oral and maxillofacial surgery — the diagnostic and operative services dealing with disease, injuries, and defects in the jaw and related structures; (3) endodontics — the diagnosis, prevention and treatment of diseases of the pulp and other dental tissues that affect the vitality of the teeth; (4) periodontics — the diagnosis and treatment of diseases that affect the oral mucous membranes and other soft tissues that surround and support the teeth; (5) pediatric dentistry — the treatment of children and adolescents; (6) prosthodontics — the replacement of missing natural teeth with fixed or removable substitutes; (7) oral and maxillofacial pathology — the provision of diagnostic and consultative biopsy services to dentists and physicians; (8) dental public health — the control and prevention of dental disease through organized community efforts, and (9) oral and maxillofacial radiology, a specialty area using the images and data produced by all modalities of radiant energy to diagnose and manage diseases, disorders and conditions of the oral and maxillofacial regions.

The Decision to Pursue Dentistry

Most students (70%) make the decision to attend dental school either during or after college, thus making it imperative that students and health professions advisors be cognizant of the profession and admission procedures. Surveys of graduating dental students indicate that the about 30% entered college with the intention of attending dental school. Factors influencing decisions to pursue a career in dentistry include the ability to deliver healthcare, awareness of emerging research about connections between oral health and overall health, and lifestyle considerations such as the flexibility to balance a professional and a personal life.

Dentistry provides an opportunity for an excellent income (in the top 5% among U.S. citizens), a satisfying professional career, and time for a personal life. Recent surveys indicate that the mean annual net income of owner general dentists in private practice is $203,000 and $336,620 for specialists who own their practices. Many dentists enjoy the independence and autonomy of owning their own practices, including the flexibility of determining their practice hours. Dentists in private practice benefit from opportunities to establish one-on-one relationships with patients over time. Dentistry is viewed by the public as one of the most trusted and ethical professions in the U.S.

Aptitude for the sciences, the ability to visually perceive depth, color and shape, and possession of manual dexterity are essential to practice dentistry. Because most dentists provide care in private practice settings, knowledge of business and personal finance is also helpful.

While only 21% of all professionally active U.S. dentists are female, more women are entering dental school than ever before. In 2011, women comprised 46% of students enrolled in US dental schools. It is anticipated that by 2020, approximately 30% of all professionally active dentists will be women.

Approximately 7% of all professionally active U.S. dentists are underrepresented minorities (3.5% African American, 3.5% Hispanic/Latino, <.01% Native American/American Indian). Dental education is challenged to build a dental workforce that reflects the nation's diversity. To achieve a more balanced workforce to adequately serve the public, the dental profession seeks to increase the number of underrepresented minorities, individuals from disadvantaged backgrounds and individuals from underserved areas.

Outlook for the Future

The career outlook for new dental practitioners is good. New dentists are needed in private practice, as teachers and researchers and in public health, because large numbers of dentists are projected to retire in the next 20 years. Increasing numbers of older adults are keeping their teeth longer; there is a greater awareness of oral health care, including links between oral and overall heath, and there is a greatly increased demand for cosmetic services such as bonding and veneers. Technological advances such as digital radiology, laser systems, computer designed restorations and informatics allow dentists to provide treatment more effectively.

Planning a Program of Study

As of May 2013, there are 65 dental schools in the U.S that are fully accredited by the Commission on Dental Accreditation of the American Dental Association. Plans are underway for several new dental schools to begin accepting students within the next few years.

The best reference about dental school programs of study is the ADEA *Official Guide to Dental Schools* which is updated annually and provides descriptive information and statistics from each of the U.S. and Canadian dental schools. A complimentary copy of the ADEA Official Guide to Dental Schools is provided annually to NAAHP members; additional copies may be ordered through the American Dental Education Association (ADEA) at www.adea.org.

Students and advisors may also wish to explore GoDental.org, ADEA's website for current and future dental students. Updated daily, this site contains valuable information about applying to dental school, financing a dental education, and the dental school experience. It also features blogs, forums, and its own YouTube channel, DenTube. The American Student Dental Association (www.asdanet.org) also offers membership and provides resources for predental students (see Resources at end of this section).

Admission requirements to the dental schools vary by school. It is important for pre-dental students to be aware of the specific requirements of the schools to which they may apply. The majority require a minimum of 8 semester hours (or 12 quarter hours) each of biology, general chemistry, organic chemistry and physics. Increasingly, some dental schools seek applicants who have completed additional upper-level courses such as biochemistry, microbiology and genetics. Many also require courses in English, mathematics and social sciences.

Most dental schools give preference to candidates who will have earned a baccalaureate degree prior to matriculation in dental school. Although a minimum of two years of preprofessional study is required by most dental schools prior to admission, typically less than 1% of the class matriculating has such minimum preparation.

Choice of Undergraduate Major

The majority of dental students majored in the biological and natural sciences. However, it is not necessary to major in a science. Dental admission committees do not look for a particular undergraduate major as long as applicants have completed course requirements and demonstrate sufficient academic preparation. Other academic majors of pre-dental students include business, social sciences, engineering, architecture and the humanities.

The Admissions Process: Factors Evaluated by Admission Committees

Dental schools use admission committees for selection of entering classes. The size and composition of committees vary from school to school, but they are typically composed of clinical and basic science faculty, and in many schools, dental students, alumni and practicing dentists. Schools seek to select applicants exhibiting evidence of high intellectual competence, demonstrated knowledge and interest in the profession, cultural sensitivity, and personal traits to relate compassionately to patients. Communication skills, leadership ability, good character, motivation and knowledge of the field of dentistry are all evaluated by admissions committees.

The strength of academic preparation, as demonstrated by courses completed, grades earned, and DAT scores are important factors in admissions decisions. However, other factors can influence admissions decisions. Many admissions committees encourage the holistic review of applicants, considering factors such as challenges faced in pursuing a college education, improving performance, and successfully balancing academics, work, and extra-curricular activities.

1. Academic Record

    The undergraduate record is usually considered the single most important factor in admissions decisions. The academic record includes the cumulative grade point averages, courses completed, academic rigor, and trends in performance (i.e., improving grades during the undergraduate program). A strong undergraduate academic record is considered evidence of both ability and academic preparedness. Grades are not evaluated alone, but in the context of the total academic program, along with such factors as employment, participation in extra-curricular activities, and other demands on study time. Applicants with special interests, i.e., research, teaching, commitment to serving underserved or disadvantaged populations, etc. are often favorably considered.

2. The Standardized Test (DAT)

    The Dental Admission Test (DAT) is required by all U.S. dental schools. The DAT measures general academic ability, comprehension of scientific information, and perceptual ability.

    The DAT is conducted by the American Dental Association, and is administered throughout the year at test centers operated by Prometric, Inc. Procedures for applying to take the DAT and making appointments to take the test are provided on the ADA website. The DAT fee covers the cost of sending official scores to selected dental schools, an unofficial personal copy of scores issued at the testing center, and scores to the pre-dental advisor if the examinee selects this option on the original DAT application.

    Examinees are required to submit a new application and fee for each test and must wait at least 90 days before retaking the DAT; the test may be taken up to three times. Results from all DATs are released on the official reporting of scores and forwarded to dental schools that are selected by examinees on the application.

    An examinee will receive an unofficial DAT score report at the Prometric test center immediately after completing the entire DAT battery. Dental schools (selected on the examinee's application to receive DAT scores) will receive official DAT scores approximately three weeks after the test. Official DAT scores will also be transmitted to ADEA AADSAS—and reported to all dental schools selected in the ADEA AADSAS application—as long as the examinee requested score results to be sent to at least one ADEA AADSAS-participating dental school. Pre-dental advisors receive reports of their students' DAT scores on a quarterly basis if their students indicated on their DAT applications that their scores can be forwarded to their pre-dental advisors. The DAT battery with the multiple-choice item format takes five hours to complete and consists of four tests: *survey of natural sciences, perceptual ability, reading comprehension, and quantitative reasoning.*

The material tested in the sciences is at the introductory level, i.e., topics that would normally be covered in a rigorous one-year introductory sequence in general chemistry, organic chemistry and biology. It is not necessary, or typically beneficial, to study from advanced textbooks in a subject. Test questions are often posed so that the application of general principles is stressed more than regurgitation of facts. The facts must be known, but the examinee must also be able to apply these facts to solve problems.

The DAT Program Guide, located on the ADA's website, contains an outline of the topics to be tested. A careful review of these areas is recommended. The four areas are:

- *Survey of Natural Sciences* (longest test) includes biology, general chemistry and organic chemistry
- *Reading Comprehension* (taken from basic science subjects usually with a dental emphasis)
- *Quantitative Reasoning* (a basic four function calculator is available on the computer screen in this test only;math problems test mathematical reasoning)
- *Perceptual Ability* (two- and three-dimensional spatial problem solving)

The Program Guide, the DAT Practice Test, and the application information are available at www.ada.org. Examinees may register for the test on-line. A tutorial is also available that familiarizes the examinee with the process of taking the computerized DAT. In the event an examinee has a dispute with the testing program, the examinee agrees to submit the dispute to arbitration if dissatisfied with the outcome of the program's standard appeal process.

Typical questions and answers regarding the DAT:

What can be done to assure acceptable scores on the DAT?
Experience has shown that an organized and systematic review of the topics tested on the DAT can result in a considerable, sometimes dramatic, improvement in DAT scores. Examinees are strongly encouraged to be familiar with both the format and the subject content of the test before sitting for the test.

Are sample tests available?
A DAT Practice Tests available at the ADA website, www.ada.org.

There are a number of companies that offer review courses for the DAT. The NAAHP does not endorse any of these commercial enterprises, but the pros and cons of enrolling in such courses are discussed elsewhere in this book. It is not necessary to take a commercial review course in order to score well on the DAT. Many disciplined students review the DAT Practice Test and prepare by reviewing their personal notes and textbooks.

No matter what method is chosen to review the material for the DAT, the candidate should begin several months before the test date with a specific block of time set aside to study, preferably daily. It is much better to study on a daily basis rather than attempt to review huge blocks of material at a time. Old notes and textbooks are particularly valuable resources since the emphasis should be on reviewing familiar concepts rather than learning new material. Examinees are encouraged to check the registration form that will allow distribution of test scores to their health professions advisors. To maintain a strong advising program, these scores must be available to the advisor, both for use in advising individual students and for the preparation of summary reports. Individual scores are protected by federal legislation (The Family Educational Rights and Privacy Act) and are never released without written authorization by the student concerned.

3. Letters of Evaluation

Most dental schools require three or four letters of evaluation (or recommendation) to consider an application complete. There are three general methods used to compile and submit letters of evaluation: 1) a predental committee report/letter, 2) a composite letter submitted by a health profession advising office, and 3) individual letters of evaluation sent to the application service. A pre-dental committee report generally consists of an evaluation of the applicant that is a composite of opinions of the members of the committee; it is sometimes composed after an in-depth interview with the applicant; supporting letters of evaluation from other faculty are frequently appended. A composite letter consists of a collection of individual letters of evaluation that are collected by a health professions advisor or advising office and supplied to the application service under a cover letter from the advising office. If these services are not available, applicants may opt to have individual letters of evaluation submitted directly to the application service.

Most dental schools prefer at least three faculty evaluation letters, with two from science faculty. A letter of support from a dentist with whom the applicant has shadowed and/or discussed the profession is strongly encouraged. Admissions committees seek insight into an applicant's ability and motivation to pursue advanced education, special experiences or qualities, special challenges the applicant may have overcome, awareness of issues in the profession, and the potential to adhere to a strong code of professional conduct.

4. The Interview

Most dental schools require the individuals they are seriously considering for admission to participate in a personal interview. Interview formats vary by dental school, from traditional one-on-one interviews with members of the Admissions Committees to small group interviews where groups of applicants discuss a particular ethical dilemma or related issue, sometimes in the Multiple Mini Interview format. Applicants invited for interview are usually provided information about the type of interview in which they will be expected to participate, either through their invitation notification, or by being directed to special websites.

Applicants should be prepared to discuss their motivation for a career in dentistry as well as their personal and professional goals, and possess awareness of oral health issues. Participating in mock interviews is strongly encouraged.

At many dental schools, the interview process includes opportunities for applicants to tour the school, meet with current students, and learn about special aspects of the program, including financial aid. The interview visit is an opportunity both for the applicant to develop a sense of "fit" with the school and for the Admissions Committee to assess the potential for the applicant to be successful if admitted.

Applicants should anticipate the cost of participating interviews, including travel, hotel stays and a suit or other professional clothing.

5. Extracurricular Activities and Work Experience

Extracurricular activities and work experience can enhance an application in many ways: demonstrating commitment to helping others, heightening awareness of oral health issues, serving in leadership positions, and the demonstrating the ability to manage multiple priorities along with academics. Admission committees are much more interested in the demonstration of leadership and genuine commitment over time than they are to an exhaustive list of activities that require one-time or occasional participation. The extent of participation in extracurricular activities will vary by applicant, depending on work and other personal demands. It is not necessary for extracurricular activities or work experience to occur in a dental setting, although such

experiences can be quite valuable. Many dental schools require specified shadowing hours to be documented as a part of the application. Applicants should be encouraged to shadow general dentists, taking the time to discuss those qualities they find both most rewarding and least satisfying. Admissions committees seek assurance that the applicant understands the profession.

The Application: When and Where to Apply

ADEA AADSAS (the Associated American Dental Schools Application Service) www.adea.org, is a centralized application service of the American Dental Education Association (ADEA). As of the 2014 application cycle, 65 dental schools participate in ADEA AADSAS, (64 U.S. schools and one Canadian school). Applicants submit a single application to ADEA AADSAS; transcripts are verified, grade point averages are calculated, and AADSAS sends a standard applicant packet to each of the dental schools the applicant designates. AADSAS also collects and disseminates letters of evaluation that are submitted on behalf of applicants. As of April 2013, only the University of Mississippi School of Dentistry does not participate in AADSAS. Texas residents applying to Texas dental schools must utilize the Texas Application Service (www.utsystem.edu/tmdsas).

The on-line ADEA AADSAS application becomes available around June 1 for the next entering class. For example, the AADSAS 2014 application cycle begins on June 3, 2013. Each dental school has its own AADSAS application deadlines, which range from September 1 to February 1. Consult the AADSAS application and individual dental school websites for current deadlines.

Applicants are <u>strongly encouraged to apply early</u>. Depending on application volume, ADEA AADSAS processing takes three to five weeks. Dental schools begin receiving applications in late June, and generally begin interviews in August and September. Many — but not all — dental schools have supplemental applications and fees that must be submitted to consider the application complete.

Factors such as residency, mission, and location of the dental school can be important factors in the section of dental schools. Applicants are encouraged to become acquainted with the dental schools by reviewing the ADEA Official Guide to Dental Schools, GoDental.org, and dental school websites. Because admission to dental school is competitive, applicants are encouraged to apply to more than one school.

ADEA AADSAS applicants can track the status of their applications by monitoring their on-line AADSAS application, and by utilizing a mobile web portal on their smartphones. Applicant data is sent to the dental schools electronically on a weekly basis. Refer to the AADSAS website (www.adea.org) for more complete information about application processing.

Acceptance

Dental schools begin sending offers of acceptance, starting December 1. Individuals accepted in December and January have 30 days to accept offers; those accepted in February 1 or later have 15 days; those accepted after July 15 or two weeks before the start of dental school classes (whichever is sooner) may be asked for an immediate response. Most dental schools require a tuition deposit (often non-refundable) to hold a position in a class. Deposits can vary by school, ranging from $100 to more than $2,000.

Most dental schools develop a wait list or alternate list of candidates who will be considered for admission if a previously confirmed applicant withdraws. The size each school's wait list varies, as does each school's policy of selecting candidates from the wait list. Starting April 1 each year, dental schools report to ADEA AADSAS the names of their confirmed acceptances and AADSAS provides each school with the names of those applicants who hold positions at more than one school. Dental schools may contact such individuals and may rescind an offer of admission if there is no resolution after 15 days. Other than list of applicants holding acceptances at multiple institutions, ADEA AADSAS does not share lists of accepted students with the dental schools.

Special Programs

Many dental schools offer summer enrichment and other programs for pre-dental students from disadvantaged backgrounds and underserved areas. Frequently, these programs are co-sponsored with other health professions or the main university. For the most up-to-date list of such programs, consult explorehealthcareers.org.

The Summer Medical and Dental Education Program (smdep.org) is a summer enrichment program coordinated by ADEA and the Association of American Medical Colleges (AAMC) and funded by the Robert Wood Johnson Foundation. College freshmen and sophomores from disadvantaged backgrounds can apply to participate in one of 12 sites throughout the U.S. The six-week program provides science academic enrichment, career development, learning skills orientation, clinical experiences, and financial planning workshops. Outcomes demonstrate that SMDEP participants are accepted at high rates to medical and dental schools, as well as to other professional programs. Applications for SMDEP generally become available in November each year, with a March 1 application deadline.

Joint Degree Programs

Joint degree programs provide applicants the opportunity to earn a Master's or PhD degree in combination with their DDS or DMD. These degree programs are particularly appealing to individuals considering a career in research and academic dentistry, or those who are considering specialty training. Joint degree programs can include Master's and PhD degrees in oral biology and the basic sciences, as well as Master's in Public Health and Master's in Business Administration degrees. Check the ADEA Official Guide to Dental Schools for a current listing of schools that offer joint degree programs.

Financing a Dental Education

The best single reference for financial aid for dental students is Chapter 4 of the ADEA Official Guide to Dental Schools, Financing Your Dental Education. This chapter includes information about how to apply for financial aid, how financial aid is awarded, and details the various types of financial aid awarded to dental students. Because more than 90% of dental student receive financial aid and because the majority of financial aid to dental students is in the form of student loans, most colleges and universities have financial aid administrators — either in the dental school or on the health sciences campus — who work specifically with dental students.

Most dental school websites offer detailed information about costs and financial aid resources at their dental schools. Applicants should initiate contact with the financial aid office early, because types, terms and deadlines for dental student financial aid programs vary.

Schools and Colleges of Dentistry

As of April 2013, there are 65 accredited U.S. dental schools. Several additional dental schools are currently in development and anticipate accepting entering classes in upcoming years. Consult the ADEA website (www.adea.org) for a current list of dental schools and links to their websites.

Resources

1. *ADEA Official Guide to Dental Schools* is published annually (in January-February) by the American Dental Education Association and contains the latest available program descriptions, selection criteria and the credentials of admitted students for each dental school in the U.S. and Canada. The *ADEA Official Guide to Dental Schools* may be purchased on-line at the ADEA website (www.adea.org) and can also be found in many libraries and health professions advising offices.

2. www.GoDental.org (sponsored by the American Dental Education Association) is a resource for current and future students that features blogs, forums, and other forms of social networking. It also offers up-to-date information about applying to dental school, financing a dental education, and the dental school experience.

3. www.ExploreHealthCareers.org (sponsored by the American Dental Education Association) provides up-to-date information about all health-related occupations including information about summer enrichment programs, special opportunities and postbaccalaureate programs.

4. Dental Admission Test (www.ada.org/prof/ed/testing/dat). Students must register on-line for the DAT. This site includes a DAT Practice Test and complete information about registering for and taking the test.

5. Dentistry career information (www.ada.org/goto/careers). Targeted career information for predental students and health advisors on job shadowing, career exploring programs and additional resources.

6. The American Student Dental Association (ASDA) is the premiere resource for students pursuing a career in dentistry. With 62 dental schools currently open and three starting in fall 2013, there will be more than 20,000 dental students in the U.S. and Puerto Rico. Among these students, 89% are ASDA members, making ASDA the largest student-run dental organization in the nation.

Why should predental students join ASDA?

- Involvement in ASDA makes them a more competitive applicant for dental school admissions. Joining ASDA can set them apart from others and show their commitment to organized dentistry early in their career.

- Check out the website at www.ASDAnet.org/predental for information catering exclusively to predental students' needs (like tips for choosing a school and taking the DATs).

- Predental members receive a hard copy handbook—Getting Into Dental School: ASDA's Guide for Predental Students—that saves them time by providing detailed information on all 62 dental schools.

- Members receive 10% off Kaplan DAT prep courses. Using this member discount with Kaplan pays for the $58 membership dues and then some.

- Prepare for dental school interviews by being current in what is happening in the dental world. Utilize ASDA's publications—Mouth, ASDA News, Word of Mouth and The Legislative Ledger—written for students by students to understand what is going on in today's fast moving dental climate.

- Access to 19,000+ current dental students through events and social media for predentals to ask questions, find mentors and find out what dental school is really like.

HEALTHCARE MANAGEMENT/ADMINISTRATION

General Description of Profession

Healthcare is a business and, like every other business, it needs good management to keep it running smoothly. The term "healthcare administrator/healthcare manager" applies to those professionals who plan, direct, coordinate, and supervise the delivery of healthcare.

Today, an estimated 303,000 people serve in healthcare management from middle management to CEO positions at organizations that range in size from 1-2 staff members to major international companies employing hundreds of thousands of employees.

The Decision to Pursue a Career in Healthcare Management

Students who are caring and compassionate, who want to make a real difference in the lives of others, and who want to make the world a better place may be attracted to healthcare management. Health administrators are also adaptable and able to think clearly and strategically on complex problems. The field attracts those drawn to the professionalism, to the application of leadership skills in organizations which can clearly improve the lives of others, and to the challenging mission of healthcare management.

Making a Difference/Social Mission — Decisions made by healthcare executives can help improve life for hundreds, even thousands of people every day. Healthcare executives have a sense of social mission—they deeply care about the people they work with and serve. Further, our hospitals and healthcare organizations provide opportunities for those who want to "do well by doing good."

Career Opportunities — Employment of medical and health services managers is expected to grow 22 percent from 2010 to 2020, faster than the average for all occupations. The healthcare industry will continue to expand and diversify, requiring managers to help ensure smooth business operations.

Furthermore, unlike many traditional management programs, graduates of healthcare management programs can find significant opportunities in areas ranging from small rural communities to large metropolitan areas and throughout the world.

Excellent Earning Potential — Students pursuing healthcare management careers have excellent earning potential. For the most recent figures and information, see the U.S. Bureau of Labor Statistics website at www.bls.gov/oco/ocos014.htm.

Career Flexibility — An education in healthcare management can take you in many different and exciting directions. In addition to more traditional careers in healthcare management, graduates work in many other areas including: pharmaceutical companies, health insurance companies, management consulting, banks and other financial institutions, long-term care facilities, professional societies and state and Federal agencies.

The core skill set you develop in a healthcare management program provides a competitive advantage within the healthcare sector. In addition, these skills transfer readily across a variety of industries, providing flexibility for non-health sector positions as well.

Management and Advancement Potential — There is an excellent career ladder — and many people also take on roles in different sectors of the field over the course of their careers.

Visible and Valued Role in the Community — Healthcare executives typically are highly respected members of their communities. Hospitals and other healthcare organizations are among the largest employers in many communities and their organizations positively impact the health of the populations they serve and the well-being of their community.

Continual Self Improvement — Healthcare management is a career that values continual self improvement and education, and most employers encourage continued professional development. Many organizations often support tuition remission or in-service training for new skills. Innovation and continuous learning will be a part of the job from the day you start.

Which Degree is Right for You

Once you have made the decision to pursue a career in this profession, you need to determine what degree will best prepare you to begin your career and enhance your opportunities in the future. The answer should be a degree from an accredited graduate healthcare management program or a certified undergraduate healthcare management program.*

An accredited or certified healthcare management degree can provide both an in depth understanding of the health sector and the essential competencies needed for the practice. A graduate of a healthcare management program is uniquely prepared to manage a broad spectrum of healthcare organizations. At the same time, a healthcare management degree program offers mentoring and field experiences with senior healthcare executives that are rarely duplicated in other degree programs. You gain a competitive advantage both in launching your career and in learning applied competencies that are essential for success.

Moreover, an accredited or certified degree has earned the highest respect among most healthcare organizations as they recruit for new management talent. Graduates have the advantage of understanding the specialized language, financing, and politics of the healthcare system. The critical thinking skills in healthcare management and knowledge of this dynamic and complex sector will provide the graduate with a significant advantage in professional preparation.

The career opportunities with a healthcare management degree are expansive and invigorating — including hospital and health systems management, medical groups, pharmaceutical and biotechnology companies, care management organizations, health information technology firms, supply chain companies, government/policy organizations, health insurers, banks, and healthcare management consulting firms. The healthcare management community and program alumni provide many advancement opportunities and a network of contacts that is invaluable.

Planning a Program of Study

Degrees in healthcare management are available at baccalaureate, master's and doctoral level. Most baccalaureate programs offer students three options: 1) general management; 2) specialist training in a specific discipline such as financial management or 3) focus on a specific segment of the industry such as ambulatory care or long-term care. The Association of University Programs in Health Administration (AUPHA) conducts a certification process for undergraduate programs in healthcare management.

An undergraduate degree in healthcare management can serve students in a variety of ways. For the student confident in wanting an administrative career in a sector of the healthcare industry, the undergraduate program can provide the basic knowledge, skills and applied studies needed for certain entry-level positions. It can also be the springboard to a graduate program for those seeking higher-level positions in healthcare management. For the clinician, the undergraduate program can provide a course of study in healthcare management and prepare them for leadership positions within their clinical specialty. For the student who wants to be a clinician, the undergraduate program can provide the foundation in learning they need to go on to their chosen area. Lastly, the undergraduate degree can also serve as a general management program which can be applied to other service industries.

A B.S. or B.A. degree - in any field of study — is the primary prerequisite for admission to a graduate program. In the past most students chose the traditional route of a master's degree in health administration or public health. Today, however, students are investigating other options, including degrees in business with course concentration in health services management. Some schools offer a joint degree--—a master's degree in both business administration and public health, or in both healthcare management and law, for example. Graduate programs generally last two years and lead to a master's degree. They include coursework in healthcare policy and law, marketing, organizational behavior, healthcare financing, human resources, and other healthcare management topics. This program may also include a supervised internship, residency, or fellowship.

The Commission on Accreditation of Healthcare Management Education (CAHME) accredits master's level programs that prepare healthcare administrators according to established criteria. Only CAHME-accredited graduate programs may become full graduate members of AUPHA.

Executive education and continuing education programs in healthcare management are available for those currently employed in the field who want to broaden their knowledge and improve their skill base.

A doctoral degree in healthcare management, administration, research and policy, which is offered by many AUPHA member universities, or a doctoral degree in a related discipline — economics, political science, accounting, etc. — is the highest academic credential that can be earned.

What is graduate accreditation of a healthcare management program?

The CAHME accreditation is designed to foster high-quality, professional healthcare management education. "Healthcare Management" is an inclusive term describing skills and competencies utilized by individuals working to support and improve the delivery of health services. The definition involves many market segments, including (but not limited to) acute and non-acute providers, medical practices, community health organizations, insurers, pharmaceutical and equipment suppliers, professional societies and trade associations, consultants, health policy organizations, and the academic community.

Students can identify graduate management education programs that meet their chosen profession's standards by connecting to the CAHME website (www.cahme.org) and reviewing the requirements and curriculum of the CAHME accredited programs. The accrediting process assures students that the programs meet rigorous academic standards that prepare them for meaningful professional careers. All education programs seeking accreditation by CAHME, regardless of the setting for the graduate program, are evaluated by CAHME Criteria for Accreditation.

What is undergraduate accreditation of a healthcare management program?

Hundreds of schools across the U.S. advertise undergraduate programs in health administration, healthcare management or health policy. The academic offerings for these programs range from a couple of electives in the subject added to a business degree on one end of the spectrum to a Bachelor of Health Administration with required field experience on the other. Within this wide range of available options, how does a program set itself apart from the others in terms of overall quality? How can prospective students gain the confidence and assurance that the academic program they choose is of the highest quality and relevant in today's healthcare industry? How can employers have confidence in the quality and competence of program graduates? All of this can be accomplished by turning to an AUPHA Certified Undergraduate Program.

For undergraduate healthcare administration programs, AUPHA has established a peer review process for those programs willing to undergo the rigors of external review in the interest of program excellence. Successful completion

of the panel review process leads to Certification by AUPHA and attainment of Full Certified membership status. For a full list of Certified undergraduate programs go to www.aupha.org/certification/.

The Admissions Process

The admissions process varies from school to school, largely dependent on whether school is housed in a school of business, a school of public health or a school of nursing, among others. In September 2011, AUPHA launched the Healthcare Administration, Management & Policy Centralized Application Service (HAMPCAS). HAMPCAS is the first national centralized application service designed for students applying to graduate programs in health administration, healthcare management and health policy. The service enables applicants to apply to multiple colleges and schools through a single web-based application.

Students may visit www.hampcas.org to research HAMPCAS school information, view FAQ's, upcoming deadlines, announcements regarding the portal, and to begin an application

Resources

1. Association of University Programs in Health Administration (www.aupha.org)

2. American College of Health Care Administrators (www.achca.org)

3. American College of Healthcare Executives (www.ache.org)

4. ACHE's Healthcare Management Careers (www.healthmanagementcareers.org) American College of Medical Practice Executives (www.mgma.com/acmpe)

5. American College of Physician Executives (www.acpe.org)

6. American Organization of Nurse Executives (www.aone.org)

7. Asian Healthcare Leaders Association (www.asianhealthcareleaders.org)

8. Canadian College of Health Services Executives www.cchl-ccls.ca

9. ExploreHealthCareers.org (www.explorehealthcareers.org)

10. Healthcare Financial Management Association (www.hfma.org)

11. Healthcare Information and Management Systems Society (www.himss.org)

12. Medical Group Management Association (www.mgma.com)

13. National Association of Advisors to the Health Professions (www.naahp.org)

14. National Association of Health Services Executives (www.nahse.org)

15. U.S. Department of Labor, Medical and Health Services Manager (www.bls.gov/oco/ocos014.htm)

16. Health Resources and Services Administration (bhpr.hrsa.gov/kidscareers/)

17. "Your Career as a Healthcare Executive" (ACHE) (www.ache.org/carsvcs/ycareer.cfm)

For additional information on a career in healthcare management, contact the Association of University Programs in Health Administration (AUPHA) at aupha@aupha.org or (703) 894-0940.

MEDICINE (DO-GRANTING, OSTEOPATHIC MEDICINE)

General Description of Profession

The philosophy and practice of osteopathic medicine developed in reaction to the frequently harmful medicine being practiced in the United States in the late 1800s. Osteopathic medicine is a uniquely American branch of medicine that has continued to evolve in the United States through the scientific method of discovery. Today, U.S. osteopathic physicians (who hold the Doctor of Osteopathic Medicine degree and are known as DOs) are fully licensed, patient-centered medical doctors. They have full medical practice rights throughout the United States and in over 45 countries abroad.

Today, more than 20 percent of U.S. medical school students are training to be osteopathic physicians, and their numbers are increasing each year. The nation's approximately 69,000 fully-licensed practicing osteopathic physicians practice the entire scope of modern medicine, bringing a patient-centered, holistic, hands-on approach to diagnosing and treating illness and injury.

Osteopathic medicine also emphasizes primary care. Approximately 57 percent of all osteopathic physicians practice in one of the primary care areas of family practice, general internal medicine, or pediatrics. Osteopathic physicians can be found in virtually all types of medical practice across the United States, ranging from general practice in small towns to highly specialized practice in the country's largest cities. However, the emphasis the profession places upon primary care bodes well for the future. Medical policy-making organizations, including the U.S. Department of Health and Human Services, agree that primary care is the area of greatest medical need, now and in the foreseeable future.

The vast majority of osteopathic medical students spend four years in undergraduate school and receive a bachelor's degree prior to entering medical school. Osteopathic medical education consists of four years of professional education, generally organized as two years of basic science courses and two years of clinical training. Much of the clinical training is composed of "clinical clerkships," where the student spends time in a clinical setting under the supervision of licensed physicians in preceptor roles. Clerkships are a part of the osteopathic medical school program and are separate and distinct from internship and residencies, which occur after graduation. It is possible to complete clerkships in a variety of clinical settings throughout the United States.

After receiving the DO degree, graduates may serve a 12-month internship approved by the American Osteopathic Association. Completion of this internship allows the new DO to begin the general practice of medicine in some states. Alternatively, graduates may apply for entry into specialty training in a variety of DO or MD residency programs that range in length from two to six additional years. Graduates may enter residency programs either directly on graduation from medical school or following the one-year osteopathic internship (in some cases depending on state licensing regulations).

Licensure of the DO is established in each state, District of Columbia or U.S. territory by a medical examining board that accepts the results of the national licensure examination. To become licensed as an osteopathic physician, one must successfully complete the Comprehensive Osteopathic Medical Licensing Examination (COMLEX), Levels I, II (a 2-part exam) and III. This examination is administered by the National Board of Osteopathic Medical Examiners (NBOME). Osteopathic medical students also are eligible to take the United States Medical Licensure Examination (USMLE).

The Decision to Pursue Osteopathic Medicine

You may have heard of osteopathic medicine but have not had the opportunity to encounter sufficient detail to fully understand and appreciate the profession. Many applicants come face-to-face with the profession only when they reach the point of applying to osteopathic medical school. You should make a serious effort early in your undergradu-

ate years to enhance your knowledge and understanding of the field.

A good way to learn about osteopathic medicine is to talk with or observe one or more osteopathic physicians. Many DOs are happy to help prospective applicants learn about the field. Interaction with several DOs provides a good understanding of what the profession might offer.

Outlook for the Future

The future of osteopathic medicine is bright. DO and MD medicine continue to move closer together in modes of practice and philosophy. DOs and MDs are collaborators in joint practices or in hospital settings, but osteopathic medicine will continue to retain those aspects of training, modes of practice and philosophy that make it distinct.

Planning a Program of Study

There are 29 U.S. osteopathic medical colleges, four of which have branch campuses, and three of which maintain additional teaching sites — in Fall 2013, there will be 37 separate locations available for the first two years of osteopathic medical education. The past 20 years have seen dramatic growth in the number of osteopathic medical schools. Nearly half of the colleges have been established during that time. While the colleges are geographically spread across the U.S, they feature a remarkable consistency of philosophy and commitment to osteopathic medicine.

The pre-professional course requirements for every U.S. osteopathic medical college are listed in *The Osteopathic Medical College Information Book* (CIB), which is updated annually and can be viewed on-line at www.aacom.org/resources/bookstore/cib/Pages/default.aspx. Most osteopathic medical colleges require one academic year (two semesters or three quarters) of the following courses as prerequisites for admission: biology, with laboratory; general chemistry, with laboratory; organic chemistry, with laboratory; general physics, with laboratory; and English Composition. Several specify one academic year of behavioral sciences. You should become familiar with this resource early in your pre-professional program and determine precise course requirements for the specific osteopathic medical colleges to which you plan to apply. The required science courses typically should be completed by the end of the junior year of your undergraduate program if you plan to begin medical school directly after college. These courses also are needed to prepare you for the Medical College Admission Test (MCAT). You have only three years to prove yourself academically if you plan to enter osteopathic medical school immediately after graduation with a bachelor's degree. The admission committees generally will not see your senior year transcript (especially the spring semester or quarter) before they make admission decisions. You may, of course, have more than three years of academic work if you are a returning student who is changing fields, or if you are pursuing a nontraditional academic schedule. Consult your health professions advisor regarding nontraditional course and application scheduling.

Some osteopathic medical colleges recommend coursework in addition to the required courses. Other recommended courses may include biochemistry, genetics, histology, cell biology, embryology and comparative anatomy. On the other hand, osteopathic schools stress the importance of a well-rounded undergraduate curriculum. Most recommend courses in the behavioral sciences, social sciences, humanities and fine arts. Extracurricular activities, volunteer work and clinical exposure to medicine are also important.

Choice of Undergraduate Major

In what should I major? Osteopathic medical college admission committees look for students who demonstrate proficiency in the sciences and have pursued a well-rounded curriculum.

Most health professions advisors agree that you should select a major based upon your interests and aptitudes; you are more likely to enjoy your courses and do well in them. If you change your mind about going into medicine or are unable to gain admission to medical school, a major can also provide preparation for an alternative career.

The Admissions Process

The admissions process should become an integral part of your thinking about 18 to 24 months prior to the time you anticipate matriculating into osteopathic medical school. The submission of your application through the centralized on-line application service can begin as early as June of the year before the year of entry. AACOMAS on-line is available at aacomas.aacom.org. Regardless of the individual college application deadlines, it is to your advantage to begin the application process as early as possible. All osteopathic medical colleges operate on a rolling admissions basis, so decisions are made throughout the application cycle. Classes may be filled and/or interview spots may be taken long before application deadlines are reached. Your health professions advisor can help you plan your application strategy, and you are encouraged to contact him/her early in the process.

Factors Evaluated by Admission Committees

- Academic Record

  Admission committees at osteopathic medical schools are interested in admitting students who are well-suited to becoming osteopathic physicians and have the academic ability to complete the program. You must recognize that you are competing with other applicants for a position in the class. Thus, it is to your advantage to establish an excellent academic record, but not at the expense of breadth. Achieve a good balance between time and effort spent on your academic work and extracurricular experiences. Consult your health professions advisor for an evaluation of your academic record within the context of an osteopathic medical school application.

- The Standardized Test (MCAT)

  All osteopathic medical schools require the Medical College Admission Test (MCAT) to consider an applicant for admission. It is recommended that the MCAT be taken no later than summer of the calendar year prior to the year of planned medical school matriculation. This allows you time to assess your performance and retake the test if necessary. For a more detailed discussion of the MCAT, see the section under medicine (MD- granting) in this chapter. While some osteopathic medical schools will accept MCAT scores from the January administration in the year of matriculation, most will accept these scores only as an additional score.

- The Letters of Evaluation

  Most osteopathic medical colleges require a minimum of three letters of evaluation. Often, one of these letters must be from an physician, in many cases the preference is for a letter from an osteopathic physician. The other two should be from science faculty who have taught you. Schools often prefer a letter of evaluation from a health professions committee, which may be a composite of other letters in your file. Individual schools may have varying supplemental materials requirements, so be sure to examine each school's application procedures for directions as to the number and type of letters required.

  Although not all osteopathic medical colleges require a letter of evaluation from an osteopathic physician, it is to your advantage to become acquainted with one or more DOs. Ask your health professions advisor if s/he could introduce you to a DO. Many state osteopathic medical associations maintain lists of DOs who are willing to talk with prospective osteopathic medical students. Colleges of osteopathic medicine are also excellent resources and may be able to refer you to a DO in your area. To locate your state osteopathic medical association address, contact the American Osteopathic Association www.osteopathic.org or contact the

American Association of Colleges of Osteopathic Medicine (AACOM) at www.aacom.org.

- The Interview

  Most osteopathic medical colleges require a personal interview before admitting an applicant. The interview is an opportunity to demonstrate your knowledge and commitment to osteopathic medicine. It is also an opportunity to visit the school and determine whether the school is "right" for you. The interview is an opportunity for both the applicant and the college to assess each other.

  It is essential that you become familiar with the profession and can honestly say "I want to be an osteopathic physician because…" If you have just recently become aware of the profession, a good decision can be made only after you have read extensively about the profession and talked with osteopathic physicians.

- Extracurricular Activities and Work Experience

  You are encouraged, to the extent allowed by your academic work, to gain some experience outside the classroom. This will give you a broader perspective and will help you put your academic work and long-range professional goals into perspective. Gaining exposure to the general field of medicine will help you gain knowledge about the field, what it will demand of you, what its rewards and shortcomings are, and what its future holds.

The Centralized Application Service

The centralized application service for osteopathic medical schools is on-line at aacomas.aacom.org. Although there are 29 osteopathic medical schools (and four branch campuses), only 28 participate in AACOMAS (The University of North Texas Health Sciences Center — TCOM uses TMDSAS). The initial application to these schools is the standardized application submitted directly to AACOMAS, a web-based application. After AACOMAS has processed your application, application data are sent to each osteopathic school you designate.

After initial review and screening by an osteopathic medical college, you may receive a supplemental application to be returned directly to the college. Supplemental applications ask you to provide information that is unique to your interest in and application to a particular school. A request for letters of evaluation usually accompanies the supplemental application. You may also receive an invitation to interview either along with the supplemental application request or after the supplemental application is completed and reviewed.

Acceptance

- What You Can Expect from the Osteopathic Medical Colleges
  Most osteopathic medical college admission committees practice "rolling admissions"; some students are accepted before all applications have been processed or even received. Most osteopathic schools will inform you of a decision (acceptance, alternate status, or denial) within a few weeks following your interview. If you find yourself on one or more alternate lists, most admission committees are willing to keep you informed of your status.

- What the Osteopathic Medical Colleges Expect from You
  Most letters of acceptance will specify a time by which you must respond to the offer. If you plan to decline the offer, it is helpful to the school and to other applicants to do so promptly. On the other hand, you may plan to accept the offer, or you may need more information before you can make a final decision. You may

need time to evaluate the financial picture, including financial aid availability at the schools to which you have been accepted. You will be asked to place a deposit (the amount varies from college to college) to secure your seat in the class. If you hold a position in more than one osteopathic or allopathic medical school, it is your responsibility to withdraw at the earliest possible date from all but the one where you plan to matriculate.

You may be informed that you are on one or more alternate lists. Movement on such lists is active up to the day classes begin. If you are on one or more lists, you are advised to have alternative plans in mind so that you can make a quick decision should this become necessary. Be aware, however, that you are no longer considered to be on an alternate list once you have matriculated at a medical college. Once matriculated, however, courtesy dictates that you inform all schools.

AACOMAS maintains guidelines and protocols for the application process. These are updated and published annually in the Osteopathic Medical College Information Book (CIB) and on-line.

Special Programs

Even though an individual osteopathic medical school may not publicize a special program, if you have a desire to include a special component in your program, it is to your advantage to ask whether this will be possible. For example, you may want to delay your date of matriculation or to work on a graduate degree at the same time you are working toward your DO degree. Each of these situations (and possibly others) may not be publicized but may be available upon request.

- Joint Degree Programs
  Most of the 29 colleges of osteopathic medicine offer a variety of joint degree programs. The listing for these programs is quite extensive and can be found in the CIB.

- Early Decision Programs
  Several of the colleges of osteopathic medicine have official Early Decision Programs (EDP). Colleges offering EDP programs are listed in the CIB. Contact each school's Admissions Office for additional information.

Resources

1. American Association of Colleges of Osteopathic Medicine (AACOM), 5550 Friendship Boulevard, Suite 310, Chevy Chase, MD 20815-7231; (301) 968-4100; www.aacom.org.

2. AACOM is the organization that serves the nation's colleges of osteopathic medicine and their students. A wide variety of literature about the field of osteopathic medicine is available from AACOM.

3. AACOM's website addresses many important issues, including a discussion of the similarities and differences between the DO and MD.

4. For a complete list of the 29 colleges of osteopathic medicine and branch campuses, visit www.aacom.org/about/colleges/Pages/default.aspx.

5. American Association of Colleges of Osteopathic Medicine Application Service (AACOMAS), 5550 Friendship Boulevard, Suite 310, Chevy Chase, MD 20815-7231; (301) 968-4190.

6. The AACOMAS application is a centralized, web-based application that can be accessed at the AACOM website, Aacomas.aacom.org.

7. American Osteopathic Association (AOA), 142 East Ontario Street, Chicago, IL 60611-3269; (312) 202-8000 or (800) 621-1773; www.osteopathic.org. This is the osteopathic physician professional organization.

References about osteopathic medicine include:

8. *The DOs: Osteopathic Medicine in America* by Norman Gevitz, PhD.

9. *Osteopathic Medicine: A Reformation in Progress* by R. Michael Gallagher, DO, FACOFP and Frederick J. Humphrey, II, DO, FACN.

10. *Fire on the Prairie: The Life and Times of Andrew Taylor Still*, Founder of Osteopathic Medicine by Zachary Comeaux, DO.

11. *A Brief Guide to Osteopathic Medicine, For Students, By Students* by Patrick Wu and Jonathan Siu (available free online at www.aacom.org/resources/bookstore/Pages/BriefGuide.aspx.

MEDICINE (MD-GRANTING)

General Description of Profession

A physician's responsibilities cover a wide range of functions in the maintenance of health and the treatment of disease, including caring for patients with both acute and chronic conditions and promoting preventive approaches involving substantial patient education. These include diagnosing disease, supervising the care of patients, prescribing medications and other treatments, and participating in the improved delivery of health care. Although most physicians provide direct patient care, some concentrate on basic or applied research, become teachers and/or administrators, or combine various elements of these activities.

According to the American Medical Association (AMA), among the 817,850 practicing physicians in the United States in 2012, 282,969 were primary care physicians, as defined by practices in family medicine, general practice, general internal medicine, and general pediatrics. Other active MDs specialized in obstetrics/gynecology, psychiatry, various medical specialties (e.g., allergy and asthma, cardiology, dermatology, gastroenterology, neurology, and pulmonology), general surgery, various surgical specialties (e.g., colon and rectal surgery, neurosurgery, ophthalmology, orthopedics, otolaryngology, and plastic, thoracic, and urological surgery), support specialties (e.g., anesthesiology, pathology, and radiology), emergency medicine, and other clinical areas.

Physicians practice in a variety of settings, including group practices, health maintenance organizations, outpatient clinics, inpatient hospitals, laboratories, and academic settings, as well as in industry, the military, and government. Medicine offers a wide variety of career options. New opportunities emerge with each advance in medical knowledge and with each development in the organization of medical services. During the course of a typical day, the activities of many physicians include performing two or more of these professional roles and providing professional services in two or more settings. Most physicians are actively engaged in their profession on a full-time basis throughout most of their lives.

Most medical students graduate after four years of medical school ("undergraduate medical education") and enter residency programs of three to eight years for additional training in a specific medical specialty ("graduate medical education" or "GME"). Training in family practice, general internal medicine, and general pediatrics takes three years; general surgery requires five years; and subspecialty training in disciplines such as plastic or neurological surgery may involve another two or three years. Residents are trainees in the clinical facility in which the training program is located; they earn salaries that, in 2012-2013, averaged $49,651 for the first year of residency and increased to $55,750 for the fourth year of residency.

The Decision to Pursue the Profession

An increasingly diverse mix of individuals is choosing medical careers. For example, the proportion of women in the applicant pool has increased dramatically over the last several decades. Whereas in the 1960s and 1970s, the proportion of women applying to and matriculating at medical schools nationally was relatively small, in 2011-2012, women represented approximately 45 percent of medical school applicants and 48 percent of graduating medical students. More specifically, applicants to the 2012 entering class were comprised of 45.1% women and 54.9% men. First-year matriculants in 2012 included 9,064 women (46.3%) and 10,453 men (53.7%).

Students from racial and ethnic groups that are underrepresented in medicine are strongly encouraged to apply. Consistent with the Office of Management and Budget Directive 15, the AAMC has, in recent years, been collecting self-reported race and ethnicity data about applicants and matriculants in such a way that they are able to identify themselves as members of multiple racial and ethnic groups. Comprehensive information about applicants and matriculants from these multiple racial and ethnic groups for the 2003-2012 entering classes can be found on the

Association of American Medical Colleges (AAMC) website at: www.aamc.org/data/facts.

As part of a continuing effort to enhance the diversity of medical school classes, the AAMC initiated, in October 2006, the AspiringDocS program. The cornerstone of this effort is the Aspiring Docs websitwww.aamc.org/aspiringdocs), which is free and features a variety of resources for prospective medical students, including information about career options in medicine, preparing for the Medical College Admissions Test (MCAT), applying to medical school, and financing a medical education. In addition to the resources and information on the website, the campaign also provides a dose of inspiration for potential applicants by highlighting real-life stories of medical students, residents and practicing physicians who have overcome a variety of obstacles and barriers on their way to medical school.

Neither age nor marital status is a consideration in the assessment and selection of medical school applicants, and the number of older applicants and matriculants has increased in recent years. In 2012, there were 3,925 applicants whose age at expected matriculation was 28 years or older. (The largest contingent of applicants, 40,865, was between 21 and 28 at the time of anticipated matriculation.) Many medical students are married with children.

What is the Unique Role and Responsibility of the Physician?

Medicine is both an art and a science. A physician develops the skills to interact with a patient, obtain a medical history, perform a physical examination, and conduct and interpret diagnostic and laboratory studies. The results of these efforts are synthesized into a comprehensive diagnosis and treatment plan. Since patients' diseases manifest themselves in idiosyncratic ways, the physician must become skilled in the application of science to solve medical problems, often within short time frames and with limitations on the data that can be obtained within the time available.

A physician's first responsibility is to her/his patient. Of necessity, many patient work-ups will require long hours and an unpredictable schedule. There is great satisfaction for the physician in knowing that s/he has taken care of a patient's medical needs. The spouse and family of medical students need to appreciate the long and demanding work schedules required of busy physicians. By the same token, physicians must learn to be considerate of the personal and social needs of their families.

It is also a physician's responsibility to educate his/her patients and promote healthy lifestyles. Practicing physicians speak of the privilege they feel in being permitted to care for patients and to be of service to the community. The care of a patient throughout the lifespan is a particular privilege and requires the utmost from the physician.

What are the Characteristics of Those for whom Medicine is a Good Choice?

The responsibilities of being a physician require maturity, integrity, perseverance, and character of the highest order. Honesty is critical. Being able to recognize your limitations is also essential. Respecting the rights of others, being tolerant of personal belief systems and life experiences different from your own, and respecting the dignity of each person are some of the qualities that the successful physician will embody.

Critical thinking and problem-solving skills are central. A basic background in science is necessary, although it is not necessary to major in a science. It is important to choose a college major you enjoy and to take sufficient advanced course work to develop skills in critical thinking, analysis, and communication.

A love of learning is important. Medicine continues to evolve as new research is completed and new findings are incorporated into everyday medical practice. Physicians learn from every patient as they advance the boundaries of medical knowledge. Medicine is an intellectually challenging field that requires the individual physician to be intellectually curious and to continue to learn virtually throughout his/her lifetime. Reading current journals, attending medical seminars, and/or contributing to the research literature are important activities for physicians. While many specialties require completion of a minimum number of continuing medical education credits annually to maintain professional credentials, a commitment to lifelong learning is an ethical and moral responsibility of all physicians.

Interpersonal skills and empathy are important in a physician. To be successful in medicine, a person must have strong communication skills (both oral and written) and enjoy communicating with others (both giving and receiving information), working in teams to achieve consensus, providing leadership to a group, and maintaining emotional stability, discipline, and a sense of calm in the midst of crisis.

It is important to be able to handle stress and to cope with adversity. During medical school, most students experience a greatly accelerated workload and demands on their stamina and emotional equilibrium. The practice of medicine entails significant demands on the physician's time and involves critical decision-making, often in life-threatening situations. Therefore, individuals considering a medical career are encouraged to develop appropriate stress and time-management skills.

Outlook for the Future

1. The Bureau of Labor Statistics projects that employment for all physicians and surgeons will grow faster than the average for all other occupations through the year 2014.
    Discussion continues about the number and type of physicians that will be needed to serve the health needs of the country in the future. Experts studying the physician workforce believe that the United States may experience a deficit of physicians in future decades if the size of medical school classes does not increase or if additional medical schools are not established in the near future, and that population demographics may result in the need for more physicians trained in the medical and surgical specialties. However, U.S. medical schools are on track to increase their enrollment 30 percent by 2017, according to results of the annual Medical School Enrollment Survey conducted by the AAMC (Association of American Medical Colleges) Center for Workforce Studies. According to results of the survey, first-year medical school enrollment is projected to reach 21,434 in 2017-18.
2. Demand for physician services is expected to continue to rise with the passage of the Affordable Care Act as well as the ongoing increase in the population in the United States, especially among those over the age of 65. In addition, one-third of current physicians are over the age of 55 and likely to retire by 2020, and recently graduated physicians are not expected to work the same number of hours per day that prior generations of physicians reportedly worked. You will want to be a well-informed observer about, and perhaps a participant in, these discussions as they progress, as well as about efforts at multiple levels to ensure that adequate health care is available to all citizens and especially to those who are currently medically underserved.

Planning a Program of Study

There are 141 MD-granting institutions in the United States and 17 in Canada. While there are some individual variations among schools, most require at English, general biology, general chemistry, organic chemistry, and physics for admission; the sciences must include relevant laboratories. Although not in the majority, some schools also have a mathematics requirement, and the most frequently mentioned mathematics courses are college math, calculus, statistics, and/or computer science. Although these core sciences are required, no specific major is preferred or required. Over the last few years, several schools have begun to recommend or to require biochemistry, social sciences and humanities courses as well.

All required science courses are typically completed by the end of the junior year of college, the time when application to medical school generally begins in earnest for undergraduate students who seek to enroll in medical school directly after college graduation. Also, these science courses are required for adequate preparation for the MCAT, described in detail in the Introduction. This means that you have only three years of undergraduate study to "prove" yourself if you plan to enter medical school immediately after graduation from college.

Entrance requirements for every medical school in the United States and Canada are listed in *Medical School Admission Requirements (MSAR®)* Online, a database-driven web site that is comprehensively updated each spring by the Association of American Medical Colleges in collaboration with medical school staff (www.aamc.org/msar). You should become familiar with this excellent resource early in your academic program to determine the specific admission requirements of medical schools in which you are potentially interested. The MSAR® may be available in your premedical advisor's office, but it is a good idea to purchase your own subscription. It can be ordered directly from the AAMC (See Resources).

It is also important to check the policies of medical schools regarding Advanced Placement (AP) and College Level Examination Placement (CLEP) credits. Not all medical schools will accept AP or CLEP units. Generally, if you tested out of one of the basic requirements, a medical school will accept an equivalent amount of credits in more advanced courses in that same discipline. If you have these credits in science or English courses, discuss your academic record with your premedical advisor or with medical school admission officers. The MSAR Online lists school's policies for accepting AP credits as well as community college and online course work in the Selection Factor's section of each individual school profile.

Choice of Undergraduate Major

Since the choice of an undergraduate major is not an issue for medical schools, on what basis should you select an undergraduate course of study? Most premedical advisors and medical school admission officers agree that you should select a major based on your interests and aptitudes, so that you will enjoy your courses and do well in them. Should you change your mind about medicine or not gain admission to medical school, your major might also prepare you for an alternative career choice. Many applicants forget that alternative doctoral-level health careers are available that require the same science coursework and same general academic preparation as that required for medical school, and that these careers can offer the same personal and professional rewards originally sought in medicine.

The Admissions Process

Medical schools seek students who will make good medical students and altruistic, knowledgeable, dutiful, and skillful physicians. They are not inclined to take great risks in selecting members of their classes; they have made a large investment, both economic and social/political, in seeing that the people whom they select for entrance become successful students and practitioners.

Medical school curricula have undergone significant revision during the past two decades as medical schools have made substantial efforts to place greater emphasis on modes of active and clinically relevant learning (e.g., problem-based learning, case-based instruction, small-group discussion) and to reduce passive approaches to medical education (e.g., lecture formats, large-group learning). Substantial investments have also been made to enhance the ways in which students' mastery of content and acquisition of clinical skills are assessed. The use of Objective Structured Clinical Evaluations (OSCEs), simulated and standardized patients, mannequins, and videotaped and computerized clinical scenarios are now standard at many medical schools.

During the first two years of the medical curriculum, students learn scientific material basic to the practice of medicine (i.e., anatomy, biochemistry, physiology, pathology, neuroscience, pharmacology, microbiology, immunology), as well as behavioral science, preventive medicine, medical ethics, human sexuality, and other clinically relevant content. They also master the skills associated with medical interviewing, history-taking, and physical examination. The substantial biomedical science content during these two years results in admission committees being interested in your science GPA, overall course load, and scientific and written communication skills as measured by the MCAT.

During the second two years of the medical curriculum, students participate in required clinical rotations called "clerkships." Each clerkship is typically four to ten weeks in length. Core clinical training usually involves rotations in internal medicine, surgery, obstetrics and gynecology, pediatrics, and psychiatry; many schools also have a required rotation in family medicine or primary care. These core clerkships are supplemented by elective rotations, in which students pursue individual interests and begin the process of identifying their future specialty choice. During the clinical curriculum, students exhibit their personal attributes and personality skills, as well as their abilities in the areas of communication, problem-solving, stress management, and leadership, which will be critical to their success as effective practicing physicians. Suitability for this phase of medical education is assessed by means of information regarding the applicant's extracurricular activities, involvement with others, and communication skills as discussed in letters of recommendation and exhibited in personal essays and interviews with admission committee members.

Factors Evaluated by Admission Committees

Each medical school's entering class is selected by an admissions committee appointed by the dean of the medical school. While the size and composition of the committee varies from school to school, it is usually composed of basic science and physician faculty members and medical school administrators. Many schools also include alumni, local physicians, medical students, and non-medical citizens from the surrounding community. The composition of the committee usually changes somewhat from year to year as some members complete their terms of office and new members are identified.

Admission committee members strive for objectivity in making their decisions. In general, medical schools select for admission those individuals who present evidence of strong intellectual ability, a record of accomplishments, and personal traits indicative of the ability to communicate and relate to patients in a realistic, professional, and compassionate manner. There is emphasis on academic achievement over time, MCAT scores, and multiple personal characteristics and experiential variables, including maturity, judgment, empathy, altruism, persistence, motivation, commitment to service, resilience, and concern for others. Some important determinants of whether or not you will be accepted for admission are:

- academic record
- scores on the MCAT
- content of letters of evaluation and recommendation
- personal statement
- the impression made in your personal interview(s)
- experience in a medical setting, and
- evidence of community involvement and volunteer and extracurricular activities.

Academic Record. Your undergraduate record will be a significant factor in predicting admission to medical school. Studies show that the quality of work in subjects taken leading to the baccalaureate degree is a very important predictor of success in basic science classes in medical school. The academic record includes the overall GPA and the science GPA (biology, chemistry, physics and mathematics), as well as performance in each individual course and trends in performance over time. Trends are an important consideration; a poor freshman year followed by improvement during the sophomore and junior years is preferred to a good freshman year followed by a declining record. A good academic record is evidence of high motivation, ability, and persistence — all factors necessary for the successful completion of a medical education.

Grades and academic load are not evaluated in a vacuum, but rather in context of your total time commitments. If during college you worked part-time, played a varsity sport, or otherwise devoted significant time to serious extracurricular activities (journalism, performing arts, community service, student government, etc.), these activities will be taken into account. However, it is necessary for the medical school admission committee to have evidence of your ability to do medical school-level work at an acceptable level. The best way to present this type of evidence is to

already have done well during your undergraduate years.

The Medical College Admission Test (MCAT®) (www.aamc.org/mcat). The Medical College Admission Test (MCAT®) is another important factor in evaluating an applicant for medical school. During and after medical school, you will have to pass nationally standardized licensure and certification examinations. Since many of these tests show high correlation with each other, medical schools are interested in those candidates who have demonstrated content mastery and proficiency in testing by doing well on the MCAT®. In addition, studies have shown that MCAT® scores are statistically reliable and valid predictors of a number of other indicators of academic success, including grade point average (GPA), likelihood of withdrawing (or being dismissed) from medical school for academic reasons, or graduating in four years. While it is important to realize that satisfactory GPA and MCAT® scores may be important factors in the consideration of one's application to medical school, they are not the only factors; qualitative factors also play a very important role in the admissions process. All applicants, with the possible exception of some students enrolled in baccalaureate-MD programs or applying to Early Assurance Programs, must present MCAT® scores as a necessary part of the materials supporting their application.

The Letters of Evaluation. Letters of evaluation are discussed in detail in chapter 2. Medical school admission committees generally prefer a composite or committee evaluation to individual letters of evaluation. Many will insist on such an evaluation if you are from a school where a composite or committee evaluation is prepared. Most schools require letters be printed on letterhead, signed and submitted electronically. Follow the guidelines described earlier, and, by all means, keep in close touch with your health professions advising office in collecting these important supporting documents.

The Interview. Once again, the discussion found in earlier pages can serve as a guideline. At the medical school interview, you should be prepared to answer some rather personal questions about your own background, beliefs, and experiences, as well as questions about moral and ethical issues affecting medicine. Review your record and expect to be asked about your interest in medicine, community and campus activities in which you have participated, and examples of ways you have exhibited leadership, faced up to challenges, and solved difficult problems.

Extracurricular Activities and Work Experience. Medical schools view extracurricular activities as positive signs that you can handle a rigorous curriculum and still participate in campus or community affairs. The level and sustained involvement of your participation is more important than the number and diversity of your activities. Commitment, leadership, service, responsibility, and the ability to interact effectively with diverse people are among qualities that medical school admission committees seek in applicants. These activities include community service, campus involvement, participation in research, outside jobs, interests, hobbies, etc. It is a myth, however, that extensive involvement in meaningful extracurricular activities will compensate for a modest academic performance. It may instead indicate to an admissions committee that you have poor judgment, skewed priorities, and/or inadequate time-management skills.

Health-Related Experience. In addition to the service component, an important value of volunteering in a hospital, doctor's office, nursing home, or health clinic is to help clarify the validity of your decision to pursue a career in medicine. You will have an opportunity to observe trained professionals in action (often referred to as *shadowing,*) and may get a chance to perform simple tasks yourself. You will find out if you feel comfortable in a hospital and around sick people, as well as how well you manage stress. The person to contact at a hospital is the director of Volunteer Services, who coordinates the efforts of volunteers, arranges their assignments, and conducts their orientation and training. While working in a health care facility is not a stated prerequisite for admission, many medical school admission committees prefer that candidates have this experience. It can show committee members that you have tested your career choice and that your commitment has been reinforced.

Research Experience. In the same way as gaining hospital experience can assist in your career decision, research involvement in a laboratory at your college, a medical school, or a medical research institute can help you decide whether you might be interested in pursuing the PhD degree in addition to the MD degree. You might pursue research just because it is interesting and will be a good experience. You might pursue research because medicine is a profession that emphasizes problem-solving. Even if you are not interested in pursuing research as a profession, it is important that you understand such concepts as the scientific method, statistical significance, and the experimental process so that you are capable of critically reviewing research reports in the professional literature and using relevant and valid results in your practice.

The Value of Work. Paying jobs unrelated to medicine may give you experience to help you develop better management and interpersonal skills. Jobs that require considerable contact with the public, for example, can help you develop interaction modes useful in patient care. Jobs that involve management of both work and personnel help develop responsibility and a mature attitude. If you do not have the luxury of volunteering and cannot find a paying job in a hospital, try to use whatever position you find, in a constructive manner, to develop some of these essential "people skills."

Study Abroad. Study Abroad programs can present excellent opportunities for expanded intercultural experiences, both curricular and extracurricular. Medical schools tend to regard Study Abroad participation favorably. However, most schools prefer that the required science coursework, if taken abroad, be strictly comparable to science courses taught in the United States. To avoid the risk of ambiguous interpretation of your academic report, it is a good idea to take all of the required premedical courses in the U.S., either before or after going abroad to study. This can be accomplished by completing all courses necessary for the MCAT and taking the MCAT before going abroad for your junior year, or perhaps going abroad and then applying to medical school after your senior year. There are some other possible variations that can be worked out on an individual basis. If possible, you should begin appropriate planning in your freshman year, in consultation with your prehealth advisor, taking into account all aspects of the medical school application and admission process before making your final decision regarding whether and/or when you will study abroad. If you have started an AMCAS application prior to going abroad, you may want consider listing a parent as an *Alternate Contact* Person in the *Biographic Information* section of your application. This will allow your parent to call the AMCAS Support Center for information about your application. Your parent's name must be listed for AMCAS to be able to share information about the application. However, an applicant is not required to enter an *Alternate Contact Person.* (Note: check with non-AMCAS schools for their policies or procedures, i.e. regarding alternate contacts.)

The Application Process

Your application is your first contact with the medical school admissions office staff and with members of the admission committee. It is therefore a good idea to make a positive first impression by preparing a well-organized application.

1. When and Where to Apply

    The medical school application process is a complex one, typically 14 or 15 months in length. The timing of the medical school application is therefore an important consideration. Those who want to begin medical school in the year they graduate from college will apply during the summer between their junior and senior college years. As a general rule, the earlier you apply in the application cycle, the better off you will be. AMCAS (American Medical College Application Service, the central application service for MD medical schools) will accept applications beginning on or about June 1, although applicants may begin preparing their on-line applications on or about May 1. Consult the MSAR® Online (www.aamc.org/msar) for application dates for those schools that have alternate application processes (e.g., the public medical schools located in Texas.)

    The majority of medical schools select their students on a "rolling admissions" basis. This means that schools do not wait until all of their application deadlines have passed prior to reviewing and assessing completed applications. Instead they review and accept applicants as their applications and interviews are completed. Thus, if you submit an application later rather than earlier in the application period, fewer seats in the class will be available. The first notification date for Regular Decision Program (RDP) acceptances is after October 15th; Early Decision Program (EDP) applicants must receive notification of the outcome of their application by October 1. In this scenario, it is possible that some applicants may be accepted before other applicants have even received the results of their August or September MCATs. If you plan to take the MCAT® in August or September, it is best to submit all other application materials well before MCAT® scores are returned. This approach places you in the best position to have your application reviewed in a timely manner, since your application will be complete at each school once MCAT® scores arrive.

You may tend, as many applicants do, to treat medical school application as a one-shot, "do-or-die" situation, based on the assumption that you must be enrolled in medical school immediately after you graduate from college. Medical schools do not care how many years you have spent out of, or away from, school, as long as your academic record, MCAT® scores, and other application materials are acceptable to them when you actually apply. There are favorable statistics for those persons who apply after their senior year, as well as for those who apply or reapply to medical school following college graduation.. If you took the MCAT® only once and did not do as well as you might have hoped, or if your senior year grades would raise your GPA to a more competitive level, you might contemplate waiting to make your first medical school application until after you have completed your college education. Increasingly, many applicants are choosing to take a "gap year" or longer prior to applying to strengthen their academic record, get more medically-related experience, participate in research, save money or pay off debt.

2. Early Decision Program

The Early Decision Program (EDP) is available at many medical schools. This allows an applicant to file an application to a single medical school well before the usual deadline (the deadline for submission of an EDP application is August 1) and to receive a decision from that school by October 1. If you plan to apply as an EDP candidate, you should take the MCAT® no later than the spring of the year in which you apply. If accepted, you agree not to apply to any other schools. If not accepted, you are immediately placed in the RDP applicant pool at that school, and you will be able to apply immediately to any other schools of interest. It is quite possible to be denied admission as an EDP candidate and then be accepted during the RDP process at the same school. One disadvantage of the EDP is that, if you are not accepted via EDP to the one school to which you applied, your application to other schools will be delayed until that school notifies you of its decision or October 1, at the latest. If accepted, however, you are free to concentrate on your studies during your senior year and/or consider Study Abroad programs or other options.

You should make an EDP application only to a school that you would be pleased to attend. You should understand that you will probably be competitive for EDP only if your credentials match those of the members of the previous year's entering class at that school. This information for individual medical schools is available in the MSAR Online web site (www.aamc.org/msar).

3. Deferred Matriculation

Many medical schools allow accepted applicants to delay matriculation for one year and will reserve a place for them in the next year's entering class. Each participating school has a policy identifying legitimate reasons for seeking deferred matriculation, and policies vary from school to school. Depending on individual school policies, you will either be required to attend the school that granted the deferral the following year or you may be permitted to make application to other schools in the interim. It is therefore extremely important, if you are considering the option of deferred matriculation, that you consult with the individual schools to which you are applying for additional information and that that you not sign any deferred matriculation contract until you are certain about any and all possible conditions.

4. State Residency Considerations

When deciding where to apply to medical school, a sensible place to begin is with the MSAR® Online site. Included in the descriptions of each medical school are data concerning the number of applicants and matriculants who are state residents and out-of-state residents as well as if the school can accept applications from out-f-state residents or international applicants. State residency is an important determinant of your chances for medical school acceptance at all public and some private schools. Public medical schools give preferential treatment to residents of their own state; some do not even consider out-of-state residents for admission. If a state has a policy of restricting its class to its own state residents, do not waste your time and money applying there if you are not a resident of that state.

Most private medical schools recruit from the national pool of applicants, rather than primarily from their state pool. At many private schools, however, preferential treatment is also given to in-state residents for a percentage of the class because these schools also receive support from state tax revenues. Some private schools are highly competitive in terms of applicants' GPA and MCAT® scores. Other private schools are somewhat less competitive. Check the MSAR® Online for information about selection factors, tuition costs, and the breakdown on state of legal residence. In the MSAR® you will also be able to determine how many resident and non-resident applicants make application to each school, how many are interviewed, and how many actually enter in the first-year class. Ascertain that schools of interest to you do not have special requirements. MSAR® Online also provides information of interest to potential applicants whose states do not have a medical school. In these instances, special arrangements have frequently been made by state governments with medical schools in neighboring states.

Before making final decisions, check with your premedical advisor, who understands the "track record" of your school and the best chances of acceptance for an applicant with your credentials. It is no surprise that once a medical school has admitted some students from a particular institution and has been pleased with their performance, there is a greater likelihood that students from that school will be accepted in the future. If this is the case for your college, you need to be aware of it.

Wherever you apply and to however many schools you apply, include the public schools in your state of legal residence in your application plans. If you are genuinely interested in attending a public school outside your own state, the EDP may be a good strategy. However, it is good idea to check with individual schools about their EDP policies; some require that EDP candidates be state residents, while a smaller number require EDP candidates to be non-residents.

5. AMCAS®: The Centralized Application Service

The American Medical College Application Service (AMCAS) is a centralized application processing service sponsored by the Association of American Medical Colleges (AAMC). For the 2014 entering class, 143 medical schools and programs will participate in AMCAS. Information about each institution's primary and secondary applications can be found in MSAR® Online. (Note: While Texas public MD/PhD programs participate in AMCAS, the Regular M.D. public medical schools in Texas use a centralized application of their own—the Texas Medical and Dental School Application Service, www.utsystem.edu/tmdsas.) (See Resources).

When applying to AMCAS-participating schools, you will submit one application, letters of evaluation, and official transcripts, regardless of the number of schools to which you apply; these must be submitted to AMCAS. AMCAS is an entirely Web-based application, accessed at: www.aamc. org/amcas. On this website, you will find links to key steps in initiating an application, video tutorials that will help you navigate the application, important frequently asked questions (FAQs), and other resources to assist you with the application, including a comprehensive instruction manual.

You must arrange for the registrar of every postsecondary school at which you have ever been registered to forward a complete set of official transcripts to AMCAS. Be aware that you may need to follow up with some institutions to be certain that all transcripts have actually been sent. In order to fill out the Course Work portion of the application, you will find it useful to have your own official copies of your transcripts. AMCAS uses your official transcripts to verify the courses and grades you have entered in your application; AMCAS also will transmit your MCAT® scores to all schools designated by you. Once processing has been completed, the application is sent to all schools designated in AMCAS. You will receive an email indicating that this has been done.

AMCAS also accepts letters of evaluation for medical schools participating in the AMCAS Letter Service. This service allows letter authors to send all letters to AMCAS rather than to each school and enables medical schools to receive all letters (along with all other applicant data) electronically from AMCAS. There are 141 schools that participate in the AMCAS Letter Service. Remember that under no circumstances will AMCAS provide applicants access to letters of evaluation.

At this point, AMCAS is finished with your application; from now on, you are in communication with each individual school. While some post-submission changes can be made, any other supplemental application materials should be sent to the individual medical school. Based on school policies, schools may send you a supplemental application and request an additional application fee, as well as some supporting documents. Once you have received supplemental application materials, the process of applying is similar for both AMCAS and non-AMCAS schools.

A section of the AMCAS application, the Essays section, appears to puzzle many applicants, but this is a very important component of the application. Applicants should consider carefully how they wish to present themselves in their Personal Comments essay. This is your first opportunity to inform an admissions office staff person or admission committee member about yourself: who you are, how you decided upon a medical career, what challenges you have overcome on your path to medical school, your unique characteristics and abilities, and personal experiences that have had a significant impact on your life and career choice. Try to be positive and confident in this section, without appearing arrogant or overconfident. Include concrete examples of your accomplishments, when appropriate, without appearing boastful. It is frequently a good idea to compose your Personal Comments, then put it aside for a few days before re-reading, evaluating, and possibly editing it. The final version should be very carefully checked for spelling, punctuation, grammar, and organization. Keep a hard copy of your Personal Comments essay for your own records.

6. Follow Up

Keep your records organized for all schools to which you have applied, with a checklist for each of the items that you are expected to supply to each school. Medical schools send you complete information regarding the supporting materials they require; these items should be checked off as they are sent. Most medical schools have an on-line mechanism for applicants to track the completion of their applications. If there is no mechanism and you do not receive notice of completion, you may wish to call the school's admissions office to inquire as to the status of your file.

It is your responsibility to see that your file is complete at each medical school to which you have applied. While supplementary materials differ for each school, they typically include faculty evaluations (or a composite prehealth committee letter). It is suggested that you supply the number of letters requested and not inundate the admission committee with more than it has requested.

New transcripts of your college coursework should be sent by the registrar's office to those schools at which your application is pending, if the new grades are higher than those on your initial application. Many schools will require grade reports for academic work completed during the application cycle. A personal note along with photocopies of the new grade report will usually suffice. A final official copy of your transcript will be required only after acceptance.

Finally, a number of medical schools require a recent passport size picture as a component of their supplementary application materials. Photos are also needed for MCAT® registration. These photographs help to identify you at interviews and can later be used to confirm your identity at the time of matriculation.

Acceptance

1. What You Can Expect from the Medical Schools

    AAMC-member medical schools agree to abide by a uniform set of recommendations to govern the process of accepting first-year students. These are sometime referred to as the admission "traffic rules." Accordingly, medical schools agree not to inform candidates of acceptance prior to October 16th, except for EDP applicants who will be informed of the outcome of their EDP application by October 1. By March 30, each school is required to have issued a number of acceptances equal to or greater than the number of places in the first year class. Prior to May 15, accepted applicants have at least two weeks to respond to an offer of acceptance and can hold acceptance offers from any other schools without penalty. After May 15, medical schools may implement school-specific procedures for accepted applicants who, without adequate explanation, continue to hold one or more places at other schools. These procedures may require applicants to respond to acceptance offers in less than two weeks and/or submit a statement of intent, a deposit, or both. The acceptance deposit for most medical schools is $100 or less, and it is often refundable until May 15. After June 1, any school that plans to make an acceptance offer to an applicant already known to have been accepted by another school for that entering class should ensure that the other school is advised of this offer at the time that the offer is made. Once accepted applicants have enrolled in medical school or have begun an orientation period immediately prior to enrollment, no additional acceptances may be offered the student by another medical school.

    A complete statement of the "AAMC Recommendations for Medical School and MD-PhD Admission Officers" can be found on the AAMC web site at: https://www.aamc.org/students/applying/recommendations/.

2. What the Medical Schools Expect from You

    In a letter of acceptance, medical schools will tell you how much time you have to respond to their offer, as well as any other conditions of acceptance. They expect you to respond to their offer in writing, whether you accept or decline, within the time period they designate.

    Your prompt decision and response to the notification process is important to you and other applicants, as well as to the medical schools where you have been accepted.

    AAMC-member medical schools have also developed a set of admission "traffic rules" for applicants. Applicants are expected to engage in timely communication with schools and to notify schools promptly when there are changes in their contact information. When applicants will be unavailable for an extended period of time, they are expected to identify a responsible party with authority to make decisions on their behalf. Applicants are expected to respond promptly to interview invitations. They are reminded of the importance of getting an early start on their financial aid applications. In addition, after May 15 each year, applicants are only allowed to hold a single acceptance. However, they are permitted to remain on any alternate (waiting) lists that they wish to continue to consider until the time that they matriculate at a medical school or begin the school's pre-matriculation or orientation program immediately prior to matriculation. When an applicant has matriculated at a medical school or has begun a pre-matriculation or orientation period immediately prior to matriculation, s/he must withdraw any applications from consideration at all other schools at which they remain active until that time.

A complete statement of the "AAMC Recommendations for Medical School and MD — PhD Applicants" can be found on the AAMC website at: https://www.aamc.org/students/applying/recommendations/.

3. Multiple Acceptances

    The suggested procedure is as follows: after you receive your first acceptance, rank the schools to which you have applied in order of preference. Send a letter of withdrawal to all schools on your list that are lower than the school to which you have been accepted. As you receive each new acceptance either accept it or reject it, on the basis of how that school compares with the school where you are already holding a seat, and withdraw from any schools that are lower on your list. If you accept the offer, you are still free to accept an offer from a higher priority school if you later receive an offer from that school. When you receive an acceptance from your first-choice school, withdraw from all other schools. In other words, applicants should hold no more than one medical school place at any time, although the medical school at which that place is held may change.

    Usually the only legitimate reason to hold two or more acceptances at any one time involves the question of financial aid. If the financial aid package offered will determine where you can attend medical school, you may wait until you receive this information before relinquishing your alternate acceptances. Applicants are expected to have reduced the number of seats they are holding to one school and to withdraw from all other schools from which acceptances have been received immediately after May 15. They may, however, maintain their applications at those higher priority schools from which they have not received a decision (i.e., remain on the alternate list) after May 15.

4. The Alternate List

    Each year, medical schools "lose" some of those applicants to whom they have offered seats as those applicants choose to attend other medical schools. To cope with this eventuality, schools keep lists of candidates who would be acceptable to them if they had an available place. This list is usually referred to as the "alternate list" or "wait list." After initial acceptances have been sent out, applicants are informed if they are on the alternate list. Unfortunately, there is no uniformity concerning wait listing; every school appears to have its own preferred method. Nevertheless, there are several broad categories into which procedures fall.

    At some schools, the alternate list appears to be "written in stone." The list is ranked by admission committee members, and alternates are accepted from the list in strict numerical order. There is generally nothing an applicant can do to enhance his or her position on the list. At schools where alternate lists are not ranked, the lists are reviewed periodically and some movement may be possible. Applicants to these schools should inquire as to whether or not additional information may be submitted to update files.

    Those schools that divide their wait lists into sections (for example, "upper," "middle," or "lower third") usually inform applicants where they are on the list and give them guidelines as to their chance of acceptance from the list based on prior years' experience.

5. School Procedures

    All schools inform candidates when they have been placed on their alternate list. The letter may or may not contain further elaboration of the school's policy. The answers to such questions as how long the list is, where you stand on the list, and how many applicants have been accepted from the alternate list in the past depend on each school. The best way to have questions answered is to speak to a staff member in the school's admissions office and/or to your health professions advisor.

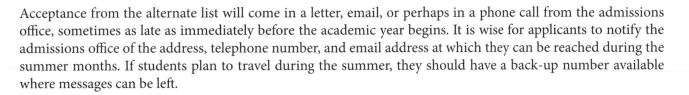

Acceptance from the alternate list will come in a letter, email, or perhaps in a phone call from the admissions office, sometimes as late as immediately before the academic year begins. It is wise for applicants to notify the admissions office of the address, telephone number, and email address at which they can be reached during the summer months. If students plan to travel during the summer, they should have a back-up number available where messages can be left.

6. Candidates' Responses

When you learn that you have been placed on an alternate list and you are interested in attending that school, the first thing to do is respond to the school electronically or in writing. Let the school know that you want to keep your place on the alternate list and that you are interested in the school. Next, find out as much as possible about your status by contacting the medical school admissions office and by speaking with your health professions advisor. Medical schools do not mind your contacting them when you have been named an alternate; if anything, it is considered a sign of your continuing interest in the school. More importantly, you should ascertain whether or not there is anything you can do that will influence your chances of acceptance. Items meaningful at some schools are your grade report from the past semester or summer session, any honors you received after your application was submitted, publications, or new experiences that might be relevant to your application.

If you are on several medical schools' alternate lists, your chances of being accepted by one of the schools increases. If you have not received an acceptance, but have been placed on an alternate list, it is a good idea to make tentative plans for the following year, should you not ultimately receive an acceptance. Psychologically, it is better to be involved in some positive action rather than merely fantasizing about receiving an acceptance. Should you actually receive that acceptance, you will probably have very little difficulty in adjusting. If you should not, then you have alternative plans already in place. The probability for success on a reapplication is usually good, especially if you begin right away to take steps to strengthen your application in some significant way during the intervening year.

Special Programs

1. Joint Degree Programs

    a. MD /PhD Degree Programs
       The MSAR Online lists joint and combined degree programs for each medical school in the "Combined Degrees and Special Programs" section of the institution's profile. These programs are sometimes administered collaboratively by the medical school and the graduate school at an institution. They provide students with the opportunity to pursue both the MD and PhD degrees in an integrated program. At present, such programs have been identified at the majority of medical schools in the United States. Depending on the program, enrollment can vary from two or three to over one hundred students. The size of the program relative to the overall enrollment in the school is another way in which programs differ. In some schools, the proportion of students pursuing combined degree programs is large, while at other schools it is very small.

       Several programs have been in operation for decades, when the National Institutes of Health established the Medical Scientist Training Program (MSTP) to encourage MD/PhD education by providing funds to medical schools to support students enrolled in MD/PhD programs, while others have been more recently established. The National Institute of General Medical Sciences maintains websites that contain general information about the Medical Scientist Training Program (www.nigms.nih.gov/Training/InstPredoc/PredocDesc-MSTP.htm) and about institutions that have received MSTP funding (publications.nigms.nih.gov/multimedia/map/mstp/).

Students in MD/PhD programs are frequently, although not always, provided with financial support, a practical necessity in light of the six to eight years of enrollment required. In addition to federal funding available for student support, funding often occurs via the medical school and/or graduate department. Several programs have received significant endowments from outside private sources.

MD/PhD programs vary with respect to the fields in which PhD's are offered and the number of different PhD programs available. Typically, the PhD can be pursued in a variety of the basic sciences, including, but not limited to, anatomy, biochemistry, cell biology, developmental biology, genetics, immunology, microbiology, molecular biology, neurosciences, pathology, and pharmacology. Medical schools that are a component of research universities are likely to enable students to pursue the PhD in graduate departments of the university and are, therefore, also likely to be able to offer more diverse areas of doctoral specialization. Reflecting the "high-tech" nature of modern medicine, several schools offer combined degree programs in medicine and the engineering sciences, physics, or computer science. In responding to the need to educate physicians to deal with the social and economic forces affecting medicine, some MD/PhD programs enable students to pursue their doctoral education in the social and behavioral sciences and the humanities, in disciplines such as anthropology, economics, philosophy, and psychology.

Students typically apply to joint degree programs at the same time they apply to the medical school, and most programs have a separate admission process in which admission to the medical school and admission to the graduate program are independent decisions. Some programs also accept applications from first- and second-year medical students at their school. The sequence of study generally begins with the medical curriculum, but there is variation and general agreement among programs that flexibility in scheduling is desirable.

Selection criteria for MD/PhD programs are generally identical to those for medical school, although higher standards may be applied to grades and test scores because of the demanding nature of combined degree education. An important additional criterion is research ability, usually evaluated on the basis of an applicant's previous experience, letters of recommendation, and discussion in interviews. If you are seeking information about MD/PhD programs, you should consider importance of research to your overall professional goals. If your primary interest is in clinical medicine, and you are considering combined degree programs because you are interested in a second field or because it might be a good "backup," the investment of an additional four years of education is probably not wise. The commitment to research must be very strong to provide a rationale and motivation to pursue both the MD and PhD degrees. There are, of course, excellent opportunities for carrying out high-level research in clinical settings. Alumni of MD/PhD programs have joined the leadership ranks in academic medicine, in government and independent research laboratories, in the corporate sector, and in public and private voluntary organizations. Many are already active in determining public policy, and it can be anticipated that those with scholarly training in the social sciences and humanities will be nationally prominent in this sphere. It is expected that there will be an ongoing need for physicians with advanced research skills and for those with the sophisticated understanding of the socio-economic forces impinging upon health care that graduate training provides.

b. Other Joint Degree Programs

It also is possible to pursue a medical degree in conjunction with another graduate or professional degree: M.P.H., M.B.A., J.D., or other Master's degree (e.g., in Education). In 2013, 24 schools were identified MD/J.D. programs in their MSAR Online profiles. An additional 69 schools noted MD/M.B.A. degree programs and 96 schools listed the availability of MD/M.P.H. programs in MSAR Online.. You can do specific searches for various available MD/graduate programs in MSAR Online (www.aamc.org/msar).

2. Baccalaureate-MD Programs

    Approximately one-quarter of the medical schools sponsor joint baccalaureate/MD programs with either their own undergraduate institutions or other schools in their geographic region. The nature of these programs varies greatly, with a small number providing accelerated programs leading to both degrees in a six to seven-year time period. Most programs provide students with the opportunity to complete their undergraduate and medical studies in seven or eight years. Typically, such programs offer the baccalaureate degree after completion of the first year of medical school. A complete listing of such programs, including 44 individual program profiles can be found in MSAR online. If you are interested in pursuing such a program, consult with your health professions advisor. Be aware, however, that many of these medical school programs are, in fact, restricted to students from their own undergraduate schools or others with which they have joint programs. For more information about these programs from the point of view of students, see the Aspiring Docs fact sheets at: www.aamc.org/students/aspiring/296544/factsheetcollection.html

Schools and Colleges of Medicine

A comprehensive listing of all medical schools granting the MD in the United States and Canada, as well as information about various criteria used to compare medical schools (e.g., amount of research funding from the National Institutes of Health, tuition and fees) can be found on the AAMC's MSAR Online website at: www.aamc.org/msar.

Resources

1. *Medical School Admission Requirements (MSAR)* Online and MSAR: Getting Started. Comprehensively updated and published annually (in early spring) by AAMC. This website contains the latest available information on selection factors and the credentials of accepted applicants for each medical school in the U.S. and Canada. The site should be consulted by every student during the time the decision is being made as to where to apply. *MSAR: Getting Started* is designed to help you prepare for and apply to medical school. *Medical School Admission Requirements,* or *MSAR*, contains chapters on deciding if a career in medicine is right for you, how to prepare for medical school during your undergraduate years, and an overview of what is learned in medical education and MD/PhD programs. You also get details about the MCAT® exam and AMCAS application, tips on choosing the right school, guidance on how to apply, information on how admissions decisions are made, diversity in medical schools, financing, applicant and matriculant data, and more. It is available in print or an ebook, which can be downloaded for your e-reader, tablet or computer. All products can be ordered from the AAMC (www.aamc.org/msar).

2. *MCAT Essentials.* Available as a PDF document from the AAMC website at: www.aamc.org/mcat.

3. *The Official Guide to the MCAT Exam.* The only guide created by the developers of the MCAT exam and developed with feedback from focus groups conducted among aspiring and current medical students. You get insight, tips, and valuable guidance to help you prepare for the exam. The latest edition of the guide is updated to reflect the changes in the 2013 MCAT exam, plus provides current data on MCAT scores and GPAs, and score changes on retake exams. Available through AAMC publications at: www.aamc.org/publications.

4. Various AAMC print and electronic publications of interest to applicants. Available on the AAMC website at: www.aamc.org/publications; click "browse by topics" and then click on "applicants".

5. AAMC Careers in Medicine Program on-line career planning program. Available on the AAMC website at: www.aamc.org/careersinmedicine.

6. *FIRST.* The AAMC has recently instituted a comprehensive program on pre-medical, medical, and post-graduate physician indebtedness entitled *FIRST* (Financial Instruments, Resources, Services, and Tools) which provides useful information and economic calculators for all levels of physicians in their careers. The website is at www.aamc.org/services/first/.

7. The AAMC student website: www.aamc.org/students/. A comprehensive site for those considering a career in medicine, those applying to medical school, medical students, and residents.

8. The website of the AspiringDocs.org program: www.aamc.org/aspiringdocs. Information for persons from groups underrepresented in medicine who are considering a career in the medical profession.

9. *The New Physician.* A monthly magazine published by the American Medical Student Association, 1910 Association Drive, Reston, VA 22091 (www.amsa.org). Membership in AMSA for premedical students is available for a fee which includes a subscription to The New Physician, a good source of information about trends in medical education, financial aid, and other timely topics.

10. *Write for Success: Preparing a Professional School Application.* A booklet written specifically to help applicants to medical school present themselves in the best possible light. Published by NAAHP, Inc., P.O. Box 1518, Champaign IL 61824-1518; (217) 355-0063; fax: 217/355-1287; www.naahp.org.

11. *Interviewing for Health Professions Schools.* A booklet offering concise, comprehensive information that helps students prepare for the interview. Published by NAAHP, Inc. (See address above.)

12. The website of the Bureau of Health Professions, Health Resources Services Administration: www.bhpr.hrsa.gov.

13. The website of the American Medical College Application Service (AMCAS): www.aamc.org/amcas. Information about making application to AMCAS-participating schools and programs.

14. The website of the American Medical Association: www.ama-assn.org. Information about becoming a physician; preparing for, applying to, and paying for medical school; and choosing a specialty.

15. The website of the Texas Medical and Dental Schools Application Service: www.utsystem.edu/tmdsas. Information about making application to the public medical schools in the state of Texas.

16. The website of the AAMC Survey of Resident/Fellow Stipends and Benefits: www.aamc.org/data/stipend/ Information about resident salaries.

17. S.E. & Etzel, S.I. (2010) Graduate Medical Education 2009-2010. JAMA, 304 (1): 1255-1270.

18. The website of the AAMC Facts 2012 Summary: www.aamc.org/facts. The AAMC FACTS tables comprise the most comprehensive and objective data on U.S. medical school applicants, matriculants, enrollment, graduates, Electronic Residency Application Service (ERAS) applicants, and MD/PhD students available to the public free of charge.

NATUROPATHIC MEDICINE

General Description of Profession

Naturopathic medicine blends centuries-old, natural, non-toxic therapies with current advances in the study of health and human systems, covering all aspects of family health from prenatal to geriatric and palliative care.

Naturopathic medicine concentrates on whole-patient wellness. Treatment and therapies are tailored to the individual patient, and emphasize prevention and self-care. The philosophy of naturopathic medicine is rooted in finding the underlying cause of the patient's condition rather than focusing solely on symptomatic treatment. Naturopathic doctors (NDs) serve as primary care providers, an area of great current and future demand. As such, NDs cooperate with all other branches of medical science to refer patients to other practitioners and specialists for diagnosis or treatment when appropriate. Patient conditions most commonly treated by naturopathic doctors include fatigue, menstruation and hormonal issues, allergies, depression/insomnia, thyroid problems, weight/appetite, cholesterol, gastrointestinal disorders, headaches/migraines, blood pressure issues, diabetes, pain and fibromyalgia. Naturopathic doctors sit for national board examinations and are licensed practitioners.

The major distinction between the ND and MD is that the ND has always been trained to approach diagnosis and treatment from a "holistic" perspective, treating the whole person rather than simply treating symptoms. Secondly, the ND receives specialized training in natural therapies such as botanical medicine and clinical nutrition, in addition to core medical training common to all licensed doctors.

Dedicated to study and celebration of nature's healing power, naturopathic medicine is not so much defined by specific methods or modalities, but rather by six fundamental principles that serve to guide every aspect of the naturopathic doctor's orientation to health and wellness:

First Do No Harm: Utilize the most natural, least invasive and least toxic therapies.

Identify and Treat the Causes: Look beyond symptoms to address the underlying cause of illness.

Prevention: Focus on promoting health, wellness and disease prevention.

Treat the Whole Person: View the body as an integrated whole in all its physical, emotional and spiritual dimensions.

Doctor as Teacher: Educate patients in the steps to achieving and maintaining health.

The Healing Power of Nature: Trust in the body's inherent wisdom to heal itself, support that process and remove obstacles to cure.

With a sound diagnostic biomedical science background, Western history and physical examination, laboratory testing and diagnostic imaging, naturopathic doctors treat patients using a wide variety of modalities, including: Clinical Nutrition; Botanical Medicine; Physical Medicine; Homeopathy; Lifestyle Counseling; Hydrotherapy; Pharmacology; Minor Office Procedures; and Acupuncture and Oriental Medicine *(only in scope of practice in a few states.)*

As evidenced by the numbers of patients seeking their care, naturopathic doctors find themselves serving a growing patient population:

- More than 80 million Americans turn to complementary and alternative medicine (CAM) every year;
- The majority of adults (68 percent) have used at least one kind of CAM therapy in their lifetime;

- At least 1/3 of cancer patients turn to a CAM therapy, most commonly in combination with allopathic treatment;
- Americans reportedly spent close to $34 billion on CAM treatments and products in 2007, a 26 percent increase from an estimated $27 billion ten years earlier;
- More specifically to naturopathic medicine, the number of adult visits to ND practitioners rose 46 percent over a recent five-year period — from 498,000 annual visits in 2002 to 729,000 visits in 2007.

Background of the Naturopathic Profession

Established as a profession at the end of the nineteenth century, naturopathic medicine came into its own in the United States in the early 1900s. In their early practices, naturopathic doctors made use of diet, exercise, hydrotherapy, osseous and soft tissue manipulation, clinical nutrition, and botanical and homeopathic medicines, drawing on traditional healing practices that had evolved over hundreds of years.

Mid-century, with the promise of new miracle cures from pharmaceutical drugs such as antibiotics and the growth of the "high tech" and pharmaceutically-based system of conventional medicine, the widespread use of holistic therapies began to decline. Resurgence then began in the 1970s and has continued throughout the past several decades, culminating in approximately 68 percent of the U.S. population now utilizing some form of integrative medicine, including naturopathic medicine.

The Decision to Pursue Naturopathic Medicine

To make a well-informed career choice it is important to learn as much about the profession of naturopathic medicine as possible. A ND school applicant should make an effort early throughout their undergraduate years to enhance his or her knowledge and understanding of the field. The best way to begin exploring naturopathic medicine is to speak with a licensed naturopathic doctor, through interviewing or shadowing in his or her practice. For more information on finding an ND near you, visit the American Association of Naturopathic Physicians (AANP) website www.naturopathic.org or the Canadian Association of Naturopathic Doctors (CAND) website www.naturopathicassoc.ca/.

Quality of Life

The core philosophy behind the practice of naturopathic medicine strives for a harmonious balance between science and nature. In practice, this philosophy offers a mutually beneficial synergy of both patients and providers. A common and collective goodwill mission is one defining characteristic found in the typical naturopathic physician. Here is a rudimentary snapshot of the ND population:

- 52% treat underserved populations
- 69% are in solo practices or are principals in a clinic environment
- 66% have instituted 'green living' into their practices
- 37% offer a sliding fee scale to their patients
- More than 60% are members of various environmental groups

The broad scope *and* flexibility of natural medicine allows naturopathic doctors to create careers and lifestyles suited to their personalities, goals, values and dreams. ND school alumni have created private and collaborative clinics, compounding pharmacies, community education programs and a range of treatment centers around the world, promoting integrative medicine, research and innovative approaches to health.

Outlook for the Future

Because of rapidly expanding interest in natural health care, there are more career opportunities in naturopathic medicine than ever before. The United States Department of Labor estimates growth for professional opportunities from 10-19% by 2020. Graduates of naturopathic programs are establishing thriving practices, with many choosing multi-faceted careers: They are working as primary care doctors in private practice and in integrative clinics. They are working as research scientists and faculty members in both alternative and conventional medical institutions. And they're filling positions as public health administrators, natural pharmacists, research and development scientists in the natural products industry, consultants to industry, insurance companies, public service, political and other organizations, wellness educators, and practitioners in medical spas in the U.S. and abroad

The number of NDs practicing has tripled over the past 10 years, no doubt in response to growing patient interest. With field expansion, the naturopathic profession continues to spark interest of those dissatisfied with conventional medicine, both patients and doctors alike. As a result, the job market for ND graduates continues to expand, with multi-disciplinary practices including MDs and DOs hiring new grads as associates. Naturopathic doctors are also working on Indian reservations, in community health centers and in specialty fields such as diabetes, allergies, cancer, pain, pediatrics and women's health. The emerging field of spa medicine is also vigorously hiring NDs at resorts, on cruise ships and in planned communities.

Currently, the practice of naturopathic medicine is regulated in 16 states, six Canadian provinces, the District of Columbia, and the U.S. territories of Puerto Rico and the U.S. Virgin Islands. Legal provisions still allow naturopathic doctors to consult with patients, making recommendations and suggestions based on prior diagnosis, in most of the yet unlicensed states and provinces. Efforts to license the practice of naturopathic medicine are currently underway in several populous states, potentially opening up additional opportunities for patients to access naturopathic medicine.

The U.S. Department of Labor (DOL) forecasts that employment of physicians in general will grow faster than average for all occupations through 2014, and predicts that consumer demand for alternative health care in particular will also continue to grow, all driven in large part by the rapidly increasing older population. The occupation of naturopathic physician specifically was named as one of the DOL's "Bright Outlook Occupations" in terms of labor force growth projections. The DOL has projected 15,300 job openings in the field of "Health Diagnosing and Treating Practitioners" in the U.S. (2008-2018). (This is a composite figure comprised of five distinct professions: Acupuncturists, Nurse Anesthetists, Nurse Practitioners, Naturopathic Physicians and Orthoptists (specialized eye care professionals).

Planning a Program of Study

An ideal candidate for a career in natural medicine is the compassionate student who exhibits a strong aptitude for medicine and the sciences, as well as a desire to treat future patients as partners in health. These students often come from eclectic backgrounds; many having already worked in another profession — health care or otherwise — and as a result bring their own rich history and insight to their 'doctor's bag.' Common character traits include:

- High level of respect for the environment and environmental causes;
- High level of social concern;
- Good communication skills (a pleasant "bedside manner");
- Inquisitive nature, likes to get to the root of the problem;
- Strong desire to make a difference, and measures personal success in terms of impact rather than status;
- Rich background in volunteerism;
- Bright, intelligent, with an aptitude for the sciences and a history of academic success;
- A keen understanding of both the art *and* the science of medicine.

Choice of Undergraduate Major

Naturopathic medical colleges look for incoming students who have pursued a well-rounded curriculum and have demonstrated

academic proficiency in the sciences. Most health professions advisors agree that a student should select a major based upon his or her interests and aptitudes; and will therefore be more likely to enjoy the courses and succeed in their chosen profession. The accredited ND programs typically require a base of undergraduate science courses that include physics, biology, and general and organic chemistry. Math and psychology courses may also be specified. Check with each school in order to ensure that all prerequisite requirements are met in advance. In addition to the required coursework, other science courses to strengthen a student's background and to better prepare him or her for a naturopathic course of study include: anatomy, physiology, biochemistry, botany and developmental psychology.

The Admissions Process

Candidates should begin planning a minimum of one to two years in advance. Application submission can begin as early as one year before the planned year of entry. Even though "deadlines" for application are later than this, it is advantageous to begin the application process as early as possible. All naturopathic medical colleges operate on a rolling admissions basis, so decisions are made throughout the application cycle.

Factors Evaluated by Admission Committees

In evaluating candidates for naturopathic medical programs, admissions counselors look for students who want to be challenged academically yet feel comfortable relying on their own intuition and creativity. They look for high-level critical thinkers who are flexible enough to deal with the challenge of formulating personalized treatment plans.

Applicants must demonstrate that they possess internal qualities essential to becoming naturopathic doctors, including excellent communication skills, concern for others, integrity, curiosity, motivation and a strong belief in the philosophy and efficacy of naturopathic medicine. An aptitude for the sciences is important, as is overall intelligence, including emotional intelligence. Prospective students must also demonstrate appropriate observational and interpersonal skills, motor function, intellectual-conceptual abilities, integrative and quantitative abilities, communication skills, and behavioral, emotional and social maturity.

1. Academic Record

    Entrance into an accredited naturopathic medical school requires a bachelor's degree, along with extensive pre-medical course work. Upon enrollment, a naturopathic medical education promises a rigorous four-year curriculum, requiring in its first two years the same biomedical sciences required at other medical schools. Some naturopathic medical schools do require more credit hours of biomedical science coursework than their MD counterparts.

    Admission committees at naturopathic medical schools are interested in admitting students who are well suited to becoming naturopathic doctors and have the academic ability to complete the program. Schools typically looks for candidates with a strong academic record, extracurricular activities, a commitment to volunteer work and exposure to the naturopathic medical profession.

2. The Standardized Testing (GRE and MCAT)

    At this time, none of the naturopathic medical schools require their applicants to sit for the GRE or MCAT. However, many applicants do submit official scores with their application for admission.

3. The Letters of Recommendation

    Most naturopathic medical colleges require a minimum of two letters of recommendation. Letters may be required from one or all of the following references: a faculty member or a previous instructor, a current or previous employer, and a naturopathic doctor or other licensed health care provider. Individual schools may

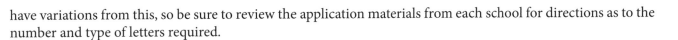

have variations from this, so be sure to review the application materials from each school for directions as to the number and type of letters required.

4. The Interview

All naturopathic medical colleges require an interview before admitting an applicant. The interview is an opportunity for the prospective student to demonstrate his or her knowledge and commitment to the field of naturopathic medicine. It also offers a good opportunity to continue exploring and learning more about the schools under consideration.

5. Extracurricular Activities and Work Experience

As part of the application process, prospective students will be asked to identify any and all extracurricular activities such as volunteer work, professional experience and community work.

6. Age

While the majority of applicants fall within the 21 to 30 age range, applicants of all ages are considered by naturopathic medical schools, and students of all ages are enrolled in the program.

The Application

1. When and Where to Apply

The schools are on a rolling admissions basis, and some offer "early decision" programs. By applying early, a student's application materials will be processed in a timelier manner. Application deadline dates are established by each college, and therefore differ slightly among the schools. Application may be made directly to the schools or through the Centralized Application Service.

2. The Centralized Application Service

Currently, four of the seven AANMC accredited member schools participate in the Naturopathic Doctor Centralized Application Service (NDCAS). NDCAS is a service designed to save time and reduce yours costs by allowing you to apply to multiple naturopathic medical schools at once using a single, web-based application and only one set of materials. More information is available at www.ndcas.org.

Resources

1. Association of Accredited Naturopathic Medical Colleges (AANMC), 818 18th Street NW, Suite 250, Washington, DC 20006; www.aanmc.org. The AANMC has seven affiliated North American ND schools — five in the U.S. and two in Canada. Prospective students may subscribe to the AANMC e-newsletter, and advisors may register for educational forums, webinars and all electronic profession updates.

2. American Association of Naturopathic Physicians (AANP), 818 18th Street NW, Suite 250, Washington, DC 20006; (866) 538-2267; www.naturopathic.org.

3. Canadian Association of Naturopathic Doctors (CAND), 20 Holly St., Ste. 200

4. Toronto, Ontario, Canada M4S 3B1. Toll free: (800) 551-4381 Canada: (416) 496-8633 www.naturopathicassoc.ca

5. Council on Naturopathic Medical Education (CNME), P.O. Box 178, Great Barrington, MA 01230; (413) 528-8877; www.cnme.org. The CNME is the recognized accreditor by the United States Department of Education for naturopathic medical programs in North America.

NURSING

General Description of Profession

Nursing is the nation's largest health care profession with more than 3.1 million registered nurses practicing nation-wide. Despite its large size, many more nurses are needed into the foreseeable future to meet the growing demand for nursing care. As you plan or consider a career as a registered nurse, you should know these facts:

- The U.S. Bureau of Labor Statistics projects that employment for registered nurses will grow faster than most other occupations through 2020.
- Nursing students comprise more than half of all health professions students.
- Nurses comprise the largest single component of hospital staff, are the primary providers of hospital patient care, and deliver most of the nation's long-term care.
- Most health care services involve some form of care by nurses. Although 62.2 percent of all employed RNs work in hospitals, many are employed in a wide range of other settings, including private practices, public health agencies, primary care clinics, home health care, outpatient surgicenters, health maintenance organizations, nursing school-operated nursing centers, insurance and managed care companies, nursing homes, schools, mental health agencies, hospices, the military, and industry. Other nurses work in careers as college and university educators preparing future nurses or as scientists developing advances in many areas of health care and health promotion.
- Though often working collaboratively, nurses do not simply "assist" physicians and other health care providers. Instead, they practice independently within their own defined scope of practice. Nursing roles range from direct patient care to case management, establishing nursing practice standards, developing quality assurance procedures, and directing complex nursing care systems.
- With more than four times as many RNs in the United States as physicians, nursing delivers an extended array of health care services, including primary and preventive care by advanced, independent nurse practitioners in such clinical areas as pediatrics, family health, women's health, and gerontological care. Nursing's scope also includes care by clinical nurse specialists, certified nurse-midwives and nurse anesthetists, as well as care in cardiac, oncology, neonatal, neurological, and obstetric/gynecological nursing and other advanced clinical specialties.
- The primary pathway to professional nursing, as compared to technical-level practice, is the four-year Bachelor of Science degree in nursing (BSN). Registered nurses are prepared either through a four-year baccalaureate program; a two- to three-year associate degree in nursing program; or a three-year hospital diploma program. Graduates of all three programs take the same state licensing exam, the NCLEX-RN. (The number of diploma programs has declined steadily — to less than 6 percent of all basic RN education programs — as nursing education has shifted from hospital-operated instruction into the college and university system.)

The Decision to Pursue Nursing

Some of the most common reasons nurses state they pursued nursing include:

- **Competitive salaries:** New RNs can earn up to $55,000+ annually; advance practice nurses can command six-figure salaries.
- **Job security:** According to the American Hospital Association, three-quarters of all vacancies in hospitals are for RNs.
- **Career outlook is bright:** The Bureau of Labor Statistics has identified registered nursing as one of the top occupation in terms of job growth through the year 2020. Government analysts also project that more than 495,000 new RN positions will be created within the next 10 years, which will account for two-fifths of all new jobs in the health care sector.

- **Endless opportunities and flexibility in workplace:** Nursing offers a wide array of professional practice opportunities in a variety of clinical settings. For example, though acute care facilities employ the highest number of nurses, home health care agencies, clinics, hospices, universities, armed forces, and large companies also employ nurses. Within these settings, nurses are educated to work with patients across the life span, from the neonate to the older adult. The choices in specialization are immense, including, pediatrics, critical care, psychiatry, dialysis, oncology, transplant, emergency room, community health, hospice/palliative care, geriatrics, among others. Nurses with advanced education also fill a variety of leadership roles including nursing faculty, administrator, researcher, policymaker, and independent practitioner.
- **No other healthcare team member spends more time at the bedside than the nurse.** The nurse is highly valued for his/her contribution to the care of patients, whether they are working in a clinic, in an acute-care facility, or out in the community as a visiting nurse. Because of their unique role in having a large amount of time with patients, their assessments are crucial to the interdisciplinary plan of care and patient safety.

Outlook for the Future

The career outlook for RNs is bright with the intensified hiring of RNs being spurred by:

- the mounting health care needs of increasing numbers of elderly;
- a growing population of hospitalized patients who are older, more acutely ill, and in need of more skilled RNs per patient;
- the rapid expansion of front-line primary care to many sites throughout the community;
- technological advances requiring more highly skilled nursing care; and
- an aging RN workforce and a projected wave of retirements.

All projections forecast accelerating demand for nursing care and for nurses with expanded education and skills. Still, the accelerating demand for RNs varies by region and market. As a result, flexibility will be key for both entering and moving within the profession. Some graduates may need to pursue employment in different parts of their home states, in another state, or even in another region where hiring in certain clinical settings or specialties may be more plentiful.

With patient care growing more complex, ensuring a sufficient RN workforce is not merely a matter of how many nurses are needed, but rather an issue of preparing an adequate number of nurses with the right educational mix to meet health care demands. Recently, the Institute of Medicine called for 80 percent of the RN workforce to hold at least a baccalaureate degree by the year 2020.

Planning a Program of Study

In 1980, almost 55 percent of employed registered nurses held a hospital diploma as their highest educational credential, 22 percent held the bachelor's degree, and 18 percent an associate degree. By 2008, a diploma was the highest educational credential for only 13.9 percent of RNs, while the number with bachelor's degrees as their highest education had climbed to 36.8 percent, with 36.1 percent holding an associate degree and 13.2 percent holding graduate degrees as their top academic preparation. In 2009, 19,606 RNs with diplomas or associate degrees graduated from BSN programs.

The American Association of Colleges of Nursing (AACN), the American Organization of Nurse Executives, the American Nurses Association, Institute of Medicine (IOM), and other leading authorities all recognize that the level of education makes a difference in nursing practice. The federal Health Resources and Services Administration is calling for baccalaureate preparation for at least two-thirds of the nursing workforce, due to evidence that clearly shows that higher levels of nursing education are linked with lower patient mortality rates, fewer errors, and greater job satisfaction among RNs. The IOM is calling for at least 80% of the RN workforce to be baccalaureate-prepared by 2020. In addition, nurse executives, federal agencies, the military, leading nursing organizations, health care founda-

tions, magnet hospitals, and minority nurse advocacy groups understand the unique value that baccalaureate-prepared nurses bring to the practice setting and their contribution to quality nursing care.

Because there are many educational variations to becoming a nurse, visit the following website for planning a program of study: www.aacn.nche.edu/students/your-nursing-career.

Additional ways of obtaining a BSN, other than going the traditional 4-year route, include:

- Accelerated programs for adults with a baccalaureate or graduate degrees in other fields (see below);
- RN to BSN degree completion programs for those with an associate degree or diploma in nursing. Many of these programs are offered on-line;
- Baccalaureate nursing programs offered at community colleges.

Rise of Accelerated Nursing Programs

Shifts in the economy and the desire of many adults to make a difference in their work have increased interest in the nursing profession among "second-degree" students. For those with a prior degree, accelerated baccalaureate programs offer the quickest route to becoming a registered nurse with programs generally running 12-18 months long. Generic master's degrees, also accelerated in nature and geared to non-nursing graduates, generally take three years to finish. Students in these programs usually complete baccalaureate-level nursing courses in the first year followed by two years of graduate study.

Graduates of accelerated programs are prized by nurse employers who value the many layers of skill and education these graduates bring to the workplace. Employers report that these graduates are more mature, possess strong clinical skills, and are quick studies on the job. Many practice settings are partnering with schools and offering tuition repayment to graduates as a mechanism to recruit highly qualified nurses.

In 2012, 244 accelerated BSN and 66 accelerated master's degree programs were offered at nursing schools nationwide. For more information on the accelerating nursing program and for a listing of schools offering this degree, go to www.aacn.nche.edu/media-relations/fact-sheets/accelerated-programs.

Graduate Nursing Preparation

Though there is a great demand for nurses to provide direct care at the bedside, nurses with graduate preparation are also in high demand as advanced practice specialists, researchers, health care administrators, policy analysts, educators, and nurse executives. For students interested in pursuing graduate nursing education, examples of these programs include:

- Clinical Nurse Specialists
- Nurse Practitioner
- Nurse Midwife
- Nurse Anesthetist
- Clinical Nurse Leader
- Variety of Doctoral Studies (i.e. PhD, Doctorate of Nursing Practice or DNP)

Prepared typically in graduate programs, these advanced practice registered nurses (APRNs) include the following categories of clinicians:

- **Nurse Practitioners (NPs)** conduct physical exams; diagnose and treat common acute illnesses and injuries;

provide immunizations; manage high blood pressure, diabetes, and other chronic problems; order and interpret X-rays and other lab tests; and counsel patients on adopting healthy lifestyles and health care options as a part of their clinical roles. In addition to practicing in clinics and hospitals in metropolitan areas, the nation's estimated 155,000 nurse practitioners also deliver care in rural sites, inner cities, and other locations not adequately served by physicians, as well as to other populations, such as children in schools and the elderly. Many NPs work in pediatrics, family health, women's health, and other specialties, and some have private practices. Nurse practitioners can prescribe medications in all states, while 25 states have given NPs authority to practice independently without physician collaboration or supervision.

- **Clinical Nurse Specialists (CNSs)** provide care in a range of specialty areas, such as cardiac, oncology, neonatal, and obstetric/gynecological nursing, as well as pediatrics, neurological nursing, and psychiatric/mental health. Working in hospitals and other clinical sites, CNSs provide acute care and mental health services, develop quality assurance procedures, and serve as educators and consultants. An estimated 72,500 clinical nurse specialists are currently in practice.

- **Certified Nurse-Midwives (CNMs)** provide prenatal and gynecological care to normal healthy women; deliver babies in hospitals, private homes, and birthing centers; and continue with follow-up postpartum care. In 2002, CNM deliveries accounted for 8.1 percent of all births in the U.S., up from 6.5 percent in 1996, according to the National Center for Health Statistics. There are approximately 13,700 CNMs nationwide.

- **Certified Registered Nurse Anesthetists (CRNAs)** administer more than 65 percent of all anesthetics given to patients each year, and are the sole anesthesia providers in approximately two-thirds of all rural hospitals in the U.S., according to the American Association of Nurse Anesthetists (AANA). Of the 34 million anesthetics given annually, about 20 percent are administered by CRNAs practicing independently and 80 percent by CRNAs in collaboration with physician anesthesiologists, says AANA. Working in the oldest of the advanced nursing specialties, CRNAs administer anesthesia for all types of surgery in settings ranging from operating rooms and dental offices to outpatient surgical centers. There are more than 45,000 CRNAs in practice nationwide.

Mounting studies show that the quality of APRN care is comparable to MDs when they have the same level of authority, responsibilities, productivity, and administrative requirements (Newhouse et al., Nursing Economics, 2011; Mundinger, JAMA, 2000; Medical Care Research and Review, 2004). For example, inpatient surgical mortality is not affected by whether the anesthesia provider is a CRNA or an anesthesiologist (Pine, AANA Journal, 2003). Data from NP's working with the elderly show that they provide effective care to hospitalized geriatric patients, particularly older and sicker patients (Lambing, Journal of the American Academy of Nurse Practitioners, 2004). Physicians know and understand that they are limited in caring for so many sick patients. Michael E. Whitcomb, MD wrote, "Since the supply of physicians will not be adequate to care for the increasing population of patients with chronic disease, academic medicine's leadership must place the needs of the patients in the forefront and work with the leadership of nursing to determine how best to provide the care those patients will need. It is simply unacceptable to have the needs of those patients go unmet." (Academic Medicine, 2006)

Though currently offered at the master's level, AACN member institutions voted to move the education level required for advance nursing specialist roles to the doctoral level by the year 2015. Doctoral preparation is the preferred level of education for nurse faculty, one of the greatest areas of need in the profession. Nurse educators play a central role in preparing new nurses and adapting curriculum in response to changing technology and professional practices.

For more details on graduate-level nursing roles and educational program options, see www.aacn.nche.edu/students/financial-aid.

The Admissions Process

Each school of nursing has its own unique admission qualifications. However, with placements in nursing school

being so very competitive, nursing schools can afford to choose exceptional students. Certain factors include excellent GPA, community service, and letters of recommendation.

In addition, baccalaureate nursing students must complete a variety of liberal arts studies, math and science courses (i.e. chemistry, anatomy and physiology, microbiology, etc) before entering nursing training. Students complete hours of clinical training in labs, hospitals, community settings, etc.

Most successful nursing students possess a common set of attributes. These include:

- Strong science, math and communication skills;
- Desire to advocate for patients and their families;
- Desire to educate the community on health awareness and disease prevention;
- Able to communicate with other members of the interdisciplinary team;
- Skilled at coordinating care across many settings (i.e. acute care facility, homecare, long-term care, etc);
- Able to provide compassionate care for patients across the lifespan and their unique needs; and
- Desire to continue to learn, as practice constantly changes in regards to treatments, medications, etc.

When and Where to Apply

Interested students should contact nursing schools as early as possible to determine program entry requirements, as they vary from school to school and competition for acceptance in nursing programs is very competitive. Interested students are also encourage to use the profession's centralized application service – NursingCAS – to apply to nursing programs nationwide. For more details, see www.nursingcas.org.

Resources

1. Career profiles in nursing
    www.discovernursing.com
    www.nursesource.org
    www.nsna.org

2. Locating nursing programs
    www.aacn.nche.edu
    www.petersons.com

3. Financial aid for nursing students
    www.aacn.nche.edu/students/financial-aid

All statistical data mentioned are from:

4. American Association of Colleges of Nursing. (2010). Nursing Shortage Fact Sheet. Accessible on-line at www.aacn.nche.edu/Media/FactSheets/NursingShortage.htm.

5. American Association of Colleges of Nursing. (2010) 2010-2011 *Enrollment and Graduations in Baccalaureate and Graduate Programs in Nursing.* Washington, DC: American Association of Colleges of Nursing (AACN).

6. Health Resources and Services Administration. (September 2010). *The Registered Nurse Population: Findings From the 2008 National Sample Survey of Registered Nurses.* Washington, DC: U.S. Department of Health and Human Services.

OCCUPATIONAL THERAPY

General Description of Profession

The practice of occupational therapy means the therapeutic use of everyday life activities (occupations) with individuals, groups, or populations to address participation and function in roles and situations in home, school, workplace, community, and other settings.

Occupational therapy services are provided for habilitation, rehabilitation, and promoting health and wellness to those who have or are at risk for developing an illness, injury, disease, disorder, condition, impairment, disability, activity limitation, or participation restriction.

The types of services that occupational therapists provide include customized treatment programs to improve people's ability to perform daily activities; evaluation and treatment to develop or restore sensorimotor, cognitive, or psycho-social performance skills; comprehensive home and job site evaluations with adaptation recommendations to make them safe, conserve energy, enhance comfort, independence and productivity; adaptive equipment recommendations and usage training; and guidance to family members and caregivers.

A wide variety of people of all ages can benefit from occupational therapy services, including, for example, those with work-related injuries including lower back problems or repetitive stress injuries; arthritis, multiple sclerosis, or other chronic conditions; birth injuries, learning problems, or developmental disabilities; mental health or behavioral problems including Alzheimer's disease, schizophrenia, and post-traumatic stress; and limitations following a stroke, traumatic brain injury, fracture, or heart attack.

Occupational therapy practitioners work in a great variety of settings, including hospitals, nursing facilities and rehabilitation centers, home health agencies, clinics, schools and early intervention centers, industry, group homes and mental health facilities, academic programs (education and research), government agencies and many others. The clients they serve range in age from the very young (infants) to the very old.

The Decision to Pursue Occupational Therapy

If you are searching for a career that is meaningful, health-related, and gives you a range of study and practice fields to choose from, occupational therapy could be the perfect fit. Occupational therapy is an exciting and growing profession that will give you the chance to help people dealing with disabilities retain their independence and live their lives to the fullest.

Occupational therapy is noteworthy because of its holistic nature. It treats the whole person and addresses the importance of people's psychological and emotional well-being as well as their physical needs. Occupational therapy enables people of all ages and abilities to engage in the activities — the occupations — that are meaningful to their lives.

Occupational therapy is an excellent career choice for those who want to contribute to society and find fulfillment in the work they do.

Outlook for the Future

Currently, school systems, hospitals, and long-term care facilities are the primary work settings for a large number of occupational therapy practitioners. Other areas of practice are becoming increasingly important, and will become new specialties. They include training workers to use proper ergonomics on the job, helping people with low vision maintain their independence, making buildings and homes accessible, promoting health and wellness, and driving

assessment and community mobility training for older adults and people with disabilities.

The job outlook for occupational therapy practitioners (occupational therapists and occupational therapy assistants) is excellent, and it is anticipated that the profession will continue to grow much faster than average. The US Department of Labor lists occupational therapy as one of the fastest growing occupations through the year 2020 with a projected growth of 33%.

There is a great deal of career flexibility. While many occupational therapy practitioners work full-time, there are opportunities for part-time employment. According to the Bureau of Labor Statistics the median annual earnings for OTs is $72,320. Salaries vary according to the specific practice settings, geographic location, and levels of advanced skills and education.

All states require occupational therapy practitioners to have graduated from an accredited occupational therapy program including passing the entry-level certification examination administered by the National Board for Certification in Occupational Therapy (NBCOT). They also must become licensed in the state where they plan to work. Entry into the profession can be either after completing an associate (occupational therapy assistant) or a postbaccalaureate degree (occupational therapist).

Planning a Program of Study

Occupational therapists (OTs.) currently earn an entry-level master's degree or doctorate degree from a university/college program. Professional programs typically require course work concentrating on the biological and behavioral sciences, including biology, anatomy, psychology, and sociology. In addition to the coursework, students complete at least 6 months of supervised clinical internships in a variety of health care and community settings.

Common prerequisite requirements for entry in to an OT program may include (but are not limited to): biology, anatomy, physiology, psychology, sociology, human development, and statistics. The Graduate Record Exam (GRE) is an admission criterion as well as some (paid or unpaid) experience in working with people in a health or OT setting..

Applicants seeking a career in occupational therapy should possess strong interpersonal skills, an ability to work in teams, and a desire to help others. Additionally, being a creative problem-solver, a good listener, and a resourceful and compassionate person with an interest in health, science, and the arts are also desirable qualities.

Occupational therapy is a highly rewarding and personally satisfying profession. Entry into occupational therapy programs is competitive. Specific programs can be found through the American Occupational Therapy Association (AOTA).

Occupational therapy assistants (OTA) earn a 2-year associate degree from an occupational therapy assistant program. They will generally work under supervision of an occupational therapist.

The Admissions Process

Entry-level programs all develop their own admission criteria. You will need to check with the individual educational programs to determine the specific admissions criteria.

Centralized Application Service (OTCAS)

OTCAS provides a full-service web-based application and admissions process for prospective occupational therapy program applicants. Currently 75 entry-level programs are part of OTCAS.

Resources

1. The American Occupational Therapy Association
   4720 Montgomery Lane
   Bethesda, MD 20814-3425
   (301) 652-2682
   www.aota.org

2. US Department of Labor
   Bureau of Labor Statistics
   Occupational Outlook Handbook 2010-2011
   www.bls.gov/oco

OPTOMETRY

General Description of Profession

"Doctors of optometry (ODs) are the independent primary health care professionals for the eye. Optometrists examine, diagnose, treat, and manage diseases, injuries, and disorders of the visual system, the eye, and associated structures as well as identify related systemic conditions affecting the eye" (American Optometric Association [AOA]).

Today, the profession of optometry involves much more than just prescribing and fitting glasses and contact lenses. ODs are trained to evaluate any patient's visual condition and to determine the best treatment for that condition. ODs are viewed as primary care providers for patients seeking ocular or visual care.

Conditions typically cared for by ODs are:

- Corneal abrasions, ulcers, or infections; glaucoma; and other eye diseases that require treatment with pharmaceutical agents, management and referral when necessary;
- Visual skill problems such as the inability to move, align, fixate, and focus the ocular mechanism in such tasks as reading, driving, computer use, and in tasks related to hobbies and employment;
- The inability to properly process and interpret information requiring perception, visualization, and retention, such as that needed for most learning tasks;
- Poor vision–body coordination when one interacts with the environment, as in sports, occupations, and other everyday activities requiring spatial judgments; and
- Clarity problems such as simple near- or far-sightedness or complications due to the aging process, disease, accident, or malfunction.

ODs also work to:

- Diagnose, manage, and refer systemic diseases such as hypertension, diabetes, and others that are often first detected in the eye;
- Provide pre- and postsurgical care of cataracts, refractive laser treatment, retinal problems, and other conditions that require pre- and postsurgical care; and
- Encourage preventative measures such as monitoring infants' and children's visual development, evaluating job/school/hobby–related tasks, and promoting nutrition and hygiene education.

Optometrists practice in many different kinds of situations and with different types of employers.

Individual Private Practice

The individual private practitioner usually is a primary care optometrist with a stand-alone practice. Such practitioners may specialize in fields such as contact lenses, pediatrics, low vision/geriatrics, and vision therapy.

An individual practice may be in a variety of settings and locations, ranging from a free-standing to a professional building.

Partnership or Group Practice

This mode of practice is similar to an individual practice except that there are two or more optometrists in the group. Each member of the group may specialize in a different area of practice. This is an increasingly popular form of practice.

Health Maintenance Organizations (HMOs)

An optometrist practicing in this setting usually is the primary eye care practitioner within a group of other types of primary health care practitioners. S/he may be employed or contracted by the HMO.

Retail/Optical Settings

In this setting, optometrists usually rent space from or are employed by a large retail outlet. However, they remain independent practitioners.

Optometric/Ophthalmologic Professional Settings

The optometrist practices in conjunction with the ophthalmologist and comanages the patients in this setting.

Military/Public Health

Optometrists are commissioned officers who work in a hospital or clinical setting with other health care practitioners.

Interdisciplinary Care

The optometrist works with other health care practitioners in a hospital-based or clinic setting, such as in a Department of Veterans Affairs (VA) hospital, as part of an interdisciplinary team.

Academic/Research

The OD either teaches about primary care or performs research in a university setting. Academics pursue additional training after optometry school and have completed a residency, masters of science, or doctoral program.

Corporate/Industrial

Optometrists are employed by large corporations to perform clinical research or to provide patient care in a clinic within the corporate setting.

Consultants

Optometrists work as consultants to the ophthalmic industry, education, sports (high school to professional), and government.

The Decision to Pursue Optometry

Before contemplating devoting your life to optometry, you will want a clear picture of the profession. For a general overview of optometry, there is the Optometry: A Career Guide produced by the Association of Schools and Colleges of Optometry (ASCO). This is an excellent introduction to the field of optometry; therefore, you will want to consult it early in your preparation. This Guide is included on the ASCO website at www.opted.org, along with other valuable information for applicants.

In addition to a realistic view of the profession, you want to have a sense of your own aptitudes and inclinations, and be positive that your motivation for optometry is not only reality-based regarding the profession, but also appropriate for your personality and value system. One way to assure this is to visit and observe an optometrist

at work; many practitioners welcome the opportunity to have potential students observe them and discuss their profession.

Personal Attributes

The desire to help others is one of the most important personality traits associated with the choice of a career in the health professions, and optometry is no exception. Skills for working with people are also important; the ability to communicate and to get along well with others is basic to the profession. You probably should enjoy working with your hands, since the optometrist must manipulate fine optical measuring devices and computer-controlled instruments. Since many optometrists are in independent practice, some business ability is desirable. In addition, if you are contemplating an optometric career you should have clear aptitude in the sciences and mathematics, since you will be studying a basic science curriculum during professional school.

Rewards of the Profession

Satisfaction from helping others is one of the primary rewards of being an optometrist. In addition to helping improve the quality of patients' lives, an optometrist is able to lead a satisfying personal life. The profession lends itself to very flexible working hours, and an optometrist's responsibilities do not normally include life-or-death decisions. Furthermore, forecasts for the profession indicate financial security in the present and opportunities in the future. Data from the American Optometric Association (AOA) shows average net incomes ranging from $129,385 for all optometrists to $203,230 for owners of group practices.

Outlook for the Future

Currently there are about 35,000 practicing optometrists across the United States. As people have come to expect improved eye care and as increasingly sophisticated technology has been developed to implement that care, the role of the optometrist is expanding. The growth of the geriatric population and the increasing vision problems that occur with age also point to an increased need for the optometrist. All of the trends mentioned above will probably continue to develop, and they are all undoubtedly responsible for the optimistic future employment prediction by the U.S. Department of Labor.

Planning a Program of Study

Doctors of optometry receive four years of specialized professional education and clinical training at an accredited school or college of optometry after completion of their undergraduate prerequisites. There are 21 accredited optometry schools in the United States. Information about all of these schools is included in the handbook, Schools and Colleges of Optometry Admission Requirements. This is updated on a biennial basis and is available on the Association of Schools and Colleges of Optometry's website at www.opted.org (see Applicant and Advisor Resources). In addition, you will also want to consult the websites of the individual schools for more exact requirements.

Although the majority of all optometric students have a college degree, the minimum requirement for all optometry schools is completion of 90 semester units of college coursework. Specific admission requirements differ widely among the schools. One sensible strategy would be to prepare for an appropriate school with the most requirements, so that you will be eligible for the majority of schools with fewer required courses.

All science courses must be those designed for pre-professional students and must include laboratories. Brief survey courses in the sciences will not prepare you for optometry school. Typical course requirements include General Chemistry with Labs, College Algebra and, Trigonometry, English, General Biology with Labs, Organic Chemistry, Calculus, Physics, Psychology and Statistics.

Choice of Undergraduate Major

In addition to the basic science requirements, optometry schools emphasize preparation in mathematics and statistics, and most of them require at least one course in psychology. Optometric training involves optics and lens design. Optometry schools emphasize the necessity for applicants to be well versed in the sciences and to have a facility for dealing with people. Beyond requiring completion of their specific requirements and pursuit of a well-rounded curriculum, including the humanities and social sciences, the majority of schools do not express a preference for an undergraduate major.

Most health professions advisors suggest that you select a major based on your interests and aptitudes, so that you will enjoy your courses and do well in them. Should you change your mind about optometry or be unable to gain admission to optometry school, a major should also provide an acceptable alternative career choice. Whatever your major, you need to be aware that the admission committee will evaluate the rigor of the program you elect along with the specific courses you undertake. Optometry schools teach you sciences at advanced levels and in heavy schedules. As an undergraduate, if you take only one science at a time, surrounded by liberal arts courses, you would not prove conclusively that you could handle the heavy science loads that are common during the first two years of optometry school. Two laboratory courses during each semester or quarter appear to be a good standard. However, you would be wise to discuss your situation with your health professions advisor.

The Admission Process

For approximately two years, optometry students are taught mainly in the lecture format and in the laboratory, in a heavily scheduled block of courses in the basic health and visual sciences. How students perform in science courses in college predicts performance at this stage. This accounts for the fact that optometry schools emphasize the science grade point average and the course loads you took as an undergraduate.

Optometry students spend the next two years of optometry school studying diagnostic and treatment techniques in clinical settings. This clinical portion of the training calls for certain personal qualities, communication skills, and an educational background that will make you an effective practitioner. These are the character traits that are evaluated by your extracurricular activities, interaction with others, and communication skills exhibited in essays and during your interview.

Factors Evaluated by Admission Committees

An admission committee selects the entering class in each optometry school. The size as well as the composition of the committee varies from school to school, but it will normally be composed of ODs from the clinical faculty as well as PhDs from the basic science faculty. It may contain some third- or fourth-year optometry students. The composition of the committee can and probably will change from year to year. In general, optometry schools select students for their entering class who show evidence of strong intellectual ability, a good record of accomplishments, and personal traits that indicate the ability to communicate with and relate to patients.

Because admission committees strive for objectivity in making their decisions, they emphasize grades, scores on the Optometry Admission Test (the admission test which will be discussed below), and other factors that can be easily quantified. The four most important factors in determining whether or not you will be accepted to optometry school will usually be: (1) your academic record, (2) your scores on the OAT, (3) letters of evaluation, and (4) your personal interview. Other factors that will affect your acceptance are your understanding of optometry as a profession based on work experience, research, and/or discussions with doctors of optometry, and your extracurricular activities. Each of these will be discussed below.

1. Academic Record

   Most optometry school admission committees feel that the quality of work in the subjects taken to earn the baccalaureate degree may be the most important predictor of success in optometry school. The academic record includes the cumulative GPA, the science GPA (biology, chemistry, physics and mathematics), the subjects taken, the rigor of the program, and trends in performance. The latter consideration is important: a poor freshman year followed by subsequently better sophomore and junior years is preferable to a good freshman year followed by a declining performance. A good academic record is considered evidence of both high motivation and ability.

   Grades are not evaluated in a vacuum, but rather in context of your total time commitments. For example, part-time work or varsity athletics will be taken into account. However, the optometry school admission committees still need evidence of your ability to perform academically at an acceptable level.

2. The Optometry Admission Testing Program (OAT)

   All schools and colleges of optometry in the United States and Canada require the Optometry Admission Test (OAT). The OAT is a standardized examination designed to measure general academic ability and comprehension of scientific information. Courses helpful in preparation for the OAT include: one year Biology/Zoology, one year General College Chemistry, one year Organic Chemistry, and one year College Physics. The tests are comprised exclusively of multiple-choice test items presented in the English language.

   The OAT is offered in a computerized format. Testing is available year round. Examinees are allowed to take the computerized format of the OAT an unlimited number of times but must wait at least 90 days between testing dates. Only scores from the four most recent attempts and the total number of attempts will be reported.

   The test consists of a total of 4 hours and 40 minutes to complete the tutorial, the four tests in the OAT battery, a 15 minute break, and the post-test survey. The four tests are:

   1. Survey of the Natural Sciences (biology, general chemistry, organic chemistry)
   2. Reading Comprehension
   3. Physics
   4. Quantitative Reasoning

   There are time limits and they are indicated on the computer screen for each section. The Survey of the Natural Sciences and the Reading Comprehension Test are administered first. The Physics Test and the Quantitative Reasoning Test are administered after an optional 15 minute rest break.

   The Survey of the Natural Sciences is an achievement test. The content is limited to those areas covered by an entire first-year course in biology, general chemistry, and organic chemistry. The test contains a total of 100 items: 40 biology items, 30 general chemistry items and 30 organic chemistry items. The time limit of the test is 90 minutes. Although the three science sections are identified, it is important that the examinees pace themselves since separate subscores will be given for each section.

   The Reading Comprehension Test contains passages typical of the level of material encountered in the first year of optometry school. Each passage is followed by 10 to 17 items, which can be answered from a reading of the passage. One should not try to answer the questions until the passage is understood thoroughly. The time limit of the test is 50 minutes. Although these materials contain only one passage, the actual Reading Comprehension Test contains three passages and has a total of 40 items.

The Physics Test is also an achievement test. The content is limited to those areas covered in a two-semester physics course. The test contains a total of 40 items. The time limit of the test is 50 minutes.

The Quantitative Reasoning Test measures the examinee's ability to reason with numbers, to manipulate numerical relationships, and to deal intelligently with quantitative materials. The test contains 40 items. The time limit of the test is 45 minutes. Calculators are permitted.

Test preparation materials are available on the OAT website (www.ada.org/oat/oat_sample_test.pdf). These materials contain samples of the four tests used in the Optometry Admission Testing Program. They are available to assist examinees in discovering possible areas of weakness in comprehension of subjects covered on the test. Sample tests also enable examinees to become familiar with the types of materials included in the test, as well as the general format of the various parts of the test battery.

    a.   Reviewing for the Test

If you know that you have poor test-taking skills on standardized/multiple-choice tests, you will want to address this problem well before the year in that you are scheduled to take the OAT exam. Have your reading, studying, and test-taking skills checked, and you might even investigate the area of test anxiety if it seems relevant. In order to work out an effective test-taking strategy, refer to the section "Standardized Tests" in Chapter 2.

A thorough review of biology, chemistry, physics and math requires a significant amount of time. It is a good idea to set aside a specific block of time each day, and adhere to this schedule. The Optometry Admission Testing electronic sample test can serve as your guide. It lists every topic for which you will be responsible.

Taking the practice test before you begin to review may help you to structure your review, as well as to gain familiarity with the test format. Your results on this test serve as a diagnostic aid and "benchmark." The test can be repeated after your review has been largely completed (perhaps three weeks before the test). You can then address any weaknesses that are still evident. Each of these tests should be taken at one sitting, with no interruptions, and with the time limits strictly observed, i.e., under conditions simulating those of the actual test. If you have been organized in your review, you can stop studying two or three days before the test.

You might also use the sample test conditions to practice the techniques outlined in chapter 2. While all of these techniques are mechanical and do not depend on actual knowledge of the subject matter (and will not replace that knowledge), they can be extremely helpful in improving your score on any standardized examination.

    b.   Scores and Their Interpretation

The raw scores (based on the number of correct answers, with no penalty for guessing) are treated statistically and become standard scores for the sake of reporting. The scaled scores are reported in a range from 200 to 400. While there are no "passing" or "failing" grades, the standard score of 300 signifies average performance on a national basis.

3.   Letters of Evaluation

Letters of evaluation are discussed in more detail in chapter 2. Optometry schools admission committees may prefer a composite or committee evaluation to individual letters of evaluation, especially if you come from a school that prepares such an evaluation. Telling the professors whom you plan to ask for evaluations that you are a pre-optometry student will help them write a more informed evaluation. Keep in close contact with your health professions advising office in collecting these important supporting documents so you can be sure that they are sent out in a timely manner.

Some schools may prefer individual letters of evaluation. The school usually specifies whether these letters should come from optometrists, employees, or others; it is a good idea to follow those guidelines. One school, for example, requires a letter from an optometrist, whereas another suggests that you send one from a faculty member. Regardless of the kind and number of evaluations required, it is your responsibility to check to see not only that they are written, but also that they have been received by OptomCAS and also at every optometry school where you have applied.

4. The Interview

All optometry schools interview their prospective students. An interview invitation represents a significant step in the selection process. Other applicants have already been screened out on the basis of their academic record and non-academic characteristics.

Once again, the general discussion contained in earlier pages can serve as your guide. You need to be prepared to talk about yourself in the interview and to have some knowledge of the field of optometry. Also helpful is information regarding the school where you are interviewing, including its particular strengths, special programs in teaching, or other innovative programs for its students. The school's website is a good source of this information, as are videos that several of the schools have available. Check with your health professions advising office to see if there are any of these available at your school.

5. Extracurricular Activities and Work Experience

Optometry schools view extracurricular activities as positive signs that you can handle a rigorous curriculum and still participate in campus or community affairs. Commitment, leadership, service, responsibility, and the ability to interact effectively with others are among the qualities that the optometry school admission committees evaluate. The level and quality of your participation is more important than the number or diversity of your activities. These activities include community service, campus involvement, research involvement and outside jobs, as well as interests and hobbies. Contrary to popular myth, however, extensive involvement in extracurricular activities, no matter how meaningful, will not compensate for an academic performance that is below par. It may instead indicate to admission committees that you have poor judgment, skewed priorities, and/or inadequate time-management skills.

6. Experience with Optometry

Working in an optometric setting can give you an opportunity not only to gain valuable experience, but also to help you in your own decision to pursue optometry as a career. You will have an opportunity to observe trained professionals in action and may have a chance to perform simple tasks. You will find out whether the professional role looks interesting, challenging, varied or whether it is different from your preconceived ideas.

Whichever is the case, this type of experience is of value. It demonstrates to the admission committees that you have taken more than a casual look at optometry as your career choice.

7. Research Experience

Research has become a significant area in optometry; optometrists now serve as members of National Institutes of Health committees — the government facility responsible for the majority of health research in the United

States. The field of optometry has also made contributions to national defense in the development of special sighting and night vision equipment. Several schools of optometry offer graduate degrees in physiological optics for optometrists who want to enter research and/or teaching. If you think you might be interested in pursuing research as an optometrist, it would be a good idea to involve yourself in a research effort. Even if you are not interested in pursuing research as a profession, understanding concepts such as the scientific method, statistical significance, and the experimental process, will enable you to evaluate the research of others.

8. The Value of Work

    Jobs unrelated to optometry may give you experience that will be beneficial in helping you develop better management and interpersonal skills. Jobs that require considerable contact with the public, for example, will help to develop interaction modes that will be useful in patient care. Jobs that involve management of both work and personnel help develop responsibility and a mature attitude. If you cannot afford to volunteer and cannot find a paying job with an optometrist, try to use whatever position you find in a constructive manner to develop some of these interpersonal skills. Any business acumen you develop will be of value to you as an optometric professional.

The Application

1. When and Where to Apply

    OptomCAS (Optometry Centralized Application Service) opens in July every year, one year before you expect to begin optometry school. Taking the OAT one year before you wish to enter will give you a chance to repeat the test if your scores are low. Use the manual, Schools and Colleges of Optometry: Admission Requirements, for a preliminary look at all schools. Considering your own state residency, grade range, and OAT scores will help eliminate those schools that appear to be unrealistic. Your health professions advisor may have suggestions concerning your choice of schools and may be able to tell you where students at your school have been successful in the past. An early application will generally benefit you, because most of the schools use "rolling admissions" (i.e., they do not wait for their deadline to pass before processing applications; instead, they evaluate and accept applicants as their files are completed).

    In deciding where to apply to optometry school, one of the prime considerations is your state of residence. Because there are so few schools of optometry, many states do not have a school but contract with specific schools to accept their residents preferentially, provide for partial tuition remission or both. You should determine whether there are places at the schools of your choice for people from your home state and whether your state has a contract with those schools. For example, many southeastern states have contracts with the University of Alabama at Birmingham and Southern College of Optometry, while Southern California College of Optometry, Pacific University College of Optometry and University of California, Berkeley have contracts via the WICHE program in western states. Consult school websites and contact individual schools for more specific information regarding contract arrangements for residents of your state. Your health professions advising office will have additional literature, videos, and other resource materials available for help with this selection process.

2. Follow Up

    It is your responsibility to see that your file is completed at OptomCAS and at each optometry school to which you have applied. Supplemental materials vary from school to school and are generally included on their websites.

Resources

1. Association of Schools and Colleges of Optometry website. This comprehensive site has information on optometric education in general, as well as resources for applicants and advisors. www.opted.org.

PHARMACY

General Description of Profession

Pharmacists are the health professionals who serve patients and other health professionals in assuring appropriate use of, and optimal therapeutic outcomes from, medications. In addition to the responsibility for professional interpretation and review of prescription orders, medication record screening and review, and the accurate dispensing of medications, pharmacists serve patients and the community by providing information and advice on health, providing medications and associated services, and by referring patients to other sources of help and care, such as physicians, when necessary.

Pharmacists must be fully acquainted with the physical and chemical properties of drugs and the way they behave in the human body. They must know how a particular drug will affect a human being, alter the course of a disease, and react in the presence of other drugs. Pharmacists must also know how a drug may react in laboratory tests of blood and other human tissues.

Pharmaceutical care encompasses the full range of pharmacists' skills, knowledge, and ability in providing medication services to patients. The principle goal of pharmaceutical care is to achieve positive intended outcomes from medication use to improve patients' quality of life. These outcomes include: (1) cure of a disease; (2) elimination or reduction of symptoms; (3) arresting or slowing a disease process; (4) prevention of disease; (5) diagnosis of disease; and (6) desired alterations in physiological processes, all with minimum risk to patients. Pharmacists are professionals committed to public service and to the achievement of this goal.

Pharmacists may also require proficiency in business matters, since they may purchase and sell hundreds of health-related items. In the hospital, pharmacists assist physicians in drug therapy decisions and may be responsible for the selection and purchase of all medicines used by the facility. In settings where hiring and supervision of personnel is required, pharmacists need personnel and fiscal management capabilities. One of the primary roles of the pharmacists is to serve as an educator in the proper use of drugs for both the public and health practitioners.

The Decision to Pursue Pharmacy

Pharmacists must have excellent interpersonal and communications skills. To perform each of the described activities well, pharmacists must read biological, medical and chemical literature as well as professional, corporate and pharmaceutical publications. Being a member of the profession of pharmacy requires commitment and dedication to life-long learning.

Pharmacists assume responsibility for human life. They are dedicated to providing conscientious and dependable services and should enjoy working with people. Meticulous regard for accuracy, orderliness, and cleanliness is essential. Pharmacists' ethics must be unquestionable. They are entrusted with the storage and distribution of dangerous and habit-forming pharmaceuticals and must be scrupulous in handling or dispensing all medications.

The proportion of actively practicing pharmacists who are female has increased from 44.8% in 2000, to 45.9% in 2004, to 46.4% in 2009. The Bureau of Health Professions projects 64% of pharmacists will be female by 2020. The demand for trained pharmacy professionals has increased in past years due the rapid growth of the healthcare and pharmaceutical industries, especially for the growing elderly population. The number of pharmacists in healthcare services is also growing, as pharmacists become more actively involved in drug therapy decision-making for patients of all ages. There is good potential for advancement and competitive salaries within a pharmacy career. Those pharmacists who pursue additional graduate study and/or residency experience have greater mobility within the profession including areas of research, administration and business. According to the Bureau of Labor Statistics, half of all pharmacists made $ 111,570 a year in 2010. The lowest 10 percent made $ 82,090 and the highest 10 percent earned $ 138,620 a year. According to a 2011 survey by *Drug Topics* magazine, pharmacist yearly salaries range from $116,000 to $140,000.

Since pharmacists have such heavy responsibilities and are so closely concerned with the health of the people they serve, all states have strict laws about licensure. These may vary from state to state; the prospective pharmacist is instructed, while still in professional college, about the regulations applying in areas where he/she may wish to practice. All of the states require graduation from a program accredited by the Accreditation Council for Pharmacy Education (ACPE).

In order to receive a license, the pharmacist must pass an examination given by the Board of Pharmacy in the state where he/she plans to practice. Most states honor licenses issued by other states through a process of reciprocity coordinated by the National Association of Boards of Pharmacy.

Outlook for the Future: Community Pharmacy

According to the 2009 Pharmacy Manpower Project report, the proportion of actively practicing pharmacists working in traditional community pharmacy practice settings (independent, chain, mass merchandiser, and supermarket pharmacies) has remained relatively stable between 2000 (55.4%), 2004 (56.4%), and 2009 (53.8%). Nearly everyone is familiar with community pharmacists and the pharmacy in which they practice.

You probably visit the community pharmacist more often than any other member of the health team. Americans make over five billion trips a year to pharmacies; the pharmacist has an opportunity to see at least one member of every family in his or her community every week. S/he talks to people when they are healthy and when they are sick, when they are "just browsing" or when they are concerned with an emergency, and when they are seeking advice or information. Pharmacists are playing an increasing role in the "wellness" movement, especially through counseling about preventive medicine and use of herbal products. According to one estimate, pharmacists get more than two billion inquiries a year from their patrons.

Advances in the use of technology in pharmacy practice now allow pharmacists to spend more time educating patients and maintaining and monitoring patient records. As a result, patients have come to depend on the pharmacist as a health care and information resource of the highest caliber.

Despite the variety of tasks performed in and out of the community pharmacy, pharmacists are specialists in the science and clinical use of medications. They must understand drug composition, chemical and physical properties manufacture and uses, activity in the normal body as well as in the person who is ill, and must be familiar with tests for purity and for strength. Pharmacists are well-prepared to compound medicines and to dispense prescription orders written by physicians, dentists, and other prescribers. More and more prescribers rely on pharmacists for information about various medications, their availability and their activity, just as patients in the pharmacy do when they ask about nonprescription medicines.

If pharmacists want to combine their professional talents with the challenge of the fast-moving retail pharmacy business, they often consider management positions in chain pharmacy practice or ownership of their own pharmacy. In a community chain practice, career paths usually begin at the store level with subsequent advancement to positions at the district, regional, and corporate levels. Many chain companies have management development programs in marketing operations, legal affairs, third party programs, computerization, and pharmacy affairs. Pharmacists interested in supervisory or clinical experiences should consider a pharmacy residency or graduate study.

Independent retail practice offers the opportunity for pharmacists to be "their own boss." The spirit of entrepreneurship and motivation has enabled many pharmacists to successfully own their pharmacy or, through establishing

consultation services, own their own pharmacy practice.

Hospitals and Other Institutional Settings

As society's health care needs have changed and expanded, there has been an increasing emphasis on provision of that care through organized health care settings. As a result, increasing numbers of pharmacists practice in large and small hospitals, nursing homes, extended care facilities, neighborhood health centers, and health maintenance organizations.

Hospital pharmacists, as members of the health care team along with physicians and nurses, have a unique opportunity for direct involvement with patient care. The clinical skills and knowledge of the contemporary pharmacist make this individual an authoritative source of drug information for physicians, nurses, and patients.

In addition to direct patient care involvement, pharmacists in hospitals are responsible for systems of total control of drug distribution, designed to assure that each patient receives the appropriate medication, in the correct form and dosage, at the correct time. Hospital pharmacists maintain records on each patient, using them not only to fill medication orders, but also to screen for drug allergies, drug interactions and adverse drug effects.

Contemporary hospital pharmacy practice includes a number of highly specialized areas, such as nuclear pharmacy, drug and poison information, and intravenous therapy. In addition, pharmacists provide specialized services in adult medicine, critical care, pediatrics, oncology, ambulatory care, and psychiatry. The nature and size of the hospital helps to determine the extent to which these specialized services are needed. Because of the diversity of activities involved in pharmacy departments, there is also an increasing demand for management expertise, including finance and budgeting, personnel administration, systems development, and planning.

About 38 percent of registered pharmacists work on a full- or part-time basis in hospitals or nursing homes. As hospital pharmacists continue to become more involved in providing patient-oriented services, the demand for practitioners in this area of pharmacy continues to grow.

Recent years have also seen dramatic growth in pharmacy services in managed health care, such as pharmacy benefit management companies and health maintenance organizations, and related organizations that offer coordinated ambulatory care by a multidisciplinary staff of health professionals, including pharmacists. In these settings, pharmacists provide primary leadership in the development of both clinical and administrative systems that manage and improve the use of medications.

Additional Opportunities in Pharmacy

Pharmacists are also employed by the U.S. Public Health Service, the Armed Forces, and the Department of Veteran Affairs (VA). Serving as commissioned officers, they can rise to the rank of colonel in the Army, and to equivalent ranks in the Public Health Service, the Navy, and the Air Force. In addition, pharmacists are employed by other governmental agencies, including the Food and Drug Administration (FDA), Centers for Disease Control and Prevention (CDC), National Institutes of Health (NIH), Indian Health Service (IHS), National Science Foundation (NSF), National Library of Medicine (NLM), and the U.S. Department of Health and Human Services.

The vast majority of the medicines pharmacists formerly compounded in their own pharmacies are now produced on a large scale by drug manufacturers. Pharmacists particularly interested in the scientific aspects of the profession can find challenging employment in the laboratories of academic institutions or pharmaceutical manufacturers. If research is a goal, pharmacy graduates usually go on to advanced study in pharmacy, pharmaceutics, pharmacology, toxicology, pharmaceutical chemistry, or other pharmaceutical sciences. A new field of research is pharmacy administration. Outcomes analysis, including cost-effectiveness of drug therapy, is one example of

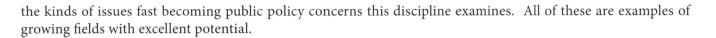

the kinds of issues fast becoming public policy concerns this discipline examines. All of these are examples of growing fields with excellent potential.

Future Prospects

Well-qualified pharmacists can be sure that the demand for their services will continue to increase in the future. They can also count on recognition for contributions to their community and to society.

Pharmacy has a direct relationship to pharmacology and other biophysical/biochemical sciences. Through the research activities of pharmaceutical manufacturers as well as of non-profit laboratories, the development of new medication therapies has become a major area of investigation and progress in the health-related sciences.

Career opportunities are available in community and hospital pharmacies, the military, in pharmaceutical research and manufacturing firms, nursing homes, public service agencies and in colleges and universities. Practice opportunities are excellent and promise to remain so.

Planning a Program of Study

All pharmacy colleges operate under one of five plans: (1) at least two years of college education followed by four academic years of professional study; (2) at least two years of college followed by three calendar years of professional study; (3) at least three years of college education followed by four academic years of professional study; (4) a bachelor's degree followed by four academic years of professional study; or (5) an integrated curriculum for high school students who successfully complete the first 2-years of pre-professional study and are guaranteed admission into the professional pharmacy program. Where preprofessional education is required for admission, the two years of study must be taken in any accredited college or university. Due to the high number of applications, many pharmacy institutions give admissions preference to students who have previously earned a bachelor's degree.

In July 2000, the accreditation standard for the pharmacy degree became the Doctor of Pharmacy (PharmD). Pharmacy schools no longer offer the BS in pharmacy degree. New students must graduate from an accredited Doctor of Pharmacy degree institution in order to be eligible to take the licensure examination of a state board of pharmacy and practice pharmacy in the U.S. Pharmacy colleges and schools are accredited by the Accreditation Council for Pharmacy Education (ACPE). A PharmD degree requires at least four academic (or three calendar) years of professional study, following a minimum of two years of pre-pharmacy study, for a total of at least six years after high school. The majority of students enter a pharmacy program with 3 or more years of college experience. More than half of all student pharmacists have earned a bachelor's degree or higher prior to matriculation.

The PharmD curriculum is designed to produce a scientifically and technically competent pharmacist who can apply this training in such a manner as to provide maximum health care services to patients. The PharmD degree program provides students the opportunity to gain experience in patient-centered learning environments and to work in close cooperative relationships with health practitioners. The goal of pharmacy education is to prepare pharmacists who can assume expanded responsibilities in the care of patients and assure the provision of rational drug therapy and optimize health care outcomes.

Choice of Undergraduate Major

Undergraduate course work should include chemistry, biological and physical sciences, English or speech communications, social and behavioral sciences and the humanities. Courses in political science, accounting and finance are recommended as electives. Students are free to pick a major of their choosing or a specialized prepharmacy curriculum as long as all pharmacy course prerequisites are fulfilled. Prepharmacy requirements do vary by school and

students are encouraged to carefully assess the requirements of the school(s) they wish to attend to ensure requisite course work is taken by the end of the fall term prior to enrollment. A summary of the course prerequisites required by each school is available on the AACP web site (www.aacp.org) under the For Students and Applicants section.

The Admissions Process

As of 2013, there were 129 colleges and schools of pharmacy in the United States and in Puerto Rico recognized by ACPE. The student should visit each pharmacy school website for information about admission requirements and deadlines. School-specific information is also available in the annual publication, "Pharmacy School Admission Requirements" (PSAR) offered on-line for free on the American Association of Colleges of Pharmacy (AACP) web site at www.aacp.org/pharmacycareers .

In high school, students should select courses designed to prepare them for entrance to college. Courses in chemistry, biology, and physics are especially helpful in preparing students for the many college courses required for admission. Colleges of Pharmacy do not typically review high school transcripts in the professional pharmacy admissions process, but students are encouraged to do well in order to prepare for the rigor of the pharmacy curriculum.

PharmCAS

In 2012-2013 103 of all pharmacy degree programs in the U.S. participated in the Pharmacy College Application Service (PharmCAS) for admission. Through this centralized service applicants complete a single application and one set of official US and/or Canadian transcripts and references to apply to multiple PharmD programs.

In addition to the PharmCAS application, pharmacy programs may require applicants to send a supplemental application and fee directly to the institution. The supplemental application deadline may be the same as the PharmCAS deadline, or at a later date. Students must complete all PharmCAS and school requirements before their application will be processed and reviewed.

PharmCAS is for first-year professional pharmacy degree applicants only. High school students, BS of Pharmacy degree graduates, and current student pharmacists who wish to transfer to another pharmacy degree program should contact institutions directly for application instructions. Visit the PharmCAS web site at www.pharmcas.org to learn more about the admissions process and requirements.

Factors Evaluated by Admission Committees

Each pharmacy admissions office evaluates applications differently based on the institution's own criteria. Pharmacy schools may evaluate one or more of the following items for college students and graduates:

1. Successful completion of pharmacy college course prerequisites

    Students should complete most or all of the pharmacy course prerequisites by the end of the fall term prior to enrollment (e.g., Fall 2013 for 2014 entering class). Some pharmacy schools will consider applicants who complete prerequisites courses during the spring semester prior to enrollment.

2. Cumulative undergraduate grade point average (GPA)

    The minimum GPA requirement may be quite low as compared to the average GPA of applicants offered admission to a particular pharmacy school. Policies regarding forgiveness of repeated coursework vary by institution. For the 2012 entering class, the average overall undergraduate GPA was 3.38.

3. Undergraduate science GPA

   For the 2012 entering class, the average undergraduate science GPA was 3.26.

4. Course prerequisite GPA

   The minimum and average course prerequisite GPA varies significantly by institution.

5. Class rank

   Colleges and schools of pharmacy, in considering applicants for admission, may give attention to the relative position of students within their class-near the top, in the middle, or near the bottom. Colleges of pharmacy are interested in enrolling students who have demonstrated exceptional work in school and have the potential to contribute to the profession.

6. PCAT test scores

   Approximately three-fourths of all pharmacy colleges require or recommend that applicants take the Pharmacy College Admission Test (PCAT). For the 2013-2014 examination cycle, this national exam will be administered four times a year and is designed to measure verbal and quantitative ability, reading comprehension, and biology and chemistry knowledge. Students should confer with the pharmacy colleges/schools to which they are interested in applying to ascertain the appropriate examination time, or visit with their health professions advisor who has experience and knowledge of pharmacy school admissions policies. For additional information on the PCAT, see your advisor or contact Pearson, Customer Relations-PCAT, 19500 Bulverde Road, San Antonio, TX 78259, 1-800-622-3231, www.pcatweb.info

7. Letters of evaluation (recommendation)

   Schools may require applicants to submit 1-4 letters of recommendation from particular individuals, such as a pharmacist, professor, or advisor. Selected pharmacy schools may require health professions advisors and evaluators to use a school-specific evaluation form in lieu of or in addition to the letter from the evaluator. PharmCAS collects electronic and paper letters of reference. School-specific information about evaluator types accepted is available on the PharmCAS website. Go to www.pharmcas.org/docs/ReqTypebySchool.pdf.

8. Results of applicant interviews

   All pharmacy schools will require competitive applicants to visit the campus for an in-person interview. Applicants who have researched and gained direct exposure to the profession will be better prepared to respond to the interview questions. Applicants may be rated on communication skills, professional behavior, knowledge of the profession, critical thinking skills, and motivation to pursue a career in pharmacy.

9. Written communication skills via an essay exercise during interview process

   Pharmacy schools may assess an applicant's writing skills through an on-campus essay exercise or by examining the applicant's PCAT score on the writing subtest.

10. Volunteer or paid experience working with patients in a pharmacy or health-related setting (hospital, nursing home, etc.)

Pharmacy colleges encourage or require applicants to have volunteer or paid experience working with patients in a pharmacy or health-related setting. On-going work or volunteer experience in a pharmacy setting may be an important factor in the admissions process. If students are unable to gain work or volunteer experience directly related to pharmacy due to state law restrictions or availability, they should contact their selected pharmacy admission offices to determine what other experiences are accepted.

11. Professionalism attributes demonstrated by portfolio or extracurricular experiences

    Pharmacy schools may require applicants to document activities that demonstrate their professional dispositions and potential.

12. Residency status (if a state-supported public institution)

    Some U.S. pharmacy institutions give preference to in-state (resident) students. Out-of-state (non-resident) and foreign applicants may vie for a limited number of positions or may be ineligible for admission, depending on institutional and state policies. Private pharmacy institutions may offer out-of-state and foreign applicants a greater number of positions within the program as compared to state-supported, public institutions.

13. Diversity of background (as defined by the institution)

Resources

1. Pharmacy School Admissions Requirements, American Association of Colleges of Pharmacy, 1727 King Street, Alexandria, VA 22314-2841; (703) 739-2330; www.aacp.org/pharmacycareers; www.pharmcas.org; www.ajpe.org

2. For a complete listing of the 129 pharmacy schools, visit this website: www.aacp.org/pharmacycareers

3. Career Information Specific to a Particular Practice Setting: American Pharmacists Association, 2215 Constitution Avenue NW, Washington, DC 20037, www.pharmacist.com.

4. American Association of Pharmaceutical Scientists, 2107 Wilson Blvd, Suite 700, Arlington, VA 22201-3042. www.aaps.org.

5. American Society of Health System Pharmacists, 7272 Wisconsin Avenue, Bethesda, MD 20814, www.ashp.org.

6. National Association of Chain Drug Stores, 1776 Wilson Blvd., Suite 200 Arlington, VA 22209, www.nacds.org.

7. National Community Pharmacists Association (represents independent retail pharmacists), 100 Daingerfield Road, Alexandria, VA 22314, www.ncpanet.org.

8. American Society of Consultant Pharmacists, 1321 Duke Street, Alexandria, VA 22314, www.ascp.com.

9. National Association of Boards of Pharmacy (Licensing Information), 700 Busse Highway, Park Ridge, IL 60068, www.nabp.net.

10. Program Accreditation Information: Accreditation Council for Pharmacy Education, 20 North Clark Street, Suite 2500 Chicago, IL 60602-5109, info@acpe-accredit.org, www.acpe-accredit.org.

PHYSICAL THERAPY

General Description of Profession

Physical therapists (PTs) are experts in movement and function of the body. Physical therapists provide services that help restore function, improve mobility, relieve pain, and prevent or limit permanent physical disabilities associated with injury or disease. Patient examinations in physical therapy include, but are not limited to, testing of muscle function, strength, joint flexibility, range of motion, balance and coordination, posture, respiration, skin integrity, motor function, quality of life, and activities of daily living. Physical therapists also determine a patient's ability to reintegrate into the workforce or community after illness or injury. Once an examination is complete and a diagnosis has been determined, the physical therapist designs a plan of care that includes short and long-term functional goals and interventions that may include, but not be limited to, exercise, traction, mobilization/manual therapy, ultrasound and/or electrotherapy, vestibular training, motor learning and development, and patient and family education. Interventions will often include the use of assistive and adaptive devices such as crutches, wheelchairs, orthotics, and prosthetics. An important component of physical therapist patient management involves teaching the patient appropriate ways to move or perform particular tasks to prevent further injury and to promote health and wellness.

Physical therapists practice in a variety of settings including hospitals, clinics, private physical therapy offices, home health agencies, skilled nursing facilities, rehabilitation centers, school systems, sports medicine facilities, industrial settings, academic settings (education and research), and government agencies. About two-thirds of physical therapists are employed in private outpatient offices or group practices, health system or hospital-based outpatient facility, hospitals, or academic institutions. Designated areas with board specialty certification for physical therapists include cardiovascular and pulmonary, clinical electrophysiology, geriatrics, neurology, orthopaedics, pediatrics, sports physical therapy, and women's health. Additional areas of focused clinical practice for physical therapists include acute care, aquatic physical therapy, education and clinical education, hand rehabilitation, health policy and administration, home health, oncology, research, private practice, and veteran's affairs.

Physical Therapist Practice

All states require physical therapists to have graduated from an accredited physical therapist educational program as well as pass a national physical therapist examination (NPTE) for licensure. Physical therapist practice is governed by state licensure laws and as such there may be additional requirements and fees beyond the required national licensure examination to practice in a specific state or jurisdiction.

Outlook for the Future: Vision 2020

Physical therapy is a dynamic and progressive profession that is intentionally shaped by a focused vision. In 2000, the governing body for the profession approved Vision 2020 in physical therapy. This Vision serves to provide short, intermediate, and long-term guidance and direction for the profession. The Vision statement states that:

"Physical therapy, by 2020, will be provided by physical therapists who are doctors of physical therapy and who may be board-certified specialists. Consumers will have direct access to physical therapists in all environments for patient/client management, prevention, and wellness services. Physical therapists will be practitioners of choice in patients'/clients' health networks and will hold all privileges of autonomous practice. Physical therapists may be assisted by physical therapist assistants who are educated and licensed to provide physical therapist directed and supervised components of interventions.
Guided by integrity, life-long learning, and a commitment to comprehensive and accessible health programs for all people, physical therapists and physical therapist assistants will render evidence-based services throughout the

continuum of care and improve quality of life for society. They will provide culturally sensitive care distinguished by trust, respect, and an appreciation for individual differences. While fully availing themselves of new technologies, as well as basic and clinical research, physical therapists will continue to provide direct patient/client care. They will maintain active responsibility for the growth of the physical therapy profession and the health of the people it serves."

The six elements that are described in the Vision 2020 Statement include the Doctor of Physical Therapy, Evidenced-based Practice, Autonomous Practice, Direct Access, Practitioner of Choice, and Professionalism. These six elements are critical to the future direction of the practice of physical therapy as well as how practitioners will be providing evidenced-based and patient/client-centered care. Thus, potential applicants should thoughtfully consider the role and responsibilities of the physical therapist within the framework of Vision 2020, given that this vision continues to guide the future direction of the profession and the individual practitioner within the profession.

Although 2020 is still several years in the future, in 2011 the profession's governing body adopted a motion prompting the Association to take steps to look beyond Vision 2020 and reflect the physical therapy profession's commitment to society. To learn more about possible future directions and vision for the profession, visit www.apta.org/BeyondVision2020/.

Employment Projections

Although federal legislation limiting therapy reimbursement has increased competition for jobs in the past few years, the U.S. Department of Labor, Bureau of Labor Statistics (BLS) projects that the employment of physical therapists is expected to grow much faster than the average. In fact, the BLS lists physical therapist as one of the growing occupations from 2010 to 2020 with a projected growth of 39%. Job opportunities for licensed physical therapists will be good for practice in all settings, especially acute hospital, skilled nursing, and orthopedic settings, and in rural practices.

According to the BLS, as of May 2010, the median annual earnings of physical therapists was $76,310. Median salaries for new physical therapist graduates with professional DPT degrees have increased by 15% from 2005 to 2010. (APTA Department of Research, 2010 APTA Median Income of Physical Therapists Summary Report, Alexandria, VA: March 28, 2011). Variation in income is dependent upon years of practice experience, geographic location, employment setting, highest earned academic degree, and supervisory responsibility.

Professional Development Opportunities

A myriad of opportunities are available to licensed physical therapists for continuing competence and lifelong professional development. These opportunities include, but are not limited to, pursuing mastery in clinical practice by completing an approved clinical residency or clinical fellowship, pursuit of clinical specialization in 8 specialty areas through the American Board of Physical Therapy Specialties, furthering one's formal academic education (eg, PhD, DScPT, ScD, DPTSc, EdD) in preparation for conducting research and teaching in an academic setting, advancing within clinical practice through additional programs that offer practice credentials, and completing continuing education courses provided through web-based distance learning (eg, APTA Learning Center), home study, and conferences (onsite and virtual) offered nationally, regionally, and locally.

Planning a Program of Study : Physical Therapist Education Preparation

With the exception of one program, professional (entry-level) physical therapist education programs award the doctor of physical therapy (DPT) degree. The Commission on Accreditation in Physical Therapy Education (CAPTE) in the fall 2009 revised the degree criterion such that by December 31, 2015, academic institutions will be required to award the Doctor of Physical Therapy (DPT) degree as the first professional degree for physical therapists. All physical therapist professional degree programs must come into compliance with this criterion by no later than December 31, 2017. As of April 4, 2012, there were 212 accredited and 24 developing PT (DPT) programs in the U.S. Specific physical therapist education programs on the APTA web directory can be accessed by clicking on education programs on the APTA website.

The vast majority of physical therapist educational programs require applicants to possess a bachelor's degree along with the successful completion of specific prerequisites that may vary between academic programs. The undergraduate degree earned varies as long as the prerequisite coursework is completed with the major course of study. Some of the undergraduate degrees earned in preparation for admission to a physical therapist program include, but are not limited to, biology, physics, exercise physiology, exercise science, health science, kinesiology, psychology, and others.

Although requirements for physical therapist programs currently vary by academic institution, prerequisite requirements common to a majority of programs typically may include (but are not limited to): biology, anatomy, physiology, chemistry, physics, statistics, psychology, and other social sciences. Many PT programs also require some paid or unpaid experience in at least one, if not more, physical therapy settings. Applicants also are typically required to take the Graduate Record Exam (GRE). Information on this computerized exam can be found at www.gre.org. Entry into physical therapist programs is competitive and applicants apply to an average of 5 programs. Applicants accepted into the 2012 entering class had an average undergraduate cumulative grade point average (GPA) of 3.5 and a combined science and math GPA of 3.4. For more information about admission prerequisites, visit www.ptcas. org/ProgramPrereqs.html.

The Admissions Process

Students seeking entry into a physical therapist program should have a clear picture of the profession and the broad spectrum of opportunities that are available. As indicated previously, volunteer or paid experiences are often required by programs for admission. The purpose of these physical therapy exposures is for the applicant to have an opportunity to personally explore the profession with its rewards and challenges, interact with physical therapists regarding their impressions about their roles and responsibilities within health care, and to determine if physical therapy is a good "fit" for the applicant. In addition, APTA's website offers information for prospective students including the Role of a Physical Therapist, Benefits of a PT Career, Physical Therapist Practice and Careers, Physical Therapist Profiles, Physical Therapist Education and the Admission Process, Directory of Accredited Physical Therapist Programs, Scholarship, Aid, and Other Financial Resources, About APTA and other information. To access Information for Prospective Students, go to www.apta.org/ProspectiveStudents/.

Personal Attributes

Students seeking entry into a physical therapist program should possess attributes that include, but are not limited to, strong interpersonal, communication, problem solving, critical thinking, and leadership skills, along with a sincere desire to enter a helping health care profession. Students should also be interested in providing physical therapy services to patients of all ages throughout the continuum of care. Provision of these services may range from patients with acutely ill conditions, through rehabilitation, and management of chronic conditions. Likewise, students should also be interested in improving the health and wellness of patients while preventing future injury or disability. In addition, applicants should be able to demonstrate behavior reflective of and integral to the profession's professionalism core values that include accountability, altruism, caring/compassion, excellence, integrity, professional duty, and social responsibility.

Program Application

The Physical Therapist Centralized Application Service (PTCAS) is available for students applying to physical therapist

programs with accredited and candidate status with CAPTE. PTCAS allows applicants to use a single Web-based application and one set of materials to apply to multiple physical therapist education programs. The majority of physical therapist programs require applicants to apply via PTCAS. To access a list of participating programs to date, refer to the PTCAS Directory at www.ptcas.org/Directory/. PTCAS offers a secure on-line Advisor Portal to NAAHP members and other authorized advisors so they may track the status and success rates of their students.

Resources

1. American Physical Therapy Association (APTA)
    1111 North Fairfax Street
    Alexandria, VA 22314-1488
    (703) 684-2782 or (800) 999-2782
    www.apta.org

2. *PT Accredited Program Information*
    For a complete list of the accredited physical therapist programs, visit www.capteonline.org/home.aspx
    2012 Fact Sheet, Physical Therapist Education Programs, Department of Accreditation, American Physical Therapy Association. Alexandria, VA: May 2010. www.capteonline.org/AggregateProgramData/

3. *PTCAS*
    Physical Therapist Centralized Application Service
    PO Box 9112
    Watertown, MA 02471
    ptcasinfo@ptcas.org
    (617) 612-2040
    Main: www.ptcas.org
    Prerequisite Summary Tables: www.ptcas.org/ProgramPrereqs/
    PTCAS Directory: www.ptcas.org/Directory/

4. Demographics and Statistics
    U.S. Department of Labor
    Bureau of Labor Statistics
    Occupational Outlook Handbook 2010-2011
    www.bls.gov/ooh/Healthcare/Physical-therapists.htm

PHYSICIAN ASSISTANT

General Description of Profession

Physician assistants (PAs) are licensed health professionals who practice medicine with physician supervision as members of a medical team. PAs deliver a broad range of medical and surgical services to diverse populations in rural and urban settings. As part of their comprehensive responsibilities, PAs conduct physical exams, diagnose and treat illnesses, order and interpret tests, counsel on preventive health care, assist in surgery, and prescribe medications. A PA's scope of practice varies, based on training, experience, and state law. A PA's clinical responsibilities correspond to the supervising physician's practice, so in general, a physician assistant will see many of the same types of patients as the physician.

The PA profession is relatively new compared to other health professions, having been founded in the mid-1960s. In 2012, the PA profession licensed their 100,000th PA.. PA educational programs graduated over 6,000 new graduates in 2012. While PAs continue their traditional role of bringing health care to the underserved in rural and inner city areas, today they practice in all urban, suburban, and rural settings. According to the 2008 census survey conducted by the American Academy of Physician Assistants (AAPA), 15 percent of clinically practicing PAs work primarily in non-metropolitan areas. According to the 2008 census survey, 37 percent of respondents reported that their medical specialty was one of the primary care fields: family/general practice medicine (26%), general internal medicine (5%), obstetrics/gynecology (2%), and general pediatrics (3%). Twenty-five percent of respondents reported they work in general surgery or a surgical subspecialty.

Outlook for the Future

The PA profession will grow much faster than the average occupation in the decade 2008 through 2018, according to the Bureau of Labor Statistics' (BLS) most recent employment projections. The BLS predicts that total employment for PAs is projected to increase by 39 percent during these years. The PA profession has consistently been listed as one of the fastest-growing occupations by the BLS. For more information on BLS economic and employment projections, go to www.bls.gov.

Planning a Program of Study

For many years the number of PA educational programs remained fairly constant, but beginning in the mid-1990s their numbers have increased dramatically. There are now 173 programs that have been awarded accreditation by the Accreditation Review Commission on Education for the Physician Assistant (ARC-PA), with over 50 in the profession pipeline. The ARC-PA is the only accrediting body for PA programs. To be accredited, programs must meet its stringent academic and professional requirements.

Although PA programs vary in their missions, requirements, and admissions processes, approximately 90% require applicants to have previous health care experience. Many applicants bring health care experience from previous careers as an emergency medical technician, orderly or a nurse's aide, nurse, x-ray technician, respiratory therapist, or military corpsman. This experience might also include volunteering a substantial number of hours in a hospital or clinic, or shadowing a PA.

Most programs are looking for people with life experience as well as medical experience, and approximately 90% of programs require that applicants have a a bachelor's degree, in addition to the health care-related experience described above.

Coursework to be completed before applying to PA programs differs according to the entrance requirements for each program, but generally includes science courses such as Anatomy, Physiology, Microbiology/Bacteriology, General Biology, General Chemistry, Organic Chemistry, and Genetics; and non-science courses like English (composition, literature, technical writing), Humanities, Math (statistics, college level algebra), Medical Terminology, Psychology (general, abnormal, developmental), and Sociology.

Chapter 5

Second-year students rotate through the various specialties, which include internal/family medicine, obstetrics/gynecology, general surgery, orthopedics, and geriatrics, in addition to other specialties with a primary care focus, and other possible elective rotations.

Following graduation from an accredited program, graduates are required to pass a national certifying examination developed by the independent National Commission on Certification of Physician Assistants (www.nccpa.net) in cooperation with the National Board of Medical Examiners. To maintain certification, individuals must log 100 hours of continuing medical education every two years, submit a certification maintenance fee to NCPA by December 31 of the certification expiration year, and pass a recertification exam every six years. In addition to passing the exam, PAs are licensed by the state in which they practice.

Admissions Process

Acceptance to a PA program is competitive. The Central Application Service for Physician Assistants (CASPA) represents approximately 85 percent of all accredited PA programs. According to CASPA, there were 2.98 applicants for each PA program seat for the class entering in 2013.

According to the annual report on PA programs for 2009-20012, the proportion of enrollees who are female is 73.3 percent. The gender distribution of first-year students has started to stabilize around 30% male and 70% female after a 20-plus-year trend of a gradually increasing percentage of female.

Competitive applicants for PA programs have completed the prerequisite coursework required by the specific schools to which they are applying. They also present a solid understanding of the profession and patient care, demonstrated by significant health-related experience. About 85% of PA programs require applicants to take the Graduate Record Exam (GRE); some programs may also require the TOEFL for international applicants, or applicants whose first language is not English. Letters of recommendation from professors, health advisors, employers, and health care providers (MD, PA, NP) are also part of the admissions process.

PAs are considered essential partners in America's medical workforce. As the country faces a growing demand for health care services, the mix of physicians, physician assistants, and other providers will be redefined to meet the structure of emerging practices.

Resources

1. Physician Assistant Education Association
    300 N. Washington Street
    Alexandria, VA 22314
    (703) 548-5538
    www.PAEAonline.org

2. American Academy of Physician Assistants
    950 N. Washington Street
    Alexandria, VA 22314
    (703) 836-2272
    www.aapa.org

3. U.S. Department of Labor
    Bureau of Labor Statistics
    www.bls.gov/oco

PODIATRIC MEDICINE

General Description of Profession

Podiatric medicine is a branch of the medical sciences devoted to the study of human movement, with the medical care of the foot and ankle as its primary focus. A Doctor of Podiatric Medicine (DPM) specializes in the prevention, diagnosis, and treatment of foot disorders, diseases and injuries. Podiatric Physicians make independent judgments and perform or order all necessary diagnostic tests. They perform surgery; administer medications, including DEA-restricted medications; and prescribe physical therapy regimens.

A DPM often detects serious health problems that may otherwise go unnoticed because of symptoms first expressed in problems of the lower extremity such as diabetes, arthritis, heart disease, or kidney disease. These doctors are educated in state-of-the-art techniques involving surgery, orthopedics, dermatology, physical medicine and rehabilitation.

Podiatrists work in general or group practices and are free to develop a practice specialty such as pediatrics, geriatrics, dermatology, wound care, or sports medicine. In addition to private practice, they serve on the staffs of hospitals and long-term care facilities, on the faculties of schools of medicine and nursing, in the armed forces as commissioned officers, in the U.S. Public Health Service, and in municipal health departments.

The degree of Doctor of Podiatric Medicine (D.P.M.) is awarded after four years of study at one of nine accredited podiatric medical colleges. The colleges differ in size and location, although the curriculum leading to the D.P.M. degree is quite similar at each institution. The first two years concentrate on classroom instruction and laboratory work in the basic medical sciences. Podiatric medical education, like that for all physicians, is characterized by course work in the basic sciences, including anatomy, physiology, biochemistry, pharmacology, microbiology, pathology, immunology, etc. In addition, the student of podiatric medicine also learns the fundamentals of specialized medicine, which include biomechanics, lower extremity anatomy, podiatric pathology, infectious diseases, orthopedics, and sports medicine. The third and fourth years of study focus on the clinical sciences and patient care; however clinical exposure begins as early as the first year. Experience is gained in some of the finest clinics in the country, including community clinics, hospitals, the Department of Veterans Affairs, and professional office settings.

After completing four years of podiatric medical education, graduates select a comprehensive Podiatric Medicine and Surgery Residency of thirty-six months in duration. A podiatric residency provides an interdisciplinary experience with rotations such as anesthesiology, internal medicine, infectious disease, surgery, orthopedics, pediatrics and emergency medicine. Many podiatric residency programs offer an additional qualification in reconstructive rear foot and ankle surgery. The AACPM assists students in the national, centralized application and residency matching process known as CASPR, in which all entry-level residency programs are required to participate. This service, modeled after the NRMP, helps students to save time and money during their residency search.

Podiatric physicians are licensed in all 50 states, the District of Columbia and Puerto Rico to treat the foot and its related or governing structures by medical, surgical or other means. State licensing requirements generally include graduation from one of the nine accredited colleges of podiatric medicine, passage of the National Board exams, which are taken in two parts while in podiatric medical school, and postgraduate training, as well as written and oral examinations. Requirements for licensure in all fifty states can be found at www.fpmb.org/memberboards.asp. Podiatric physicians may also become certified in specialty areas: primary medicine and orthopedics, or surgery.

The Decision to Pursue Podiatric Medicine

Students who do well in the basic sciences and are interested in becoming integral members of the health care team should seriously consider a career in podiatric medicine. Podiatrists are often able to provide immediate patient relief and detect serious health problems early because of their specialized training. Preventing serious illness or identifying potential problems while still in treatable stages can be most satisfying. The independence afforded any practicing physician who chooses to be self-employed is another attractive feature of this profession.

In general, the practice of podiatric medicine lends itself to flexible hours and is therefore comfortable for individuals who want time for family, friends and other involvements that characterize a balanced lifestyle. The work hours of a podiatric physician can vary from 30 to 60 hours a week.

Earnings of podiatrists depend upon geographic location, type of practice, number of patients seen per week, years of experience, etc. According to a survey by the American Podiatric Medical Association (APMA 2012 Podiatric Practice Survey), the average NET income of full-time (30+ hrs. /week) podiatric physicians in 2012 was as follows:

Net income range (after practice expenses) in 2012	Percentage of podiatrists with that level of income in 2012
Less than $100,000	23.2%
$100,000 - $174,999	38.8%
$175,000 - $249,999	18.8%
$250,000 - $324,999	10.2%
$325,000 or more	9.0%

Planning a Program of Study

As is the case with other fields of medicine, the schools and colleges of podiatric medicine accept students from any major provided that they have completed course work that fulfills the science prerequisites. Many students enter podiatric medicine from other health professions, such as nursing, pharmacy, clinical laboratory science (formerly medical technology) and physical therapy. Candidates for admission should present evidence of strong preparation for professional study. The minimum requirement for admission is completion of three academic years (90 semester hours) of study at an accredited college or university. The vast majority of students who matriculate, however, have completed a minimum of a bachelor's degree.

All podiatric medical colleges require a year of biology, chemistry, organic chemistry and physics along with a year of English. All science courses must include laboratory work. These courses should be completed by the end of the junior year, as they are good preparation for the standardized admissions tests, which should be taken before starting the senior year of college, if the applicant plans to enroll in podiatric school right after college. Students should visit the AACPM website: www.aacpm.org/html/careerzone/pdfs/AACPM%20CIB-2013%20Entering%20Class.pdf to view the "Podiatric Medical College Information Booklet" that lists each college's admission requirements, or utilize the direct links at the website to the colleges of podiatric medicine.

Interested applicants should visit the office of a practicing podiatrist to learn more about the profession and possibly to obtain a letter of recommendation. An applicant can access the DPM Mentors Network at the AACPM website to contact a podiatrist in his/her state for shadowing purposes or information about the practice of podiatric medicine. Visiting a podiatric practice both demonstrates an applicant's seriousness in applying to a college of podiatric medicine and gives an opportunity for the student to see first-hand if the profession fits his or her needs and aptitudes. A letter of recommendation or a statement made by the podiatrist can document evidence of this experience. All schools and colleges of podiatric medicine require a letter of recommendation from a practicing podiatric physician for admission consideration. To find a mentor, go to www.aacpm.org and click on the "Find a Mentor" tab. Select a state and a list of both podiatric physicians and current students will appear for your use.

The Admissions Process

The Application Service

The American Association of Colleges of Podiatric Medicine (AACPM) administers the application service, AACP-MAS, which processes all applications submitted for admission to all nine schools and colleges of podiatric medicine. AACPMAS reviews the application for completion, verifies academic coursework; received official standardized admissions test scores; and processes payment of application fees. AACPMAS then electronically transmits applicant's data to the colleges selected by the applicant. There are no secondary applications forms or fees for the schools and colleges of podiatric medicine. To complete the web application, interested students should go directly to https://portal.aacpmas.org.

Standardized Admissions Tests

All students are required to submit scores from a graduate-level standardized admissions test prior to matriculation, such as, MCAT, USDAT, GRE, etc. Candidates should consult with each school to determine which test(s) is (are) acceptable for admission consideration.

Results of these standardized admission tests taken more than three years prior to year of application are *NOT* acceptable. For fall admission, applicants are advised to take the MCAT no later than spring of the year of application. Official MCAT and DAT scores must be sent to the AACPMAS.

The Letters of Evaluation

Each of the colleges of podiatric medicine has different requirements for letters of recommendation. Typically, letters are requested from a pre-professional advisory committee or from members of the science faculty at a college or university. At least one recommendation from a podiatrist is required. Letters of recommendation are to be mailed *directly* to the individual colleges of podiatric medicine.

The Interview

Each institution invites qualified applicants for a personal interview conducted by the Admissions Committee at that school. The interview is considered to be an important tool for making final admissions decisions. For more information on interviewing, refer to chapter 2.

 *Chapter 5*

Resources

1. *"Podiatric Medical College Information Booklet"* brochure published by the American Association of Colleges of Podiatric Medicine (AACPM), www.aacpm.org 15850 Crabbs Branch Way, Suite 320, Rockville, MD 20855; 301-948-0957.

2. View books, Catalogs and other resource materials from AACPM's member colleges which are linked from AACPM's website at: www.aacpm.org.

Inquiries about podiatric medicine can be directed to the association by email: dtaubman@aacpm.org: Daniel Taubman, Career Promotion Coordinator, AACPM, 15850 Crabbs Branch Way, Suite 320, Rockville, MD 20855; or by calling: 301-948-0958. For a complete list of the nine colleges of podiatric medicine, visit www.aacpm.org.

PUBLIC HEALTH

General Description of Profession

Public health is a diverse field, encompassing a wide range of specialties from health policy to infectious disease epidemiology. Public health professionals solve population-based challenges using a variety of skills from areas such as biology, environmental science, policy, and education. Because the field is so varied, students from numerous backgrounds have the ability to contribute to improving the health of the public.

Opportunities to improve public health are possible every day and in every area of the world. Domestically and globally, people face challenges of obesity, heart disease, cancer, stroke, automobile accidents, and infectious diseases.

Examples of public health in the headlines include:

- Investigators link Salmonella outbreak to tainted alfalfa sprouts
- Officials address cholera outbreak in Haiti
- New influenza vaccine reduces shots
- Mental health awareness rises

Public health not only applies to numerous diseases, pollutants, and behavior changes, it is also applicable to many levels of society. At the local level, county and city health departments are usually the first line of communication with residents and the first line of defense against microbes and harmful environmental factors. State health departments provide coordination amongst the counties and fund many programs by way of state legislatures and federal monies. At the federal level, the Department of Health and Human Services includes key agencies such as the National Institutes for Health (NIH) and the Centers for Disease Control and Prevention (CDC). At the global level public health, often called global health or global public health, works through governmental and scores of non-governmental organizations to prevent disease, treat patients, train workers, and build sustainable health infrastructure.

Three things can be said about public health: it is relevant, it is challenging, and it is necessary. The mission of public health is the "fulfillment of society's interest in assuring the conditions in which people can be healthy" (Institute of Medicine, The Future of Public Health). The most important aspect of public health is that it focuses on the health and well being of populations. While medicine is concerned with individual patients, public health regards the community as its patient.

What are the functions of public health? According to the Public Health Functions Project site (www.health.gov/phfunctions/public.htm), public health:

- Prevents epidemics and the spread of disease
- Protects against environmental hazards
- Prevents injuries
- Promotes and encourages healthy behaviors
- Responds to disasters and assists communities in recovery
- Assures the quality and accessibility of health services

In fact, during the twentieth century, the average lifespan of individuals in the United States lengthened by thirty years. Twenty-five of this gain is attributable to advances in public health such as assuring clean water, immunizing children against infectious diseases, improving motor vehicle safety, creating safer workplaces, controlling infectious diseases, providing safer and healthier foods, providing prenatal care and well child care to ensure healthier mothers and babies, and developing major campaigns to stop smoking.

More information about the field of public health can be found at: www.whatispublichealth.org, a website designed to guide interested students and advisors alike about the public health profession. This website includes interactive games, vignettes from public health professionals, quizzes, video files and examples of public health in action.

Outlook for the Future

The demand today for public health professionals is great and is increasing in the face of new threats, new knowledge, and new demands. The opportunities are as wide and varied as the public health challenges facing society.

Public health takes place in many different career settings. Public health professionals include researchers in a laboratory, an administrative official in a public or private organization, a teacher in an educational institution, or a policy analyst with a national think-tank. Public health professionals can be basic scientists researching new viruses, health educators who work with teenage moms or who develop anti-smoking campaigns, or epidemiologists who study the emergence, frequency and geographic spread of viral diseases (e.g. H1N1) or the risk factors associated with certain cancers. They can also be biostatisticians who run clinical trials for pharmaceutical companies or work with a team to determine the impact of genetics on certain diseases, or hospital administrators or health policy experts who write or evaluate federal health legislation. Additionally, they can be health researchers who study outcomes of cardiac surgery or determinants of access to health care, or sanitarians or environmental researchers who determine the impact of car emissions on the public's health.

Environmental Health

Environmental health deals with the air we breathe, the water we drink, the complex interactions between human genetics and our surroundings. These environmental risk factors can cause diseases such as asthma, cancer, and food poisoning. Environmental health studies the impact of our surroundings on our health.

Biostatistics

Biostatistics uses data analysis to determine the cause of disease and injuries, as well as to identify health trends within communities. This field entails collecting and studying information, forecasting scenarios, and making reliable conclusions. Biostatistics involves estimating the number of deaths from gun violence or looking at trends in drunk driving injuries by using math and science.

Behavioral Sciences/Health Education

Behavioral science/health education is concerned with stopping the spread of sexually transmitted diseases, such as herpes and HIV/AIDS; helping youth recognize the dangers of binge drinking; and promoting seatbelt use. Behavioral Science/Health Education focuses on ways that encourage people to make healthy choices. This includes the development of community-wide education programs that range from promoting healthy lifestyles to preventing disease and injury, to researching complex health issues.

Epidemiology

Epidemiology is used when food poisoning or an influenza outbreak attacks a community. In that situation, "disease detectives" or epidemiologists are asked to investigate the cause of disease and control its spread. Epidemiologists do fieldwork to determine what causes disease or injury, what the risks are, who is at risk, and how to prevent further incidences. They understand the demographic and social trends upon disease and injury. The initial discovery and containment of an outbreak, such as West Nile virus, often come from epidemiologists, as well as the initial determination of the relationship between smoking and lung cancer.

Health Services Administration

Health services administration entails managing the database at a school clinic, developing budgets for a health department, creating policies for health insurance companies, and directing hospital services. The field of health services administration combines politics, business, and science in managing the human and fiscal resources needed to deliver effective public health services.

Maternal and Child Health

Maternal and child health involves providing information and access to birth control, promoting the health of a pregnant woman and an unborn child, and dispensing vaccinations to children. Professionals in maternal and child health improve the public health delivery systems specifically for women, children, and their families through advocacy, education, and research.

Nutrition

Nutrition requires promoting healthy eating and regular exercise, researching the effect of diet on the elderly, and teaching the dangers of overeating and overdieting. This field examines how food and nutrients affect the wellness and lifestyle of population. Nutrition encompasses the combination of education and science to promote health and disease prevention.

Global Health

International/global health addresses health concerns from a global perspective and encompasses all areas of public health (e.g., biostatistics, epidemiology, nutrition, maternal and child health, etc.). International health professionals address health concerns among different cultures in countries worldwide.

Public Health Laboratory Practice

Public health laboratory professionals perform tests on biological and environmental samples in order to diagnose, prevent, treat, and control infectious diseases in communities; to ensure the safety of our food and water; to screen for the presence of certain diseases within communities; and to respond to public health emergencies, such as bioterrorism.

Planning a Program of Study: Choosing a Major

There is no single recommended undergraduate major for students intending to apply to a CEPH-accredited school or program of public health. Public health students come from a variety of educational backgrounds; a quality undergraduate education is a plus for any applicant.

However, there are some undergraduate majors that can be beneficial when applying to public health. For example, to study Epidemiology or Biostatistics, a major in math or basic science is ideal. For an education in Behavioral Sciences or Health Education, consider sociology, psychology or anthropology as a major. For studying Health Services Administration, consider a business or political science background. To study Global Health, a social science degree is helpful. For those who want to study Environmental Health, consider studying either biology or chemistry. Maternal and Child Health lends itself to both biology and social sciences.

Acquiring public health experience

Schools and programs of public health do accept students without prior work experience; however, they look favor-

ably on applicants who have at least a little experience, so students should consider pursuing some experience before applying. It is also suggested that applicants contact the school or program that they are most interested in attending to ask about specific requirements.

There are many options for individuals who are looking to gain experience before applying to a school or program of public health. Examples are:

- Working part-time or full-time at a hospital or health clinic, such as working on an immunization program, a reproductive health clinic or a health promotion program.
- Volunteering for a non-profit direct services organization such as a Community Health Center, an HIV/AIDS clinic or a local chapter of the Red Cross.
- Working at a non-profit organization that is directly involved in public health advocacy and policy, either in the US or abroad.
- Working or volunteering for a local health department.

CEPH-accredited public health schools and programs recognize that it is sometimes difficult to gain experience before applying, so some schools of public health have developed programs that offer opportunities for potential applicants to get experience before applying. In addition, volunteer or community-service experience in general, even if it is not directly related to public health, will likely benefit a student's application.

Prospective students may also conduct informational interviews with members of the public health community. Many schools look upon this experience as providing at least some exposure to public health, which is helpful in the application process.

Public Health Degree Programs

At CEPH–accredited schools and programs, the most common public health degree is the Master of Public Health (MPH); however, most schools offer other master's degrees, such as the Master of Health Administration (MHA) or Master of Science (MS). Additionally, all CEPH-accredited schools of public health must offer at least three doctoral degrees, such as the PhD, Doctorate of Public Health (DrPH) or Doctorate of Science (DSc).

Professional degrees generally have a greater orientation towards practice in public health settings. The MPH, DrPH, and MHA are examples of degrees that are geared towards those who want careers as practitioners of public health in traditional health departments, managed care organizations, community-based organizations, hospitals, consulting firms, international agencies, and state and federal agencies, among others.

Academic degrees are more oriented toward students wishing to seek a career in academics and research rather than public health practice. Examples of academic degrees are the MS, PhD, and ScD. However, each school of public health can tailor its degree programs significantly, so students are encouraged to check with individual schools and programs for more information.

In an effort to ensure a well-rounded education, all MPH students are required to take at least one course in each of the five core areas of public health: biostatistics, epidemiology, environmental health, behavioral sciences/health education, and health services administration. Students take the rest of their courses either in their area of specialization or they may take additional credits in other areas such as maternal and child health, nutrition, genomics, informatics, and public health law. There is a rich menu of choices for a student to choose from when enrolling in a school of public health. First year students are encouraged to take the five core courses early on because many students find unexpected interest in another concentration. Most master's programs are generally two years in length for full-time students, though executive programs for students with significant public health experience can be completed in less time. Doctoral programs are normally three to five years in length.

Public health is an interdisciplinary field — not only does it require specialists in public health, but it also requires the cooperation and participation of other professionals, such as medical doctors, lawyers, dentists, nurses, urban planners, etc. To this end, there are over 45 joint degrees in public health, which include the MD/MPH, JD/MPH, MPH/MBA and the MPH/MSW. Joint degrees are an excellent opportunity for students who want to practice the clinical health professions while applying public health principles.

ASPPH hosts a program search found on its website (www.aspph.org) which allows applicants to search for degree programs based on area of interest, degree, enrollment term, distance learning options and other criteria.

The Admissions Process

While admissions committees look for high graduate entrance exam scores and GPA, other aspects of an applicant's record, such as career achievement, professional experience, and clarity of career goals are equally important. Admissions decisions are based on an overall assessment of the ability of applicants to successfully complete the degree track area selected. Each program or track within a given department may set additional requirements for admission; therefore, applicants should refer to the individual programs for details. All schools of public health require effective verbal and written communication; therefore, students should try to take advantage of undergraduate opportunities to hone these skills.

As of 2013, 42 of the 50 CEPH-accredited schools of public health participate in SOPHAS, the centralized application service for public health. Public health programs will be eligible to join as of September 1, 2013 and a number are likely to participate in the fall of 2013.

SOPHAS is open from September to August each year. Public health schools and programs have multiple deadlines, so applicants are asked to keep a close eye on the list of deadlines found on the SOPHAS website. Once the application has been e-submitted, applicants can monitor the progress of their application and their submitted documents. Instructions, customer service contact information and a complete check-list of items need to complete the application can be found at www.sophas.org.

A typical SOPHAS application package includes:

- Completed application and fee (some SOPHAS institutions may require a supplemental application and/or fee);
- A personal statement describing the student's interest in and potential for contributing to the field of public health;
- A resume reflecting work/volunteer history;
- Official transcripts of all academic work;
- A strong undergraduate record overall;
- Three letters of recommendation from academic or professional references;
- Submission of one standardized test scores. More schools of public health require GRE scores but many allow for the substitution of other standardized tests, such as the MCAT, GMAT, DAT or LSAT.

Financing Public Health Education

For 2010-2011, the average yearly cost of a master's level degree in public health, including tuition, fees, books, etc., is $26,117 and the median is $25,000. The range is from just under $13,000 to $56,000 per year. (Numbers are based on non-resident tuition.)
Students may wish to defray these expenses through the wide variety of assistance programs that are available to public health students, such as scholarships, grants, loans, and work programs. Students should contact the school they will be attending and ask about university-based student aid programs. Some schools and programs have endowments for student aid for which matriculating students would be eligible.

Students who are willing to pursue their degree part-time are encouraged to ask about their school's tuition remission programs. Many colleges subsidize or pay full tuition for employees that enroll in courses. These types of programs are useful in reducing reliance on student loan programs; however, students must balance that benefit against the additional time it will take to complete their degree program on a part-time basis.

The National Health Service Corps (NHSC) offers tuition assistance and living stipends for students participating in some Public Health disciplines in exchange for service in a federally-mandated health manpower shortage area after leaving school. More information about this program is available at nhsc.bhpr.hrsa.gov or by calling (800) 638-0824.

Public health students are encouraged to investigate scholarship and financial aid programs such as www.fastweb. com, www.finaid.org, www.fafsa.org and studentaid.ed.gov/PORTALSWebApp/students/english/index.jsp

Certified in Public Health (CPH) Credential

Students and graduates of CEPH-accredited schools or programs of public health are eligible to sit for a national credentialing exam which confers the credential CPH, certified in public health. The credential assures that students and graduates from schools and programs of public health have mastered the knowledge and skills relevant to contemporary public health.

To date, more than 3,000 people have people have received their CPH.. Administered by the National Board of Public Health Examiners (NBPHE), the exam consists of 200 multiple choice questions covering the core domains of public health (biostatistics, epidemiology, environmental health, the social and behavioral sciences, and health policy and management) and the cross-cutting competency domains articulated by the ASPH Masters of Public Health competencies (public health biology, leadership, communications, diversity and culture, professionalism, program planning and systems thinking). More information is available at www.nbphe.org

Resources

1. Association of Schools and Programs of Public Health
   1900 M Street NW #710
   Washington DC 20036
   (202) 296-1099
   fax: (202) 296-1252
   info@asph.org

2. www.aspph.org

3. www.asph.org/advisors

4. www.whatispublichealth.org

5. www.nbphe.org

6. www.ceph.org

VETERINARY MEDICINE

General Description of Profession

Traditionally, veterinarians have maintained healthy and productive commercial food animals and livestock, secured public health, and treated illness and disease in livestock, and sport and companion animals. Today, however, the breadth of veterinary medicine encompasses much more. The majority of veterinarians are in private small, large or mixed animal clinical practice; however, county, state and federal governments, universities, private industry, zoos, the U.S. military, wildlife organizations, racetracks, and circuses are also some of the diverse settings that employ veterinarians.

About 75% of the approximately 85,000 veterinarians in the United States work in private practice. During the past twenty years, the nature of private practice has evolved to cater to increasing demands by animal owners and production animal managers. No longer are practices focused only on large animals in the classical rural large animal or equine practice, or to dogs and cats in a suburban neighborhood small animal practice. Many large animal practitioners now consult on herd-health issues, with some traveling great distances to deliver their expertise. Emergency animal clinics service trauma victims much as do trauma centers in urban hospitals. Board Certified Specialists run referral practices in specialty fields such as critical care, dentistry, dermatology, internal medicine, ophthalmology, radiology and surgery. Mobile veterinary services come to your home, and mobile surgeons contract with general practitioners in their offices. Practices limited to dogs, cats, avian medicine, exotic animals (reptiles, amphibians, etc.), aquatic animals, cancer treatment, low-cost spaying-neutering, in vitro fertilization, geriatric care, preventive medicine (acupuncture, nutrition, etc.), and in-home euthanasia, all exist. And there are bound to be more changes in future types of practices developed due to increased specialization and to competition in the veterinary marketplace. The other 25% of veterinarians work for county and state governments, private industry, U.S. military, universities, humane associations, and other organizations.

The following federal agencies employ a large number of veterinarians: U.S. Department of Agriculture, Food and Drug Administration, National Institutes of Health Centers for Disease Control and Prevention, Department of Defense, and the U.S. Fish and Wildlife Service. Veterinarians employed by government entities enforce regulations established to protect public health and the health of animals (domestic and wild), eradicate diseases such as rabies and brucellosis, and ensure the quality, safety and wholesomeness of foods and animal-derived products. Universities and industry employ veterinarians to conduct basic and advance biomedical research with laboratory animals. Their goal is to better understand disease processes and develop methods for their control or cure in both animals and humans. Biomedical research continually produces major advances in pharmaceuticals and disease treatments. Veterinarians are also educators in universities. This list is far from complete. See your health professions advisor to discuss these and other possible veterinary careers, which may be of interest to you.

You may be interested in an area closely related to veterinary medicine that does not require a veterinary degree. Such areas include animal welfare, animal training and breeding, hospital administration, wildlife conservation, marine biology, agriculture, etc. The American Veterinary Medical Association (AVMA) Directory, published annually, lists national and international organizations associated with these activities and their addresses so you may contact them concerning additional career possibilities. Contact the AVMA for information about the AVMA Directory (see Resources) or an AVMA member veterinarian.

The Decision to Pursue a Career in Veterinary Medicine

"I have always wanted to be a veterinarian." Most veterinarians will tell you that their interest in animals and animal health began when they were very young. Perhaps the spark was lit by experiences with a beloved family pet, toiling on a farm, riding horses, visiting a zoo, or walks through the woods. For others, the spark was lit later in life and may

have focused on research, public health, animal welfare, or ecological issues. People come to veterinary medicine from all types of backgrounds with diverse goals. Many enter the profession when they are young, while others may gain their degree after a successful career in another field. A number of students enter a veterinary college with an advanced degree such as an MS or PhD. Others have yet to graduate from an undergraduate college.

Whatever your background and motivation, you have decided that you wish to prepare for a veterinary medical education. With a degree in veterinary medicine, your options for professional success and fulfillment are broad. This section will give you appropriate information for charting your course and setting realistic goals for yourself.

Outlook for the Future

The outlook for veterinary medicine, in companion and production animal practice, along with research and public practice, remains bright. The profession continues to see growth, especially in government, research, and other forms of public practice. Numerous opportunities lie outside of standard clinical practice. This is especially evident in response to the threat of bioterrorism and national security needs. At present, there is a shortage of veterinarians who enter research and public practice as a whole. Those interested in public practice and research have many open doors. Veterinarians are also being called upon to work on issues pertinent to the environment, conservation, aquaculture, wildlife management, and overall ecological health.

Opportunities and employment for veterinarians in companion animal practice, including horses, are expected to continue to grow. While the number of pets is expected to remain stable, rising incomes and the maturation of the boomers are expected to fuel the demand for high-quality companion animal care. More veterinary services are now available due to increased specialization and medical technology. There are more effective treatment modalities for acute and chronic problems and veterinary practices are becoming more flexible. More pet owners are also taking advantage of nontraditional veterinary services, including acupuncture, holistic medicine, physical therapy, behavior consultation, prophylactic dentistry, etc. With the advent of new and specialized procedures and medicines, pet owners may be willing to pay more for elective and intensive care than in the past. Pet owners are even purchasing pet insurance, increasing the likelihood that a considerable amount of money will be spent on veterinary care for their pets. The level of income of companion animal practitioners has increased in recent years and reflects the current and projected shifts in the supply and demand of veterinarians. As with most healthcare professions, practitioner salaries reflect regional demand and level of urbanization.

Food animal veterinarians have seen dramatic changes the nature of their practices over the past decades. The number of farms with animals in the U.S. has dropped precipitously, while the number of animals per farm has increased. Whereas in 1980 there were 334,000 farms with at least one dairy cow and an average of 32 head, the year 2002 saw only 92,000 farms, but an average of 99 head. This type of consolidation is seen in cattle, poultry and swine production as well. These dramatic changes were the result of a combination of low commodities prices, higher feed costs, and competition. The veterinarian's role focuses less on the individual animal and more on the health of the herd. Demand for veterinarians with specialized knowledge in herd-health issues is strong and these individuals command high salaries.

Demand for specialists, in many areas, including ophthalmology, internal medicine, toxicology, laboratory animal medicine, etc. is expected to continue to increase. Many students, during their third year of veterinary school, consider further education through internships as a lead-in to a residency program. Internships and residencies are optional and not required to become a licensed, practicing veterinarian.

Planning a Program of Study

The veterinary medical profession is much smaller than human medicine. While there are well over 100 medical schools, there are only 29 colleges and schools of veterinary medicine in the U.S. There is no distinction between a college and a school of veterinary medicine and the terms will be used interchangeably throughout the chapter. In 2012, there were 2,900 positions available for first-year students and over 6,500 applicants applied through the central application service, Veterinary Medical College Application Service (VMCAS) administered by the Association of American Veterinary Medical Colleges. Others applied directly to select individual schools. The number of seats available is not expected to significantly rise in the near future. The number of underrepresented students in Veterinary Medicine such as, African American, Hispanic, Native American and Asian applicants was 10% of the total applicant enrollment of veterinarian students in 2005.

The number of women applying and matriculating into veterinary school has changed the face of veterinary medicine profoundly, and is now nearly 80% of all veterinary students. The increase in the number of female applicants and enrolled students mirrors a less dramatic increase in women entering other professional medical fields.

In response to the changing applicant pool and national needs for veterinarians, veterinary medical schools have changed or are considering changing some of their admission practices. Many now actively recruit students by making high school and college visitations, as well as by offering special admission and summer enrichment programs for disadvantaged students. Combined DVM/VMD, PhD, MPH, and MBA programs are increasing in numbers. Colleges may recruit applicants, especially those with research interests, into one of these programs. While recruitment efforts may be increasing, the number of graduates has remained relatively constant over the past 20 years. The number of accredited veterinary colleges has increased by one since 1983, with the Western University of Health Sciences College of Veterinary Medicine admitting its first class in 2003.

Many individuals desire to enter the profession and practice medicine or pursue related interests. The individual colleges set their own admission criteria and have the sole discretion concerning student admissions. Not every qualified applicant will be accepted. Thus, part of your professional plan should consist of options should you not be accepted to a veterinary college. It is imperative that you keep your options open. Should you not gain admission and remain committed to becoming a veterinarian, do not become discouraged. You are not alone. Many students gain admission their second application cycle. Consult with your advisor — where there is a will, there usually is a way.

As with any aspect of life, having a plan to achieve a goal is essential. Your goal is to gain admission to a college of veterinary medicine and create your path to professional success. Many considerations, including academics, experience, debt load, program of study, family life and more need to be taken into account when planning your professional path. The following sections explain the requirements and steps necessary to make yourself a competitive candidate for admission into a college of veterinary medicine. A wealth of information sources exist concerning veterinary applications, colleges and careers. Use them well.

The term "preprofessional requirements" defines the characteristics and requirements necessary to submit a complete application to a college of veterinary medicine. Successful completion of your preprofessional requirements includes finishing all required coursework, maintenance of a high GPA, scoring well on required standardized exams, gaining exposure to different aspects of veterinary medicine, and taking on leadership roles in activities on campus or in the community. Applicants who are deficient in any of the above are at a disadvantage, compared to other applicants. Each of the above will be discussed in detail below.

Required Coursework

Each college or school of veterinary medicine has its own list of required courses to be completed prior to matriculation. (Some schools require that prerequisite courses be completed during the fall semester prior to matriculation; some require spring semester completion; and some allow completion of prerequisite courses during the summer semester immediately prior to matriculation.) Admission will be denied if said courses are not completed on time.

Most colleges require that all of your science and math courses be taken within the past 4–10 years. Below is a summary of courses required by many of the colleges and schools. Not all of the courses are required for each school. You may be fortunate in attending an undergraduate college that offers all of the courses required for the schools to which you plan to submit an application. If there is a course not offered by your undergraduate college, consult with the veterinary colleges to determine if another closely-related course can be substituted. This is a common occurrence with animal science courses. If no substitution can be made, you may need to consider other options, such as taking the course at a different undergraduate college (possibly during the summer), inquire if the course can be taken via a distance-learning or web-based class, or transfer to another undergraduate college. Consult the *Veterinary Medical School Admissions Requirements (VMSAR)* book, your advisor or the college to learn about the college's specific requirements. Requirements do change, so you should check annually to see if there are any changes, which may impact your academic plan.

Math and Sciences

Algebra/Trigonometry	Calculus/Precalculus
Animal sciences	Animal nutrition
Biology with lab	Cell biology
Inorganic Chemistry with lab	Organic Chemistry with lab
General Physics	Biochemistry
Embryology	Genetics
Microbiology	Statistics
Zoology	Immunology

Non-Sciences

English Composition	Literature
Humanities/Arts and	Public Speaking/Speech
Social Sciences	Behavioral Sciences

A few schools require business/finance, physiology, vertebrate anatomy, technical writing, history, economics, computer skills course.

1. Math

    If you have a weak math background or it has been a long time since you have taken math, consider taking an introductory or intermediate algebra class to prepare for upper-level math. It is important that your mathematics abilities are strong. Even if calculus is not required by your colleges of interest, analytical skills are critical to your success in chemistry, physics, statistics, and computer science.

2. Chemistry

    Most students agree — chemistry is difficult to master. If your chemistry background is weak, consider taking an introductory course. Some undergraduate colleges give placement exams in their beginning-level general chemistry course. Discuss the results with your preveterinary advisor or instructor. Be mindful that many students struggle with chemistry courses. Most of the schools currently require at least one course in biochemistry, which means you will be taking a sequence of two to three years of chemistry courses (inorganic, organic and biochemistry). Give yourself every advantage by building a good foundation in the beginning. Remember, the later you begin your chemistry sequence, the longer it will be before you may apply to veterinary school.

3. Other Sciences

    All veterinary colleges require one or more semesters of physics and biology, and many require genetics, microbiology, biochemistry, nutrition or other upper division biology courses such as embryology or immunology.

4.   English, Humanities, Social Sciences and Behavioral Sciences

The majority of veterinary schools require courses in both English and humanities, and most undergraduate institutions include varying amounts of these in graduation requirements. Several veterinary schools require courses in social sciences, business, and public speaking. In addition, all of the standardized examinations include an analysis of reading ability.

Choice of Major

The veterinary profession is broad and wide-ranging. Colleges and schools of veterinary medicine seek applicants with diverse educational backgrounds. English majors have gained admission, as have those who have majored in a variety of other fields. However, schools generally select students who have strong backgrounds in the sciences. It is important that you choose a field that interests you, but enables you to complete all of the required courses (see above). Thus, it is not essential that you have a major in a science. If you are required to take the Biology Subject GRE test, a major in Biology will prepare you for that test better than any other major.

The Admission Process

Completing your applications to veterinary colleges can be a daunting task. Each college has its own academic, examination and experience requirements, expectations and deadlines. Many also have specific application requirements. However, the schools all put emphasis on the following criteria as they review candidates.

Factors evaluated by Admissions Committees

1.   Academic Record

Although veterinary admissions committees evaluate many criteria when selecting a veterinary class, academic performance remains one of the most important factors in the committees' decisions as they are seeking evidence that you will be able to successfully complete the rigorous DVM program. If you are like most preveterinary students, you want to understand the role of your grades in the admission process. Here is a typical statement from a veterinary school catalog, "Demonstration of outstanding academic achievement is a necessary prerequisite for admission to the professional veterinary medical curriculum." How to define "outstanding academic achievement," of course, is quite another question. You will be able to glean information from *VMSAR* or the college's website. These sources contain the average GPAs and test scores from the previously admitted class.

Method of application evaluation and weight placed on various admissions criteria varies from school to school. Many schools have a point system, which gives weight to various criteria, while a few schools now use a subjective evaluation process which allows for a broad, overall evaluation of the application. In a typical admission process, academic factors count for about 50% of your score or ranking. Generally, equal weight is given to the undergraduate cumulative GPA, GPA for the last year or two of undergraduate work, GPA for the required science courses and finally, the standardized test. The other 50% of your evaluation may be based on "non-academic" factors, which will vary from school to school. It is important to be aware of the evaluation criteria and processes for the schools to which you are applying.

Most schools require that all preveterinary courses be taken for a letter grade, as admission committee members wish to see what level you achieved and evaluate all applicants equally. Therefore you place yourself a disadvantage if you take these courses pass/fail or if you attend an undergraduate institution that does not assign grades. Each veterinary school has its own policy for course repeats and GPA calculations. Some schools include repeats in the

GPA calculation, some do not. If you received a low grade and it was due to factors other than your study skills and the college does not require repeating the course, then improving your performance in a more difficult course should compensate. If you did not really master the material and other courses build on it, you should probably repeat the course. However, several low grades in required courses may mean your strategy or your goals are inappropriate. Your health professions advisor will be able to counsel you on how to proceed. Also admissions committees often view inordinate numbers of withdrawals on a transcript to be a sign of the applicant's inability to master the material, despite the final grade in the course.

While overall GPA is important, the colleges pay special attention to applicants' science-based or math/science-based GPA. Even if the overall GPA is high, a low science GPA will disadvantage an applicant. Many colleges have a minimum acceptable science GPA (see *VMSAR*). Geographical boundaries may place an added requirement on students: schools tend to have higher overall GPA requirements for out-of-state at-large applicants. A student who takes an average or greater number of units per semester, has a GPA in the range of 3.4 to 3.8 or better and has excellent non-academic factors (discussed below) will be an outstanding candidate. Remember, grades account for a significant portion of the weight of your application. Be mindful that a 4.0 is not a free ticket into veterinary school. The remainder of your application must be outstanding, as well. And yes, students with a 4.0 have been denied admission in the past.

2. Standardized Examinations

All of the colleges require scores from at least one examination. Currently, there are three different examinations utilized: The Graduate Record Examination (GRE), Medical College Admission Test (MCAT) or GRE Biology Subject test. The greatest number of veterinary colleges and schools require or accept scores from the GRE general test. The Veterinary College Admission Test (VCAT) has been discontinued. Contact individual colleges regarding their acceptance of old VCAT scores. Acceptance of particular examinations varies by college. Most require or accept the GRE General test, but a few require either the MCAT or Biology Subject test. Thus, it is important that you identify which exam(s) you will take and when it will be appropriate to take them. Deadlines for receipt of test scores vary by school. For testing dates and information, see the websites of the test administering organizations (Resources). The colleges have limits as to the oldest scores they will accept. This ranges from two to six years.

There are no specific college courses to help prepare you for the General GRE test other than mathematics through college algebra, trigonometry and introductory English. Therefore, it may be to your advantage to prepare for and take the GRE early, perhaps after your second year in college. Most applicants take the exam in the spring of the year when they are applying to veterinary school. Consult the GRE Bulletin or website for test centers and dates. When selecting a date to take the exam, be sure to allow enough preparation time before the exam, and leave yourself enough time to receive your scores from the first attempt and to strengthen your knowledge in any weak areas, so that you can improve your scores if you need to retake it.

The GRE Biology Subject Test is designed for students majoring in biology. Not only should students have completed an introductory year biology course, but also many students report that some advanced courses in subjects such as genetics and ecology are especially helpful to their preparation. There are, naturally, many courses that can be added to this list, but you should discuss your strengths and weaknesses with your advisor before planning. Thus, plan to take the Biology Subject test no later than the spring prior to submitting your application so you have time to retake it, if necessary. It is important to remember that some schools will not accept the GRE Biology Subject exam, only the GRE General exam.

3. Animal and Health-Related Experience

While academics play a significant role in the admissions process, most competitive candidates have similar GPAs and standardized test scores. Experiences and employment history can help distinguish applicants from each other. Animal and health-related experiences may account for up to one-third of the weight of an application. Admission committees utilize an applicant's experiences to:

- Demonstrate an applicant's sincere interest in veterinary medicine and the biological sciences.

- Show that an applicant has developed a realistic and accurate understanding of the veterinary medical profession. Besides the immediately obvious benefits of acquiring such a familiarity with the profession, this becomes important when an applicant is asked to discuss his/her understanding of the veterinary medical profession in the narrative portion of the application and in the interview.

- Define and reaffirm the applicant's desire to enter the veterinary profession and to formulate his/her future goals and objectives. This is where interest in nontraditional career goals can be demonstrated.

- Show that the student has a sense of confidence and comfort around a variety of animals, which is essential in handling the animals that one will encounter throughout the curriculum.

Developing breadth of experience in different veterinary settings, such as a combination of small, large and exotic animal veterinary work and research is to your advantage. Students should make every effort to acquire a basic understanding of the veterinary medical profession as a whole. Non-veterinary experiences include areas where you work with animals but are not directly supervised by a veterinarian, such as on a farm; training horses, grooming dogs and cats; at the local zoo; pet adoption programs, pet therapy, or animal shelters; and non-animal related, such as in a chemistry or computer laboratory. Other positions, non-animal related, may show other special skills or abilities that you have. The positions that you work may be formal or informal, paid, unpaid or volunteer. It is important to demonstrate that you are well-rounded and can adapt to a variety of roles. Most schools require a minimum number of hours of animal and veterinary medicine exposure. It is always a good idea to have above the minimum in order to demonstrate a high level of motivation and extensive experience.

All veterinary school applicants are requested to provide certain facts on the application about veterinary and animal/health-related experiences, including number of hours worked, inclusive dates, responsibilities and names of supervisors and advisors. If you keep accurate records of this information while obtaining the experience, you will find it much easier to completely and accurately fill out this part of the application. Plan ahead.

There are many ways to acquire experience, including:

- Internship Programs. Your campus career planning and placement office, biology, animal sciences, biochemistry, microbiology, etc. departments or preveterinary advisor may provide a list of internships where you can work on or off campus in veterinary practices, zoos, institutions, organizations, etc. Internships are usually on a volunteer basis, although some paid positions occasionally become available. Some internships may be taken for college credit.

- Private Veterinary Practices. Obtaining experience in a private practice may involve offering your services on a voluntary basis to a practicing veterinarian, but more frequently, paid positions can be arranged. This experience may vary from simply observing the veterinarian in surgery to actively participating in many aspects of day-to-day private practice. In any case, this will probably be the most important type of experience that you will obtain since it offers enormous potential for you to learn about the intricacies of the veterinary profession. Many students begin in a small animal or mixed animal practice.

- Research. Independent study programs in any area of the health sciences may be pursued by a motivated upper-division student. You must generally connect with a faculty advisor who will support your project in his/her research laboratory. Although research experience is not required by the veterinary schools, it provides a way in which you can use the knowledge you have acquired in a problem-solving environment. There are many places to consider for research experience both during the academic year and during the summer. Feel free to pursue any type of scientific research that interests you.

- Special Resources. Some undergraduate colleges are associated with veterinary schools that have primate centers, raptor centers, or commercial animal programs; some cities have large aquatic parks, wild animal parks, and zoos; and you may be able to work for a private wildlife organization or a government agency such as the U.S. Fish and Wildlife Service during the summer.

- Enrichment Programs. Several veterinary schools have summer enrichment programs to help minority and disadvantaged students prepare for and gain admission to veterinary school. These programs can help to upgrade your academic and noncognitive qualifications. Contact your preveterinary advisor or the schools individually. The *VMSAR* also has a list of these programs.

- Other possibilities for obtaining experience do exist. Use your imagination. Do not be afraid to knock on doors and sell yourself. Have you heard of horseback riding programs for people with physical-impairments? How about helping to hatch penguins at Sea World? Talk to students in your local preveterinary club. They may exchange information about positions with veterinarians. Of course, you will want to find out about opportunities in your own area.

4. Letters of evaluation

Letters of evaluation are required by veterinary schools, and are utilized as another source of information to demonstrate your special qualities and interests. Personal letters of recommendation provide the admissions committees with information which cannot be assessed by grades or academic performance alone. They showcase your personality, interests and drive to succeed. For this reason, veterinary school prefer individual letters of recommendation over committee or composite letters. Veterinary schools will only accept an electronic letter of evaluation submitted through the VMCAS evaluation portal. More information is provided about letters of evaluation in chapter 2.

5. Leadership and Communication Skills

Are you a leader or a follower? Are you a team player and get along well with others? It is of benefit to students if they have been able to demonstrate leadership qualities and strong communication skills. Holding offices on campus, such as on the student health advisory board or in the preveterinary club can be beneficial. There are many community organizations as well that afford you the opportunity for leadership experience. Skills can also be demonstrated through work experience, student government, teaching assistantships, youth mentoring, etc. Veterinarians are leaders in their practices, in the community, and in many medical and public health fields and the veterinary schools look to applicants for future leadership.

6. Commitment to Service

Veterinary schools are looking for individuals who show compassion and are interested in giving back to the community. Therefore, involvement in volunteer service is an important learning experience. Many campuses have student volunteer programs, or look around in your community for opportunities. You can get involved in volunteer service of any kind that interests you.

7. The Interview

Some veterinary schools require an interview; some only interview some portion of their acceptable applicant pool; others do not interview at all. Be prepared for the interview format and review the material in chapter 2. Interviews are unique experiences for most applicants. They are another opportunity to demonstrate your personal qualities and accomplishments and most importantly to convey your understanding of and motivation for the veterinary profession.

The Application

1. When and where to apply

   Apply when you are prepared to present yourself as a qualified applicant. In the early spring of the year you plan to apply to veterinary school, begin to prepare your application materials. Most students who want to go directly to vet school after college begin their application during the spring of their junior (third) year of their undergraduate education and submit the application in the fall of their senior year. Very well-qualified students who can complete the required coursework and credit hours, experiences and tests, may submit their application in the fall of their second or third year. A smaller number of individuals are accepted from the pool of second and third year applicants than from the pool of those who submit their application during the fall of their senior year. This is due to the fact that younger students have not had time to acquire adequate work and life experiences. You can gain practice and experience by submitting an application, but keep in mind that it is better to submit your best application the first time.

   a. Timeline for applying
   Applications are normally available early June. Applicants spend the summer months preparing the application, seeking evaluators for the required letters of recommendation, and gathering transcripts. Most applications are due early October; all are due in the early fall. Verify with each school the specific application deadlines for that school.

   b. Selecting Schools or Colleges of Interest
   In order to begin selecting schools where you will apply, there are many factors to consider: geographic location, residency requirements, personal support system (presence of family or friends), cost and financial aid, curriculum, special programs, facilities, support for disadvantaged students, preveterinary course requirements and type of admission examination required. Most students look at three or four colleges or schools of veterinary medicine, but there is no limit. It is to your advantage to educate yourself as much as possible about all of these factors.

   c. Residency Considerations and Contracts
   Geographic boundaries, such as your state or country of residence, used to limit an applicant's choice of veterinary colleges. However, many veterinary colleges, public and private, are enrolling many more non-residents. This is a shift and is to the applicant's advantage. Although all colleges accept non-residents, there are many fewer seats for non-residents than residents. Some colleges accept out-of-state students and allow them to become residents and pay resident tuition after one year.

   Most states without a veterinary college contract with one or more colleges of veterinary medicine to enroll a certain number of students from the contracting state. A specific number of seats are allotted to the state but contracts with the veterinary schools frequently change. The *VMSAR* book contains a section outlining all of the contracts available as of press time. It is best to consult the *VMSAR* book annually. Many of the contracts are only financial in nature and do not give preference to the applicant over other non-residents. You may apply to all of the colleges that contract with your state or any other college based on your strengths and perception of your chances for admission. Your advisor may have suggestions regarding contract seats. Also, be aware of residency requirements in each state, i.e. you must live in the state for so many years or months as a non-student, have a state driver's license, pay taxes, etc. You may need to be certified as a

contract student during your application process. If so, it is your responsibility to register with your state.

If you live in a state without a veterinary college it is wise to be aware of your options at several colleges outside of your state and to apply to more than one college. In the past, an applicant usually submitted one or two applications. With the advent of a centralized application service and increased acceptance of non-residents, the average number of applications submitted through the centralized application service is between three and four. Submitting more than two applications has traditionally been a strategy of many students as the success of applicants submitting three or more applications is substantially higher than for those submitting two or fewer.

2. Veterinary Medical College Application Service

Most of the colleges utilize the centralized application service through the Veterinary Medical College Application Service (VMCAS). VMCAS is sponsored by the Association of American Veterinary Medical Colleges (AAVMC) in Washington, DC. The application is web-based and is completed by the applicant only once per admission cycle. VMCAS distributes the application to the colleges designated by the applicant.

The web-based application becomes available for students in early June and may be found through the AAVMC's website (www.aavmc.org). The application can be completed at the applicant's discretion, over several months. Your personal statement and evaluations are also completed through VMCAS.

The VMCAS website contains valuable information concerning completion of the application as well as general information on the application process. Even with a centralized application, applying is quite time consuming. VMCAS saves the applicant the work of completing multiple application forms when she/he is applying to multiple schools. Some colleges prefer to utilize their own applications and do not participate in VMCAS. Others utilize the service for out-of-state applicants only. The VMCAS website details level of participation for each college. Also, many colleges require completion of supplemental application forms. Your application will not be considered if you do not also submit the supplemental application. Check the colleges' websites for specific information on submitting a supplemental application.

VMCAS maintains a staff to address questions or problems with the VMCAS process itself but all questions pertaining to specific policies of the participating schools must be directed to the schools themselves. The VMCAS website provides links to the individual colleges for your convenience. You must request applications individually from each school that does not participate in VMCAS. The applications are usually available in late May or June.

An important part of your application will be the personal statement that you will write. It is your opportunity to give the admissions committee a look into your life, aspirations and unique attributes. The committees also utilize the personal statement to assess your writing and communications skills. It usually requires you to discuss (a) the events that led you to choose veterinary medicine as a career, (b) how your background and personal interests relate to the desire to become a veterinarian, (c) your understanding of veterinary medicine as a profession and (d) your career goals and objectives. Committees are also interested in what unique qualities you will bring to the class and to the profession. Be certain to answer these questions in a well-organized, complete, and professional manner. This is especially true in supplemental application narratives. The admission committee will use this narrative in an attempt to understand the quality of animal and veterinary experiences gained by the applicant. Students should, therefore, use the narrative to convey what they have learned about the veterinary profession, not merely what they have experienced as a part of it. Avoid negative or pessimistic connotations or undertones. A well-written narrative will, instead, present you as an optimistic, positive individual. Lastly, the narrative should be unique and interesting, as well as grammatically correct and error free.

The VMCAS application also requires that you enter the names and contact information for a minimum of three evaluators through its Electronic Letters of Recommendation system (eLOR). Due to the varying evaluation requirements, applicants may need to submit more than three evaluations. The eLOR system will accept up to six evaluations. All of the schools your VMCAS application is delivered to will contain these electronic letters. If applying through VMCAS, you cannot have evaluators tailor letters to specific colleges, unless you are applying only to one college. Once you enter the evaluators' names into the VMCAS application, the evaluators will be able to complete their evaluations on-line. The system also allows applicants to check if their evaluations have been submitted. All of your VMCAS evaluations must be submitted electronically with the exception of Committee & Composite letters. The applicant is responsible for ensuring the timely submission of their evaluations. Colleges not participating in VMCAS have their own evaluation submission policies and require evaluations be sent directly to them.

Resources

1. Veterinary Medical Associations:
   Association of American Veterinary Medical Colleges (www.aavmc.org)
   American Veterinary Medical Association (www.avma.org)
   For a complete list of the 28 US veterinary schools, visit www.avma.org.

2. *Veterinary Medical School Admissions Requirements* published annually by the AAVMC. See www.aavmc.org for ordering information.

3. Services for evaluations of transcripts from foreign colleges:
   Joseph Silney and Associates, Inc. (www.jsilney.com)
   World Education Service (www.wes.org)
   American Association of Collegiate and Registrars and Admissions Officers (www.aacrao.org)
   International Education Research Foundation (IERF) (www.ierf.org)
   Educational Credential Evaluators, Inc (www.ece.org)

Appendix A
Career Summaries

CHIROPRACTOR (DC)

Summarized from the Bureau of Labor Statistics, U.S. Department of Labor, *Occupational Outlook Handbook, 2012-13 Edition*, Chiropractors, www.bls.gov/ooh/healthcare/chiropractors.htm:

I. *Career Description*

Chiropractors treat patients with health problems of the musculoskeletal system, which is made up of bones, muscles, ligaments, and tendons. They use spinal manipulation and other techniques to treat patients' ailments, such as back or neck pain.

Chiropractors typically do the following:
- Assess a patient's medical condition by reviewing his or her medical history, listening to the patient's concerns, and performing a physical examination
- Analyze the patient's posture and spine
- Provide musculoskeletal therapy, which involves adjusting a patient's spinal column and other joints by hand
- Conduct additional diagnostic tests, including evaluating a patient's posture or taking x rays
- Provide additional treatments, such as applying heat or cold to a patient's injured areas
- Advise patients on health and lifestyle issues, such as exercise and sleep habits
- Refer patients to other medical specialists if needed

II. *Career Settings*

Chiropractors held about 52,600 jobs in 2010. Most chiropractors work in a solo or group practice. Many are self-employed, meaning that they own or are partners in owning their practice. A small number work in hospitals or physicians' offices.

Employment of chiropractors is expected to increase by 28 percent from 2010 to 2020, faster than the average for all occupations.

III. *Compensation*

The median annual wage of chiropractors was $67,200 in May 2010. The lowest 10 percent earned less than $32,270, and the top 10 percent earned more than $143,670.

IV. *Educational Requirements for Practice*

3-to-4 years of undergraduate education, followed by a 4-year Doctor of Chiropractic (D.C.) degree program.

V. *Licensing*

All states and the District of Columbia require chiropractors to be licensed. Although specific requirements vary by state, all jurisdictions require the completion of an accredited Doctor of Chiropractic (D.C.) program.

All jurisdictions also require passing exams, either their own specific exams or those administered by the National Board of Chiropractic Examiners or both. These exams include written tests and, usually, a practical evaluation. States usually require continuing education to keep the license. Check with your state's board of chiropractic examiners or health department for more specific information on licensure.

VI. *Resources*

> American Chiropractic Association
> 1701 Clarendon Boulevard
> Arlington, VA 22209
> 703-276-8800
> www.acatoday.org

> Association of Chiropractic Colleges (ACC)
> 4424 Montgomery Avenue, Suite 202
> Bethesda, MD 20814
> 800-284-1062
> www.chirocolleges.org

DENTIST (D.D.S., D.M.D.)

Summarized from the Bureau of Labor Statistics, U.S. Department of Labor, *Occupational Outlook Handbook, 2012-13 Edition*, Dentists, www.bls.gov/ooh/healthcare/dentists.htm:

I. *Career Description*

Dentists diagnose and treat problems with a patient's teeth, gums, and related parts of the mouth. They provide advice and instruction on taking care of teeth and gums and on diet choices that affect oral health.

Dentists typically do the following:
- Remove decay from teeth and fill cavities
- Repair cracked or fractured teeth and remove teeth
- Straighten teeth to correct bite issues
- Place sealants or whitening agents on teeth
- Give anesthetics to keep patients from feeling pain during procedures
- Write prescriptions for antibiotics or other medications
- Examine x rays of teeth, gums, the jaw, and nearby areas for problems
- Make models and measurements for dental appliances, such as dentures, to fit patients
- Teach patients about diet, flossing, use of fluoride, and other aspects of dental care

Most dentists are general practitioners and handle a variety of dental needs. Other dentists practice in one of nine specialty areas, as dental public health specialists, endodontists, oral and maxillofacial radiologists, oral and maxillofacial surgeons, oral pathologists, orthodontists, pediatric dentists, periodontists, or prosthodontists.

II. *Career Settings*

Dentists held about 155,700 jobs in 2010. Some dentists own their own businesses and work alone or with a small staff. Other dentists have partners in their practice, and a few work for more established dentists as associate dentists. Employment of dentists is expected to grow by 21 percent from 2010 to 2020, faster than the average for all occupations.

III. Compensation

The median annual wage of dentists was $146,920 in May 2010. The lowest 10 percent earned less than $71,210, and the top 10 percent earned $166,400 or more. Earnings vary according to number of years in practice, location, hours worked, and specialty.

IV. Educational Requirements for Practice

Undergraduate Education: 3-4 years, but very few have only the minimum 3 years of undergraduate education. Most will have a baccalaureate degree before entering dental school.

Professional School: 4-year professional degree program that will earn either the D.D.S. or the D.M.D. degree. These two degrees are entirely equivalent in terms of the program taken and the rights conferred for practice.

Graduate Dental Education: Additional postgraduate training is required only for dentists wishing to specialize.

V. Licensing

Dentists must be licensed in all states; requirements vary by state. In most states, a license requires a degree from an accredited dental school and passing a written and practical exam.

VI. Resources

American Dental Association (ADA)
211 East Chicago Avenue
Chicago, IL 60611
312-440-2500
www.ada.org

American Dental Education Association (ADEA)
1400 K Street, NW
Suite 1100
Washington, DC 20005
202-289-7201
www.adea.org

DIETITIANS AND NUTRITIONISTS (R.D.)

Summarized from the Bureau of Labor Statistics, U.S. Department of Labor, *Occupational Outlook Handbook, 2012-13 Edition*, Dietitians and Nutritionists, www.bls.gov/ooh/healthcare/dietitians-and-nutritionists.htm:

I. Career Description

Dietitians and nutritionists are experts in food and nutrition. They advise people on what to eat in order to lead a healthy lifestyle or achieve a specific health-related goal.

Dietitians and nutritionists typically do the following:
- Explain nutrition issues

- Assess patients' and clients' health needs and diet
- Develop meal plans, taking both cost and clients' preferences into account
- Evaluate the effects of meal plans and change the plans as needed
- Promote better nutrition by giving talks to groups about diet, nutrition, and the relationship between good eating habits and preventing or managing specific diseases
- Keep up with the latest nutritional science research

II. Career Settings

Dietitians and nutritionists held about 64,400 jobs in 2010.

Dietitians and nutritionists work in hospitals, cafeterias, nursing homes, and schools. Some dietitians and nutritionists are self-employed and maintain their own practice. They work as consultants, providing advice to individual clients, or they work for healthcare establishments on a contract basis.

Employment of dietitians and nutritionists is expected to increase 20 percent from 2010 to 2020, faster than average for all occupations.

III. Compensation

The median annual wage of dietitians and nutritionists was $53,250 in May 2010. The lowest 10 percent earned less than $33,330, and the top 10 percent earned more than $75,480.

IV. Educational Requirements for Practice

Most dietitians and nutritionists have earned a bachelor's degree and receive supervised training through an internship or as a part of their coursework. Also, many states require dietitians and nutritionists to be licensed.

V. Licensing

Most states require licensure of dietitians and nutritionists. Other states require only state registration or certification, and a few have no state regulations.

Most states have enacted state licensure or certification for dietitians or nutritionists or both. The requirements for state licensure and state certification include having a bachelor's degree in food and nutrition or a related area, supervised practice, and passing an exam.

VI. Resources

American Dietetic Association
120 South Riverside Plaza, Suite 2000
Chicago IL 60606
800-877-1600
www.eatright.org

American Society for Nutrition
9650 Rockville Pike
Bethesda, MD 20814
301-634-7050
www.nutrition.org

GENETIC COUNSELOR (M.S.)

Summarized from the National Society of Genetic Counselors, www.nsgc.org, and material from the M.S degree program in Genetic Counseling at the University of North Carolina at Greensboro, www.uncg.edu/gen:

I. *Career Description*

Genetic counselors are health professionals who have obtained specialized graduate degrees and experience in the areas of medical genetics and counseling. Most have entered the profession from a variety of disciplines, including biology, clinical laboratory science, genetics, nursing, psychology, public health, and social work. Genetic counselors work as members of a health care team to provide information and support to families who have members with birth defects or genetic disorders and to families that may be at risk for a variety of inherited conditions. They identify families at risk, investigate the problem, investigate the problem present in the family, interpret information about the disorder, analyze inheritance patterns and risks of reoccurrence, and review available options with the family. Genetic counselors also provide supportive counseling to families, serve as patient advocates, and refer individuals and families to community or state support agencies. Some counselors work in administrative capacities. Many engage in research related to the fields of medical genetics and genetic counseling.

II. *Career Setting*

Genetic Counselors can work in a variety of setting, which may include some the following: university medical centers, private and public hospitals, diagnostic laboratories, physician private practices, HMOs, government offices, research and development/biotechnology companies. The primary work of the majority of genetic counselors takes place in a clinical setting.

III. *Compensation*

According to the National Society of Genetic Counselors, the average salary of respondents to NSGC's 2012 Professional Status Survey was approximately The average salary for a full-time genetic counselor is $68,000 but ranges up to $170,000 depending on specialty area and experience. (www.nsgc.org.)

IV. *Educational Requirements for Practice*

The master's degree in Genetic Counseling is the preferred degree in the United States. Programs are also offered in Canada, Australia, England, and South Africa. Courses often include clinical genetics, population genetics, cytogenetics, molecular genetics, psychosocial theory, ethics, and counseling techniques. Programs typically take two years of full-time study to complete, and include clinical practice in diverse clinical settings.

V. *Licensing*

Certification in Genetic Counseling is available by the American Board of Genetic Counseling (ABGC). Requirements include documentation of the following: a graduate degree in genetic counseling; clinical experience in an ABGC-approved training site or sites; a log book of 50 supervised cases; and successful completion of both the general and specialty certification examination.

VI. *Resources*

National Society of Genetic Counselors
401 N. Michigan Avenue
Chicago, IL 60611

312-321-6834
www.nsgc.org

American Board of Genetic Counseling
P.O. Box 14216
Lenexa, KS 66285
www.abgc.net

MEDICAL AND HEALTH SERVICES MANAGERS

Summarized from the Bureau of Labor Statistics, U.S. Department of Labor, *Occupational Outlook Handbook, 2012-13 Edition*, Medical and Health Services Managers, www.bls.gov/ooh/management/medical-and-health-services-managers.htm:

I. *Career Description*

Medical and health services managers, also called healthcare executives or healthcare administrators, plan, direct, and coordinate medical and health services. They might manage an entire facility, specialize in managing a specific clinical area or department, or manage a medical practice for a group of physicians.

II. *Career Settings*

Medical and health services managers held about 303,000 jobs in 2010. Most medical and health services managers work in offices in healthcare facilities, including hospitals and nursing homes, and group medical practices.

Employment of medical and health services managers is expected to grow by 22 percent from 2010 to 2020, faster than the average for all occupations.

III. *Compensation*

The median annual wage of medical and health services managers was $84,270 in May 2010. The lowest 10 percent earned less than $51,280, and the top 10 percent earned more than $144,880.

IV. *Educational Requirements for Practice*

Medical and health services managers typically need at least a bachelor's degree to enter the occupation. However, master's degrees in health services, long-term care administration, public health, public administration, or business administration also are common.

V. *Licensing*

All states require nursing care facility administrators to be licensed; requirements vary by state. In most states, these administrators must have a bachelor's degree, pass a licensing exam, and complete a state-approved training program. Some states also require administrators in assisted-living facilities to be licensed. A license is not required in other areas of medical and health services management.

VI. *Resources*

American College of Healthcare Executives

One North Franklin Street, Suite 1700
Chicago, IL 60606
312-424-2800
www.ache.org

Association of University Programs in Health Administration
2000 North 14th Street, Suite 780
Arlington, VA 22201
703-894-0940
www.aupha.org

NATUROPATHIC MEDICINE (N.D.)

Summarized from the American Association of Naturopathic Physicians (AANP), www.naturopathic.org:

I. *Career Description*

Naturopathic medicine is a distinct system of primary health care-an art, science and practice of preventing, diagnosing and treating conditions of the human mind and body. Naturopathic physicians work with their patients to prevent and treat acute and chronic illness and disease, restore health and establish optimal fitness by supporting the person's inherent self-healing process, the vis medicatrix naturae.

Prevention of disease is emphasized through public health measures and hygiene as well as the encouragement and guidance of persons to adopt lifestyles which are conducive to optimal health.

Diagnosis and evaluation of the individual's state of health are accomplished by integrated modern and traditional, clinical and laboratory diagnostic methods.

Therapeutic methods and substances are used which work in harmony with the person's inherent self -help process, the vis medicatrix naturae, including: dietetics and nutritional substances, botanical medicine, psychotherapy, naturopathic physical medicine including naturopathic manipulative therapy, minor surgery, prescription medications, naturopathic obstetrics (natural childbirth), homeopathy, and acupuncture.

II. *Career Settings*

Graduates of naturopathic programs work as primary care physicians in private practice and in integrative clinics. Others pursue careers as research scientists, faculty members, natural pharmacists, wellness educators, public health administrators, research and development scientists in the natural products industry, consultants to industry and insurance companies, and advisors to other health care professionals. Naturopathic doctors also function on hospital-based teams with other medical professionals to complement treatments by conventional physicians.

III. *Compensation*

From www.aanmc.org: There exists a very wide income range among practicing NDs. (It's important to note that many NDs are not salaried, but rather are self-employed.) On average, industry data shows that an established ND who runs or partners in a large, busy practice makes an average estimated net income of $80,000 to $90,000 per year – and may make upwards of $200,000. A beginning ND just starting up his or her practice, working part-time or building a staff, generally earns less than these averages for the first years of practice. Early residency positions reflect incomes between $20,000 and $30,000 per year.

IV. *Educational Requirements for Practice*

A licensed naturopathic physician (ND) attends a four-year, graduate-level naturopathic medical school and is educated in all of the same basic sciences as an MD, but also studies holistic and nontoxic approaches to therapy with a strong emphasis on disease prevention and optimizing wellness. In addition to a standard medical curriculum, the naturopathic physician is required to complete four years of training in clinical nutrition, acupuncture, homeopathic medicine, botanical medicine, psychology, and counseling (to encourage people to make lifestyle changes in support of their personal health). A naturopathic physician takes rigorous professional board exams so that he or she may be licensed by a state or jurisdiction as a primary care general practice physician.

V. *Licensing*

Currently, 17 states, the District of Columbia, and the United States territories of Puerto Rico and the United States Virgin Islands have licensing or regulation laws for naturopathic doctors. In these states, naturopathic doctors are required to graduate from an accredited four-year residential naturopathic medical school and pass an extensive postdoctoral board examination (NPLEX) in order to receive a license.

VI. *Resources*

American Association of Naturopathic Physicians
818 18th Street, NW, Suite 250
Washington, DC 20006
202-237-8150 or 866-538-2267
www.naturopathic.org

American Association of Naturopathic Medical Colleges (AANMC)
4435 Wisconsin Avenue, NW, Suite 403
Washington, DC 20016
202-237-8150 or 866-538-2267
www.aanmc.org

American Association of Acupuncture and Oriental Medicine (AAOM)
9650 Rockville Pike, Suite 3501
Bethesda, MD 20814
866-455-7999
www.aaaomonline.org

Council of Colleges of Acupuncture and Oriental Medicine
600 Wyndhurst Avenue, Suite 112
Baltimore, MD 21210
410-464-6040
www.ccaom.org

The Naturopathic Medicine Network
www.pandamedicine.com

NURSE (R.N., B.S.N., M.S.N., D.N.S., D.N.P. and Ph.D.)

Summarized from the Bureau of Labor Statistics, U.S. Department of Labor, *Occupational Outlook Handbook, 2012-13 Edition*, Registered Nurses, www.bls.gov/ooh/healthcare/registered-nurses.htm:

I. *Career Description*

Registered nurses (RNs) provide and coordinate patient care, educate patients and the public about various health conditions, and provide advice and emotional support to patients and their family members.

Registered nurses typically do the following:
- Record patients' medical histories and symptoms
- Give patients medicines and treatments
- Set up plans for patients' care or contribute to existing plans
- Observe patients and record the observations
- Consult with doctors and other healthcare professionals
- Operate and monitor medical equipment
- Help perform diagnostic tests and analyze results
- Teach patients and their families how to manage their illnesses or injuries
- Explain what to do at home after treatment

Some RNs choose to become advanced practice registered nurses (APRNs). APRNs work independently or in collaboration with physicians. They may provide primary care, and, in most states, they may prescribe medications.

II. *Career Settings*

As the largest healthcare occupation, registered nurses held about 2.7 million jobs in 2010. 48% worked in private hospitals, while 8% worked in physician offices, 6% in local public hospitals, 5% in home health services, and 5% in nursing care facilities. The remainder worked mainly in government agencies, administrative and support services, and educational services.

Employment of registered nurses is expected to grow 26 percent from 2010 to 2020, faster than the average for all occupations.

III. *Compensation*

The median annual wage of registered nurses was $64,690 in May 2010. The lowest 10 percent earned less than $44,190 and the top 10 percent earned more than $95,130.

IV. *Educational Requirements for Practice*

Registered nurses usually take one of three education paths: a bachelor's of science degree in nursing (BSN), an associate's degree in nursing (ADN), or a diploma from an approved nursing program.

Many registered nurses with an ADN or diploma find an entry-level position and then take advantage of tuition reimbursement benefits to work toward a BSN by completing an RN-to-BSN program. There are also master's degree programs in nursing, combined bachelor's and master's programs, and programs for those who wish to enter the nursing profession but hold a bachelor's degree in another field.

Graduate programs include Master of Science in Nursing (M.S.N.), usually two years beyond a B.S.N., and Doctor of Nursing Practice (D.N.P.), Science (D.N.S.) and Philosophy (Ph.D.) programs that usually require four years beyond a B.S.N.

V. *Resources*

American Association of Colleges of Nursing
One Dupont Circle NW, Suite 530
Washington, DC 20036
202-463-6930
www.aacn.nche.edu

American Association of Nurse Practitioners
PO Box 12846
Austin, TX 78711
512-442-4262
www.aanp.org

National League for Nursing (NLN)
61 Broadway, 33rd Floor
New York, NY 10006
800-669-1656
www.nln.org

OCCUPATIONAL THERAPIST (O.T.)

Summarized from the Bureau of Labor Statistics, U.S. Department of Labor, *Occupational Outlook Handbook, 2012-13 Edition*, Occupational Therapists, www.bls.gov/ooh/healthcare/occupational-therapists.htm:

I. *Career Description*

Occupational therapists treat patients with injuries, illnesses, or disabilities through the therapeutic use of everyday activities. They help these patients develop, recover, and improve the skills needed for daily living and working.

Occupational therapists typically do the following:
- Observe patients doing tasks, ask the patient questions, and review the patient's medical history
- Use the observations, answers, and medical history to evaluate the patient's condition and needs
- Establish a treatment plan for patients, laying out the types of activities and specific goals to be accomplished
- Help people with various disabilities with different tasks, such as helping an older person with poor memory use a computer, or leading an autistic child in play activities
- Demonstrate exercises that can help relieve pain for people with chronic conditions, such as joint stretches for arthritis sufferers
- Evaluate a patient's home or workplace and identify how it can be better suited to the patient's health needs
- Educate a patient's family and employer about how to accommodate and care for the patient
- Recommend special equipment, such as wheelchairs and eating aids, and instruct patients how to use that equipment
- Assess and record patients' activities and progress for evaluating clients, for billing, and for reporting to physicians and other healthcare providers

II. *Career Settings*

Occupational therapists held about 108,800 jobs in 2010. Forty-eight percent of occupational therapists worked in offices of physical, occupational and speech therapists, and audiologist or hospitals. Others worked in schools, nursing homes, and home health services.

Employment of occupational therapists is expected to increase 33 percent from 2010 to 2020, much faster than the average for all occupations.

III. *Compensation*

The median annual wage of occupational therapists was $72,320 in May 2010. The lowest 10 percent earned less than $48,920, and the top 10 percent more than $102,520.

IV. *Educational Requirements for Practice*

Most occupational therapists enter the occupation with a master's degree in occupational therapy. A small number of programs offer doctoral degrees in occupational therapy.

Master's programs generally take 2 years to complete; doctoral programs take longer. Some schools offer a dual degree program in which the student earns a bachelor's degree and a master's degree in 5 years. Part-time programs that offer courses on nights and weekends are also available. Both master's and doctoral programs require several months of supervised fieldwork, in which prospective occupational therapists gain real-world experience.

V. *Licensing*

All states require occupational therapists to be licensed. Licensure requires a degree from an accredited educational program and passing the NBCOT certification exam. Other requirements, such as continuing education and fees, vary by state.

VI. *Resources*

American Occupational Therapy Association, Inc.
4720 Montgomery Lane
PO Box 31220
Bethesda, MD 20824
301-652-2682
www.aota.org

OPTOMETRIST (O.D.)

Summarized from the Bureau of Labor Statistics, U.S. Department of Labor, *Occupational Outlook Handbook, 2012-13 Edition*, Optometrists, www.bls.gov/ooh/healthcare/optometrists.htm:

I. *Career Description*

Optometrists examine the eyes and other parts of the body related to vision. They also diagnose, treat, and manage diseases, injuries, and other disorders of the eyes. They prescribe eyeglasses or contact lenses as needed.

Optometrists typically do the following:
- Perform vision tests to check for sight problems, such as nearsightedness or farsightedness
- Check for eye diseases, such as glaucoma
- Prescribe eyeglasses, contact lenses, and medications
- Provide other treatments, such as vision therapy or low-vision rehabilitation
- Provide pre- and postoperative care to patients undergoing eye surgery—for example, examining a patient's eyes the day after surgery
- Evaluate patients for the presence of diseases such as diabetes and refer them to other health care providers as needed
- Promote eye health by counseling patients, including explaining how to clean and wear contact lenses

II. Career Settings

Optometrists held about 34,200 jobs in 2010. About half of optometrists work in stand-alone offices of optometry. Optometrists may also work in doctors' offices, retail stores, outpatient clinics, and hospitals. In 2010, 22% of optometrists were self-employed.

Employment of optometrists is expected to grow by 33 percent from 2010 to 2020, much faster than the average for all occupations.

III. Compensation

The median annual wage of optometrists was $94,990 in May 2010. The lowest 10 percent earned less than $49,630, and the top 10 percent earned $166,400 or more.

IV. Educational Requirements for Practice

Optometrists must complete a Doctor of Optometry program and get a state license. Doctor of Optometry programs take 4 years to complete after earning an undergraduate degree.

After finishing the O.D., some optometrists do a 1-year residency program to get advanced clinical training in a specialty. Specialty areas for residency programs include family practice, primary eye care, pediatric or geriatric optometry, vision therapy and rehabilitation, cornea and contact lenses, refractive and ocular surgery, low vision rehabilitation, ocular disease, and community health optometry.

V. Licensing

All states require optometrists to be licensed. To get a license, a prospective optometrist must have an O.D. from an accredited optometry school and must complete all sections of the National Boards in Optometry. Some states require an additional exam. Many states require optometrists to take continuing education and renew their license periodically.

VI. Resources

American Optometric Association (AOA)
243 North Lindbergh Boulevard
St. Louis, MO 63141
800-365-2219
www.aoa.org

Association of Schools and Colleges of Optometry (ASCO)
6110 Executive Boulevard, Suite 420
Rockville, MD 20852
301-231-5944
www.opted.org

PHYSICIANS and SURGEONS (M.D. or D.O.)

Summarized from the Bureau of Labor Statistics, U.S. Department of Labor, *Occupational Outlook Handbook, 2012-13 Edition*, Physicians and Surgeons, www.bls.gov/ooh/healthcare/physicians-and-surgeons.htm:

I. *Career Description*

Physicians and surgeons diagnose and treat injuries or illnesses. Physicians examine patients, take medical histories, prescribe medications, and order, perform, and interpret diagnostic tests. They often counsel patients on diet, hygiene, and preventive health care. Surgeons operate on patients to treat injuries, such as broken bones; diseases, such as cancerous tumors; and deformities, such as cleft palates.

There are two types of physicians: M.D. (Medical Doctor) and D.O. (Doctor of Osteopathic Medicine). Both types of physicians use the same methods of treatment, including drugs and surgery, but D.O.s place additional emphasis on the body's musculoskeletal system, preventive medicine, and holistic (whole person) patient care.

Physicians and surgeons typically do the following:
- Take a patient's medical history
- Update charts and patient information to show current findings
- Order tests for nurses or other healthcare staff to do
- Review test results to identify any abnormal findings
- Recommend and design a plan of treatment
- Answer concerns or questions that patients have about their health and well-being
- Help patients take care of their health by discussing topics such as proper nutrition and hygiene

In addition, surgeons operate on patients to treat injuries, diseases, or deformities.

Physicians and surgeons work in one or more of many different specialties.

II. *Career Settings*

Physicians and surgeons held about 691,000 jobs in 2010. Many physicians work in private offices or clinics, often helped by a small staff of nurses and administrative personnel.

Increasingly, physicians work in group practices, health care organizations, or hospitals where they share a large number of patients with other doctors. The group setting gives doctors backup coverage, allows them more time off, and lets them coordinate care for their patients, but it gives them less independence than solo practitioners have.

Employment of physicians and surgeons is expected to grow by 24 percent from 2010 to 2020, faster than the average for all occupations.

III. Compensation

According to the Medical Group Management Association's Physician Compensation and Production Survey, median total compensation for physicians varied by their type of practice. In 2010, physicians practicing primary care received total median annual compensation of $202,392, and physicians practicing in medical specialties received total median annual compensation of $356,885.

Median annual compensations for selected specialties in 2010, as reported by the Medical Group Management Association, were as follows:

- Anesthesiology $407,292
- General surgery $343,958
- Obstetrics/gynecology $281,190
- Internal medicine $205,379
- Psychiatry $200,694
- Pediatrics/adolescent medicine $192,148
- Family practice $189,402

IV. Educational Requirements for Practice

Almost all physicians complete at least 4 years of undergraduate school, 4 years of medical school, and 3 to 8 years in internship and residency programs, depending on their specialty.

V. Licensing

All states require physicians and surgeons to be licensed; requirements vary by state. To qualify for a license, candidates must graduate from an accredited medical school, complete residency training in their specialty, and pass written and practical exams.

All physicians and surgeons must pass a standardized national licensure examination. M.D.s take the U.S. Medical Licensing Examination (USMLE). D.O.s take the Comprehensive Osteopathic Medical Licensing Examination (COMLEX-USA).

VI. Resources

American Association of Colleges of Osteopathic Medicine (AACOM)
5550 Friendship Blvd, Suite 310
Chevy Chase, MD 20815
301-968-4190
www.aacom.org

American Medical Association (AMA)
515 North State Street
Chicago, IL 60610
800-621-8335
www.ama-assn.org

American Osteopathic Association (AOA)
142 East Ontario Street
Chicago, IL 60611

800-621-1773
www.osteopathic.org
Association of American Medical Colleges (AAMC)
2450 N Street NW
Washington, DC 20037
202-828-0400
www.aamc.org

PHARMACIST (Pharm.D.)

Summarized from the Bureau of Labor Statistics, U.S. Department of Labor, *Occupational Outlook Handbook, 2012-13 Edition*, Pharmacists, www.bls.gov/ooh/healthcare/pharmacists.htm:

I. *Career Description*

Pharmacists dispense prescription medications to patients and offer advice on their safe use.

Pharmacists typically do the following:
- Fill prescriptions, verifying instructions from physicians on the proper amounts of medication to give to patients
- Check whether the prescription will interact negatively with other drugs that a patient is taking or condtions the patient has
- Instruct patients on how and when to take a prescribed medicine
- Advise patients on potential side effects they may experience from taking the medicine
- Advise patients about general health topics, such as diet, exercise, and managing stress, and on other issues, such as what equipment or supplies would be best for a health problem
- Complete insurance forms and work with insurance companies to be sure that patients get the medicines they need
- Oversee the work of pharmacy technicians and pharmacists in training (interns)
- Keep records and do other administrative tasks
- Teach other healthcare practitioners about proper medication therapies for patients
- Some pharmacists who own their store or manage a chain pharmacy spend more time on business activities, such as inventory management. Pharmacists also take continuing education throughout their career to keep up with the latest advances in pharmacological science.

Pharmacists who work in universities or for pharmaceutical manufacturers are involved in researching and testing new medications.

With most drugs, pharmacists use standard dosages from pharmaceutical companies. However, some pharmacists create customized medications by mixing ingredients themselves, a process known as compounding.

II. *Career Settings*

Pharmacists held about 274,900 jobs in 2010. Pharmacists work in pharmacies, including those in grocery and drug stores. They also work in hospitals and clinics.

Employment of pharmacists is expected to increase by 25 percent from 2010 to 2020, faster than the average for all occupations.

III. *Compensation*

The median wage of pharmacists was $111,570 in May 2010. The lowest 10 percent earned less than $82,090, and the top 10 percent earned more than $138,620.

IV. *Educational Requirements for Practice*

Applicants need at least 2 to 3 years of undergraduate study; for some programs, applicants must have a bachelor's degree. For most programs, applicants also must take the Pharmacy College Admissions Test (PCAT).

Pharm.D. programs usually take 4 years to finish, although some programs offer a 3-year option.

V. *Licensing*

All states license pharmacists. After they finish the Pharm. D., prospective pharmacists must pass two exams to get a license. One of the exams is in pharmacy skills and knowledge. The other is in pharmacy law in the state giving the pharmacy license.

VI. *Resources*

American Association of Colleges of Pharmacy (AACP)
1727 King Street
Alexandria, VA 22314
703-739-2330
www.aacp.org

American Society of Health-System Pharmacists (ASHP)
7272 Wisconsin Avenue
Bethesda, MD 20814
301-657-3000
www.ashp.org

American Pharmacists Association (APhA)
1100 15th St. NW, Suite 400
Washington, DC 20005
202-628-4410
www.pharmacist.com

PHYSICIAN ASSISTANT (P.A.)

Summarized from the Bureau of Labor Statistics, U.S. Department of Labor, *Occupational Outlook Handbook, 2012-13 Edition*, Physician Assistants, www.bls.gov/ooh/healthcare/physician-assistants.htm:

I. *Career Description*

Physician assistants, also known as PAs, practice medicine under the direction and supervision of physicians and surgeons. They are formally trained to examine patients, diagnose injuries and illnesses, and provide treatment.

Physician assistants typically do the following:
- Work under the supervision of a physician or surgeon
- Review patients' medical histories
- Do physical exams to check patients' health
- Order and interpret diagnostic tests, such as x rays or blood tests
- Make preliminary diagnoses concerning a patient's injury or illness
- Provide treatment, such as setting broken bones and giving immunizations
- Counsel patients and their families; for example, answering questions about how to care for a child with asthma
- Prescribe medicine, when needed
- Record a patient's progress
- Complete insurance paperwork

II. *Career Settings*

Physician assistants held about 83,600 jobs in 2010, and most worked in physicians' offices or hospitals.

Employment of physician assistants is expected to increase 30 percent from 2010 to 2020, much faster than the average for all occupations.

III. *Compensation*

The median annual wage of physician assistants was $86,410 in May 2010. The lowest 10 percent earned less than $57,450, and the top 10 percent earned more than $117,720.

IV. *Educational Requirements for Practice*

Physician assistants typically need a master's degree. Most applicants to master's programs already have a bachelor's degree and some work experience. Then, they must complete an accredited educational program for physician assistants. That usually takes at least 2 years of full-time study and typically leads to a master's degree.

V. *Licensing*

All states and the District of Columbia require physician assistants to be licensed. To become licensed, they must pass the Physician Assistant National Certifying Examination from the National Commission on Certification of Physician Assistants (NCCPA). After they pass the exam, they may use the credential "Physician Assistant-Certified."

VI. *Resources*

Physician Assistant Education Association
300 North Washington Street, Suite 505
Alexandria, VA 22314
703-548-5538
www.paeaonline.org

American Academy of Physician Assistants
950 North Washington Street
Alexandria, VA 22314
703-836-2272
www.aapa.org

 *Appendix A*

PHYSICAL THERAPIST (M.P.T., D.P.T.)

Summarized from the Bureau of Labor Statistics, U.S. Department of Labor, *Occupational Outlook Handbook, 2012-13 Edition*, Physical Therapists, www.bls.gov/ooh/healthcare/physical-therapists.htm:

I. *Career Description*

Physical therapists, sometimes referred to as PTs, help people who have injuries or illnesses improve their movement and manage their pain. They are often an important part of rehabilitation and treatment of patients with chronic conditions or injuries.

Physical therapists typically do the following:
- Diagnose patients' dysfunctional movements by watching them stand or walk and by listening to their concerns, among other methods
- Set up a plan for their patients, outlining the patient's goals and the planned treatments
- Use exercises, stretching maneuvers, hands-on therapy, and equipment to ease patients' pain and to help them increase their ability to move
- Evaluate a patient's progress, modifying a treatment plan and trying new treatments as needed
- Educate patients and their families about what to expect during recovery from injury and illness and how best to cope with what happens

II. *Career Settings*

Physical therapists held about 198,600 jobs in 2010. Physical therapists typically work in private offices and clinics, hospitals, and nursing homes.

Employment of physical therapists is expected to increase 39 percent from 2010 to 2020, much faster than the average for all occupations.

III. *Compensation*

The median annual wage of physical therapists was $76,310 in May 2010. The lowest 10 percent earned less than $53,620, and the top 10 percent earned more than $107,920.

IV. *Educational Requirements for Practice*

Physical therapists are required to have a postgraduate professional degree. Physical therapy programs usually award a Doctor of Physical Therapy (DPT) degree, although a small number award a Master of Physical Therapy (MPT) degree. Doctoral programs typically last 3 years; MPT programs require 2 to 3 years of study.

V. *Licensing*

All states require physical therapists to be licensed. Licensing requirements vary by state but typically include passing the National Physical Therapy Examination or a similar state-administered exam. A number of states require continuing education for physical therapists to keep their license.

VI. *Resources*

American Physical Therapy Association (APTA)
1111North Fairfax Street

Alexandria, VA 22314
703-684-2782 or 800-999-2782
www.apta.org

PODIATRIC PHYSICIAN (D.P.M.)

Summarized from the Bureau of Labor Statistics, U.S. Department of Labor, *Occupational Outlook Handbook, 2012-13 Edition*, Podiatrists, www.bls.gov/ooh/healthcare/podiatrists.htm:

I. *Career Description*

Podiatrists provide medical and surgical care for people suffering from foot, ankle, and lower leg problems. They diagnose illnesses, treat injuries, and perform surgery. For example, podiatrists treat calluses, ingrown toenails, heel spurs, and arch problems. They also treat foot and leg problems associated with diabetes and other diseases; they may set fractures.

Podiatrists typically do the following:
- Listen to a patient's concerns about their feet, ankles, or lower legs
- Diagnose foot, ankle, and lower-leg problems, through physical exams, x rays, medical laboratory tests, and other methods
- Provide treatment for foot, ankle, and lower-leg ailments, such as prescribing special shoe inserts (orthotics) to improve a patient's mobility
- Perform foot and ankle surgeries, such as removing bone spurs
- Offer advice and instruction on foot and ankle care
- Prescribe medications
- Refer patients to physicians or specialists if they detect larger health problems, such as diabetes
- Read journals and attend conferences to keep up with advances in podiatric medicine
- Podiatrists who own their practice may also spend time on business related activities, such as hiring employees and managing inventory.

II. *Career Settings*

Podiatrists held about 12,900 jobs in 2010. Most podiatrists work in offices of podiatry, either on their own or with other podiatrists. Some work in hospitals. Others work in group practices with other physicians or specialists. Many podiatrists are self-employed; they own or are partners in their medical practice. Podiatrists also work in health maintenance organizations (HMO's), the U.S. Department of Veterans Affairs, the military, and academic health science centers and universities.

Employment of podiatrists is expected to increase 20 percent from 2010 to 2020, faster than the average for all occupations.

III. *Compensation*

The median annual wage of podiatrists was $118,030 in May 2010. The lowest 10 percent earned less than $50,150, and the top 10 percent earned more than $166,400.

IV. *Educational Requirements for Practice*

Becoming a podiatrist requires completing an undergraduate college education, a 4-year postgraduate degree, and a 3-year medical and surgical residency.

V. Licensing

Podiatrists must be licensed in every state. Licensure usually requires passing a state exam (written or oral) and paying a fee. In most states, podiatrists also must have completed a residency program to be licensed. Licenses must typically be renewed periodically, and podiatrists must take continuing medical education.

VI. Resources

American Association of Colleges of Podiatric Medicine (AACPM)
15850 Crabbs Branch Way, Suite 320
Rockville, MD 20855
800-922-9266
www.aacpm.org

American Podiatric Medical Association (APMA)
9312 Old Georgetown Road
Bethesda, MD 20814
301-581-9200
www.apma.org

PUBLIC HEALTH (M.P.H., Ph.D.)

Summarized from the Association of Schools of Public Health, www.asph.org:

I. Career Description

Public Health is the science and art of improving the health of communities through education and promotion of healthy lifestyles, and research for disease and injury prevention. Rather than focusing on individuals, public health care workers endeavor to protect and improve the health of whole groups of people. They assess and monitor the health of populations, educate decision makers and the public, and develop and implement policies and programs. Public health is a multi-disciplinary field involving many different kinds of professionals, including physicians and nurses, as well as graduates of formal public health programs. There is also a wide variety of specialty areas within the field, including biostatistics, epidemiology, environmental health, health education, health services administration, international public health, nutrition and occupational health and safety.

II. Career Settings

Depending on their specialty, public health workers may be employed by government agencies and health departments, insurance companies, community wellness centers, public school systems, colleges and universities, hospitals, private businesses or other facilities.

III. Compensation

ASPH notes that because public health professionals work in such a wide variety of settings and often work in multi-disciplinary capacities, the salaries vary significantly from job to job. There are currently no national data available through ASPH on the average starting salary that is representative of what a graduate can expect. ASPH refers potential MPH students to www.publichealthjobs.net for information on particular positions.

IV. *Educational Requirements for Practice*

A master's degree in public health (M.P.H.) or related area is a typical credential in this field, although educational requirements vary depending on the profession and specialty area.

V. *Licensing*

Licensure and certification requirements vary, depending on the specialty area.

VI. *Resources*

Association of Schools of Public Health
1900 M Street NW, Suite 710
Washington, DC 20036
202-296-1099
www.asph.org

American Public Health Association
800 I Street NW
Washington, DC 20001
202-777-2742
www.apha.org

RECREATIONAL THERAPIST

Summarized from the Bureau of Labor Statistics, U.S. Department of Labor, *Occupational Outlook Handbook, 2012-13 Edition*, Recreational Therapists, www.bls.gov/ooh/healthcare/recreational-therapists.htm:

I. *Career Description*

Recreational therapists plan, direct, and coordinate recreation programs for people with disabilities or illnesses. They use a variety of techniques, including arts and crafts, drama, music, dance, sports, games, and field trips. These activities help maintain or improve a client's physical and emotional well-being.

II. *Career Settings*

Recreational therapists held about 22,400 jobs in 2010. Recreational therapists work in a variety of settings and may arrange to have activities both indoors and outdoors. Therapists often work in hospitals or nursing and residential care facilities.

Employment of recreational therapists is expected to grow by 17 percent from 2010 to 2020, about as fast as the average for all occupations.

III. *Compensation*

The median annual wage of recreational therapists was $39,410 in May 2010. The lowest 10 percent earned less than $24,640, and the top 10 percent earned more than $62,670.

IV. Educational Requirements for Practice

Most recreational therapists need a bachelor's degree in therapeutic recreation or a related field. Though less common, associate's, master's, or doctoral degrees are also available.

V. Licensing

Most employers prefer to hire certified recreational therapists. Hospitals and other clinical settings often require certification by the NCTRC. The council offers the Certified Therapeutic Recreation Specialist (CTRS) credential to candidates who pass a written certification exam and complete a supervised internship of at least 480 hours.

NCTRC also offers specialty certification in five areas of practice: geriatrics, behavioral health, physical medicine/ rehabilitation, developmental disabilities, or community inclusion services. Although therapists typically need at least a bachelor's degree in recreational therapy, in some cases therapists may qualify for certification with an alternate combination of education, training, and experience.

Some states require recreational therapists to be licensed; requirements vary by state. As of 2010, only Oklahoma, North Carolina, Utah, and New Hampshire required recreational therapists to hold a license. For specific requirements, contact the state's medical board.

VI. Resources

American Therapeutic Recreation Association
629 North Main St
Hattiesburg, MS 39401
601-450-2872
www.atra-online.com

National Therapeutic Recreation Society (now a branch of the National Recreation and Park Association)
22377 Belmont Ridge Road
Ashburn, VA 20148
703-858-0784 or 800-626-6772
www.nrpa.org

RESPIRATORY THERAPIST

Summarized from the Bureau of Labor Statistics, U.S. Department of Labor, *Occupational Outlook Handbook, 2012-13 Edition*, Respiratory Therapists, www.bls.gov/ooh/healthcare/respiratory-therapists.htm:

I. Career Description

Respiratory therapists care for patients who have trouble breathing; for example, from a chronic respiratory disease, such as asthma or emphysema. Their patients range from premature infants with undeveloped lungs to elderly patients who have diseased lungs. They also provide emergency care to patients suffering from heart attacks, drowning, or shock.

Respiratory therapists typically do the following:
- Interview and examine patients with breathing or cardiopulmonary disorders
- Consult with physicians to develop patient treatment plans

- Perform diagnostic tests such as measuring lung capacity
- Treat patients, using a variety of methods, including chest physiotherapy and aerosol medications
- Monitor and record the progress of treatment
- Supervise respiratory therapy technicians during tests and evaluate the findings of the tests
- Teach patients how to use treatments

II. Career Settings

Respiratory therapists held about 112,700 jobs in 2010. Most respiratory therapists work in hospitals. Others may work in nursing care facilities or travel to patients' homes.

Employment of respiratory therapists is expected to grow by 28 percent from 2010 to 2020, faster than the average for all occupations.

III. Compensation

The median annual wage of respiratory therapists was $54,280 in May 2010. The lowest 10 percent earned less than $39,990, and the top 10 percent earned more than $73,410.

IV. Educational Requirements for Practice

Respiratory therapists need an associate's or bachelor's degree.

V. Licensing

Respiratory therapists are licensed in all states except Alaska, although requirements vary by state. Licensure requirements in most states include completing a state or professional certification exam.

Many employers prefer to hire respiratory therapists who have certification. Certification is not always required, but it is widely respected throughout the occupation. Certification usually requires graduating from an accredited program and passing a certification exam and is often required in order to get a state license.

The National Board for Respiratory Care (NBRC) is the main certifying body for respiratory therapists. The Board offers two levels of certification: the Certified Respiratory Therapist (CRT) and the Registered Respiratory Therapist (RRT).

VI. Resources

American Association for Respiratory Care
9425 N. MacArthur Blvd, Suite 100
Irving, TX 75063
972-243-2272
www.aarc.org

Commission on Accreditation for Respiratory Care
1248 Harwood Road
Bedford, TX 76021
817-283-2835www.coarc.com

SPEECH-LANGUAGE PATHOLOGIST

Summarized from the Bureau of Labor Statistics, U.S. Department of Labor, *Occupational Outlook Handbook, 2012-13 Edition*, www.bls.gov/ooh/healthcare/speech-language-pathologists.htm:

I.   *Career Description*

Speech-language pathologists, sometimes called speech therapists, assess, diagnose, treat, and help to prevent communication and swallowing disorders in patients. Speech, language, and swallowing disorders result from a variety of causes such as a stroke, brain injury, hearing loss, developmental delay, a cleft palate, cerebral palsy, or emotional problems.

When diagnosing patients, speech-language pathologists typically do the following:
   • Communicate with patients to evaluate their levels of speech or language difficulty
   • Determine the extent of communication problems by having a patient complete basic reading and vocalizing tasks or by giving standardized tests
   • Identify treatment options
   • Create and carry out an individualized treatment plan

When treating patients, speech-language pathologists typically do the following:
   • Teach patients how to make sounds and improve their voices
   • Teach alternative communication methods, such as sign language, to patients with little or no speech capability
   • Work with patients to increase their ability to read and write correctly
   • Work with patients to develop and strengthen the muscles used to swallow
   • Counsel patients and families on how to cope with communication disorders

II. *Career Settings*

Speech-language pathologists held about 123,200 jobs in 2010. Almost half of all speech-language pathologists work in schools. Most others work in healthcare facilities. Some work in patients' homes.

Employment of speech-language pathologists is expected to grow by 23 percent from 2010 to 2020, faster than the average for all occupations.

III. *Compensation*

The median annual wage of speech-language pathologists was $66,920 in May 2010. The lowest 10 percent earned less than $42,970, and the top 10 percent more than $103,630.

IV. *Educational Requirements for Practice*

Speech-language pathologists typically need at least a master's degree.

V.   *Licensing*

Speech-language pathologists must be licensed in almost all states. A license requires at least a master's degree and supervised clinical experience. Some states require graduation from an accredited program to get a license.

Speech-language pathologists can earn the Certificate of Clinical Competence in Speech-Language Pathology (CCC-SLP) offered by the American Speech-Language-Hearing Association. Certification satisfies some or all of the requirements for licensure and may be required by some employers.

VI. *Resources*

American Speech-Language-Hearing Association
2200 Research Boulevard
Rockville, MD 20850
301-296-5700
www.asha.org

VETERINARIAN (D.V.M.)

Summarized from Bureau of Labor Statistics, U.S. Department of Labor, *Occupational Outlook Handbook, 2012-13 Edition*, Veterinarians, www.bls.gov/ooh/healthcare/veterinarians.htm:

I. *Career Description*

Veterinarians care for the health of animals. They diagnose, treat, or research medical conditions and diseases of pets, livestock, and animals in zoos, racetracks, and laboratories.

Veterinarians typically do the following:
- Examine animals to diagnose their health problems
- Treat and dress wounds
- Perform surgery on animals
- Test for and vaccinate against diseases
- Operate medical equipment such as x-ray machines
- Advise animal owners about general care, medical conditions, and treatments
- Prescribe medication
- Euthanize animals

II. *Career Settings*

Veterinarians held about 61,400 jobs in 2010, of which 81 percent were in the veterinary services industry. Others held positions at colleges or universities; in private industry, such as medical or research laboratories; or in federal, state, or local government.

Employment of veterinarians is expected to grow 36 percent from 2010 to 2020, much faster than the average for all occupations.

III. *Compensation*

The median annual wage of veterinarians was $82,040 in May 2010. The lowest 10 percent earned less than $49,910, and the top 10 percent earned more than $145,230.

IV. *Educational Requirements for Practice*

Although not required, most applicants to veterinary school have a bachelor's degree. Veterinarians must complete a Doctor of Veterinary Medicine (D.V.M. or V.M.D.) degree at an accredited college of veterinary medicine. A veterinary medicine program generally takes 4 years to complete and includes classroom, laboratory, and clinical components.

V. *Licensing*

All states and the District of Columbia require veterinarians to have a license. Licensing requirements vary by state, but all states require prospective veterinarians to complete an accredited veterinary program and to pass the North American Veterinary Licensing Exam.

Most states require not only the national exam but also have a state exam that covers state laws and regulations. Few states accept licenses from other states, so veterinarians who want to be licensed in a new state must usually take that state's exam.

VI. *Resources*

American Veterinary Medical Association (AVMA)
1931 North Meacham Road, Suite 100
Schaumburg, IL 60173
800-248-2862
www.avma.org

Association of American Veterinary Medical Colleges (AAVMC)
1101 Vermont Avenue NW, Suite 301
Washington, DC 20005
202-371-9195
www.aavmc.org

FOR OTHER HEALTH CAREERS, including those not requiring an undergraduate degree (often aids, assistants, technologists or technicians), see www.bls.gov/ooh/healthcare.

Appendix B
HEALTH PROFESSIONS RESOURCES

Acupuncture and Oriental Medicine Master of … / Doctorate of … (various), DAOM		
Professional Organization	AAAOM	www.aaaomonline.org
Association of Schools/Colleges	CCAOM	www.ccaom.org
Admission Requirements	see individual programs	www.acaom.org/accdtd_cndtdschls.htm
Entrance Exam	none	
Application Service	none	
Student Organization	none	

Audiology Au.D.		
Professional Organization	AAA	www.audiology.org
Association of Schools/Colleges	none	programs listed: www.asha.org/students
Admission Requirements	see individual programs	individual schools' websites
Entrance Exam	GRE (most commonly)	www.ets.org/gre
Application Services	CSDCAS serves 25% of programs	www.csdcas.org/index.html
Student Organizations	Student Academy of Audiology	www.audiology.org/saa/pages/default/aspx

Chiropractic D.C.		
Professional Organization	ACA	www.acatoday.org
Association of Schools/Colleges	ACC	www.chirocolleges.org
Admission Requirements	ACC website	www.chirocolleges.org
Entrance Exam	none	
Application Service	ChiroCas	https://portal.chirocas.org
Student Organization	SACA	www.acatoday.org/sudents/index.cfm

Dentistry D.M.D., D.D.S		
Professional Organization	ADA	www.ada.org
Association of Schools/Colleges	ADEA	www.adea.org
Admission Requirements	ADEA Official Guide	hardcopy only
Entrance Exam	DAT	www.ada.org/dat.aspx
Application Service	AADSAS	https://portal.aadsasweb.org
	TMDSAS	www.utsystem.edu/tmdsas
Student Organization	ASDA	www.asdanet.org

Health Administration Master of/Doctorate of... (varies)		
Professional Organization	AUPHA	www.aupha.org
Association of Schools/Colleges	none	programs listed: www.aupha.org
Admission Requirements	see individual programs	individual schools' websites
Entrance Exam	GRE	www.ets.org/gre
	GMAT	www.mba.com/mba/thegmat
	LSAT	www.lsac.org/JD/LSAT/test-dates-dead-lines.asp
	MCAT	www.aamc.org/students/applying/mcat
Application Service	none	
Student Organization	Upsilon Phi Delta Honor Society	www.aupha.org

Medicine M.D. -granting		
Professional Organizations	AMA	www.ama-assn.org
	NMA	www.nmanet.org
Association of Schools/Colleges	AAMC	www.aamc.org
Admission Requirements	MSAR	www.aamc.org/students/applying/requirements/msar
Entrance Exam	MCAT	www.aamc.org/students/applying/mcat
Application Services	AMCAS	www.aamc.org/students/applying/amcas
	TMDSAS	www.utsystem.edu/tmdsas
Student Organizations	AMSA	www.amsa.org
	SNMA	www.snma.org/

Medicine D.O.-granting (osteopathic medicine)		
Professional Organization	AOA	www.osteopathic.org
Association of Schools/Colleges	AACOM	www.aacom.org
Admission Requirements	Osteopathic Medical College Information Book	www.aacom.org (downloadable pdf)
Entrance Exam	MCAT	www.aamc.org/students/applying/mcat
Application Service	AACOMAS	https://aacomas.aacom.org
Student Organization	SOMA*	www.studentdo.com

Naturopathic Medicine N.D.		
Professional Organization	AANP	www.naturopathic.org
Association of Schools/Colleges	AANMC	www.aanmc.org
Admission Requirements	AANMC website	www.aanmc.org
Entrance Exam	none	
Application Service	NDCAS	www.ndcas.org
Student Organization	NMSA	www.naturopathicstudent.org

Nursing L.P.N., R.N., B.S.N., M.S.N., D.N.P., Ph.D.		
Professional Organizations	ANA	www.nursingworld.org
	NLN	www.nln.org
Association of Schools/Colleges	AACN	www.aacn.org
Admission Requirements	see individual programs	individual schools' websites
Entrance Exams	NLN	www.nln.org/testingservices/index.htm
	TEAS - NET	www.atitesting.com/Home.aspx
	SAT	www.collegeboard.com
	ACT	www.act.org
Application Service	Nursing CAS	www.nursingcas.org
Student Organization	NSNA	www.nsna.org

Occupational Therapy O.T.		
Professional Organization	AOTA	www.aota.org
Association of Schools/Colleges	AOTA	www.aota.org
Admission Requirements	AOTA website	www.aota.org
Entrance Exam	GRE	www.ets.org/gre
Application Service	OTCAS	www.aota.org/educate/edres/otcas.aspx
Student Organization	AOTA	www.aota.org/students.aspx

Optometry O.D.		
Professional Organization	AOA	www.aoa.org
Association of Schools/Colleges	ASCO	www.opted.org
Admission Requirements	ASCO website	www.opted.org
Entrance Exam	OAT	www.ada.org/oat/index.html
Application Service	OptomCAS	www.optomcas.org
Student Organization	AOSA	www.aosa.org

Pharmacy PharmD		
Professional Organization	APhA	www.pharmacist.com
Association of Schools/Colleges	AACP	www.aacp.org
Admission Requirements	PSAR	www.aacp.org/resources/student/pharmacyforyou/admissions/admissionrequirements/Pages/default.aspx
Entrance Exams	PCAT	www.pcatweb.info
	SAT	www.collegeboard.com
	ACT	www.act.org
Application Service	PharmCAS	www.pharmcas.org
Student Organization	ASP	www.pharmacist.com

Physical Therapy P.T.		
Professional Organization	APTA	www.apta.org
Association of Schools/Colleges	APTA	www.apta.org
Admission Requirements	PTCAS website	www.ptcas.org/ProgramPrereqs
Entrance Exam	GRE	www.ets.org/gre
Application Service	PTCAS	www.ptcas.org
Student Organization	APTA	www.apta.org/students

Physican Assistant P.A.		
Professional Organization	AAPA	www.aapa.org
Association of Schools/Colleges	PAEA	www.paeaonline.org
Admission Requirements	PAEA website	www.paeaonline.org
Entrance Exam	GRE	www.ets.org/gre
	MCAT	www.aamc.org/students/applying/mcat
Application Service	CASPA	https://portal.caspaonline.org
Student Organization	AAPA-SA	www.aapa.org/students

Podiatric Medicine D.P.M.		
Professional Organization	APMA	www.apma.org
Association of Schools/Colleges	AACPM	www.aacpm.org
Admission Requirements	AACPM College Information Booklet	www.aacpm.org/html/careerzone/pdfs/ AACPM CIB-2013 Entering Class.pdf
Entrance Exam	MCAT	www.aamc.org/students/applying/mcat
Application Service	AACPMAS	www.e-aacpmas.org
Student Organization	APMSA	www.apmsa.org

Public Health M.P.H.		
Professional Organization	APHA	www.apha.org
Association of Schools/Colleges	ASPH	www.asph.org
Admission Requirements	see individual programs	access online through www.asph.org
		www.asph.org
Entrance Exam	GRE	www.ets.org/gre
	MCAT	www.aamc.org/students/applying/mcat
	GMAT	www.mba.com/mba/thegmat
	DAT	www.ada.org/dat.aspx
Application Service	SOPHAS	www.sophas.org
Student Organization	APHA-SA	www.aphastudents.org

Veterinary Medicine D.V.M.		
Professional Organization	AVMA	www.avma.org
Association of Schools/Colleges	AAVMC	www.aavmc.org
Admission Requirements	VMSAR	www.aavmc.org/publications/VMSAR.aspx (paperback/kindle/nook)
Entrance Exam	GRE	www.ets.org/gre
	MCAT	www.aamc.org/students/applying/mcat
Application Service	VMCAS	www.aavmc.org/vmcas/vmcas.htm
Student Organization	SAVMA	www.avma.org/about/savma/

Application Services Chart

	AACOMAS	**AACPMAS**	**ADEA AADSAS**
Application Service Name	American Association of Colleges of Osteopathic Medicine	American Association of Colleges of Podiatric Medicine Application Service	ADEA Associated American Dental Schools Application Service
Association	American Association of Colleges of Osteopathic Medicine www.aacom.org	American Association of Colleges of Podiatric Medicine www.aacpm.org	American Dental Education Association www.adea.org
Number of Schools	28 colleges, 4 branch campuses and 1 additional teaching location participate in AACOMAS.	All 9 schools and colleges participate in AACPMAS	65 Schools participate in AADSAS (63 US, 1 Puerto Rico, 1 Nova Scotia)
Contact Information	(301) 968–4190 aacomas@aacom.org	(617) 612–2900 aacpmasinfo@aacpmas.org www.e-aacpmas.org/ info@aacpm.org	Applicant Contact: (617) 612–2045 aadsasinfo@aadsasweb.org
Opening Date*	May 1	August 1	June 3
Submission Date**	June 3	August 1	June
Deadlines	Range from October – April 2013	April 1st is the priority deadline. Pending available seats, final deadline is June 30th	Different according to each school
Letters of Recommendation	Letters of recommendation sent directly to colleges following the processes outlined by each college.	Letters of recommendation sent directly to designated colleges or through VE or Interfolio – see chart in the FAQ section on www.aacpmas.org for details.	Up to four individual letters of evaluation or one Committee Report plus one individual letter of evaluation. Most dental schools strongly prefer that letters be submitted to AADSAS as either an online electronic document or as a paper letter that is mailed to AADSAS.
Standardized Test Scores	Scores should be sent directly to AACOMAS. Applicants must use MCAT's THx system to release their MCAT scores to their AACOMAS application. Students must provide their 8-digit MCAT number, beginning with 1, on the MCAT section of the AACOMAS application.	MCAT and US DAT scores (no older than 3 years) must be sent directly to AACPMAS.	Official DAT scores are downloaded by dental schools through a DAT website. When registering for the DAT, applicants should indicate all the schools where they want their official DAT scores sent. There is no longer a restriction on the number of schools an applicant can select in the DAT registration process.
Transcripts	No data provided.	Send official transcripts directly to AACPMAS.	Send official transcripts directly to ADEA AADSAS.

*   Opening refers to the opening date of the application for this cycle
**   Submission refers to the first date that applicants may submit the application for this cycle.

	AMCAS	CASPA	ChiroCAS
Application Service Name	American Medical College Application Service	Central Application Service for Physician Assistants	Chiropractic Centralized Application Service
Association	Association of American Medical Colleges www.aamc.org	Physician Assistant Education Association www.paeaonline.org	Association of Chiropractic Colleges www.chirocolleges.org
Number of Schools	143 schools and programs will participate in AMCAS. The only exceptions are the Regular M.D programs at Texas Public Schools and the UMKC BA/MD program.	161 programs participate in CASPA	All 17 US programs participate in ChiroCAS, although most also accept direct applications as well.
Contact Information	(202) 828–0600 amcas@aamc.org www.aamc.org/amcas	(617) 612–2080 caspainfo@caspaonline.org	(617) 612–2870 chirocasinfo@chirocas.org
Opening Date*	May 8	Mid-April (to be announced)	No data provided.
Submission Date**	June 1	Mid-March (to be announced)	No data provided.
Deadlines	Early Decision Program deadline including transcript is August 1. All other program deadlines range Oct. 1 - Dec. 31st.	Individual deadlines per school, 8 options: June 15; August 1; September 1; October 1; November 1; December 1; January 15; March 1	Rolling: Individual deadlines vary by program, some of which have multiple start dates. In most cases, students should plan to apply at least 6 months before desired start date.
Letters of Recommendation	Most medical schools receive letters through AMCAS (5 schools/programs do not participate). Evaluators submit letters electronically directly to AMCAS, or through VirtualEvals, Interfolio, U.S. Mail, or the AMCAS Letter Writer Application.	Three LORs are processed by CASPA and disseminated to programs. CASPA will verify all applications with a complete status, which is defined as 'payment, all transcripts, and at least two of the three required LORs are received by CASPA.' Please note, that some programs may not review applications until all three LORs have been received. CASPA LORs are completely electronic in the 2013-2014 application cycle.	A maximum of three references can be uploaded to Chiro CAS. References may submit an online (preferred) or paper reference to ChiroCAS. LORs may also be sent directly to designated programs. Check with each college to determine number and kind of letters required or recommended.
Standardized Test Scores	MCAT Scores are automatically sent to AMCAS for distribution to applied participating schools once the applicant scores are available.	Official GRE scores can now be uploaded directly into the CASPA application. Programs must have a CASPA-specific GRE code in order for scores to be sent electronically to CASPA. If your program(s) does not have a CASPA code, then you must continue tofollow their procedures and send official GRE scores directly to the program and not to CASPA. All official TOEFL scores should continue to be sent directly to the program, and not to CASPA.	ALL official test scores must be sent directly to designated programs. Test requirements vary by institution. Not all programs require GRE scores. Check with designated schools for which tests are required. Information about CCAT, TOEFL, or TSE tests taken or planned can be entered into ChiroCAS.
Transcripts	Send official transcripts directly to AMCAS.	Send official transcripts directly to CASPA.	Send official transcripts directly to ChiroCAS.

*   Opening refers to the opening date of the application for this cycle
**   Submission refers to the first date that applicants may submit the application for this cycle.

	HAMPCAS	**NDCAS**	**NursingCAS**
Application Service Name	Health Administration, Management & Policy Centralized Application Service	Naturopathic Doctor Centralized Application Service	Nursing's Centralized Application Service
Association	Association of University Programs in Health Administration www.aupha.org	Association of Accredited Naturopathic Medical Schools www.aanmc.org	American Association of Colleges of Nursing www.aacn.nche.edu
Number of Schools	37 schools participate in HAMPCAS (constantly adding more)	4 of the naturopathic colleges participate in NDCAS	115 schools of nursing participate in NursingCAS
Contact Information	(703) 894–0940, x-130 hampcasinfo@hampcas.org	Applicant Contact: (617) 612–2950 ndcasinfo@ndcas.org	Applicant Contact: (617) 612–2880 nursingcasinfo@nursingcas.org
Opening Date*	September	September 3	August 10
Submission Date**	August	September 3	July 1
Deadlines	Closes August, but schools have individual deadlines for the applicant to follow	Individual deadlines per school will be published on www.ndcas.org.	Deadlines vary by school
Letters of Recommendation	Submitted to HAMPCAS reference portal (typically 3 letters of evaluation).	Three e-letters of recommendation are submitted to NDCAS and processed for dissemination to the designated programs. Committee and composite letters are accepted.	References should come directly from the evaluator to NursingCAS electronically.
Standardized Test Scores	GREs are self reported into application, then sent directly to schools.	Not required (TOEFL is required in some cases, those results are sent directly to the schools)	Test requirements vary by program. Official test scores should be sent directly from the testing agency to the school if required.
Transcripts	Send official transcripts directly to HAMPCAS.	Send official transcripts directly to NDCAS.	Send official transcripts directly to NursingCAS.

*   Opening refers to the opening date of the application for this cycle
**   Submission refers to the first date that applicants may submit the application for this cycle.

	OptomCAS	OTCAS	PharmCAS
Application Service Name	Optometry Centralized Application Service	Occupational Therapy Centralized Application Service	Pharmacy College Application Service
Association	Association of Schools and Colleges of Optometry www.opted.org	American Occupational Therapy Association www.aota.org	American Association of Colleges of Pharmacy www.aacp.org/pharmacycareers
Number of Schools	21 schools and colleges participate in OptomCAS	67 OT programs with 6 additional locations	111 pharmacy programs participate in PharmCAS
Contact Information	(617) 612–2888 optomcasinfo@optomcas.org	(617) 612–2860 otcasinfo@otcas.org	(617) 612–2050 (617) 612–2060 TTY info@pharmcas.org
Opening Date*	July 1	July 17	June
Submission Date**	July 1	July 17	June
Deadlines	Deadlines vary by school and range from December -June.	Deadlines vary by program.	Ranges by program from November- March.
Letters of Recommendation	Recommendation letters must be sent directly to OptomCAS by the evaluator electronically.	References should come directly from the evaluator to OTCAS electronically.	Send up to four references to PharmCAS which will disseminate to colleges. Letters must be sent directly to PharmCAS by the evaluator, either electronically or hard copy, or to the program, if required. www.pharmcas.org/applicants/eval.htm
Standardized Test Scores	Official OAT scores must be sent to optometry schools and colleges when the exam is taken. Applicants are asked to self-report OAT scores on the OptomCAS application.	If required by program, GRE and TOEFL test scores must be entered on the OTCAS application. Any other scores should be sent directly to the program.	Send PCAT, TOEFL, & TSE scores to PharmCAS, if required. (PCAT not required by all pharmacy schools) www.pharmcas.org/applicants/tests.htm
Transcripts	Send official transcripts directly to OptomCAS by the schools or college's deadline.	Send official transcripts directly to OTCAS.	Send official U.S. transcripts to PharmCAS. Policies for Int'l transcripts vary. www.pharmcas.org/applicants/transcripts.htm

*   Opening refers to the opening date of the application for this cycle
**   Submission refers to the first date that applicants may submit the application for this cycle.

	PTCAS	**SOPHAS**	**TMDSAS**
Application Service Name	Physical Therapist Centralized Application Service	Schools of Public Health Application Service	Texas Medical and Dental Schools Application Service
Association	American Physical Therapy Association www.apta.org	Association of Schools of Public Health www.asph.org	Texas Medical and Dental Schools www.utsystem.edu/tmdsas.
Number of Schools	164 programs participate in PTCAS	42 schools participate in SOPHAS	8 medical, 3 dental and 1 veterinary schools participate in TMDSAS
Contact Information	Applicant Contact: (617) 612-2040 ptcasinfo@ptcas.org	(202) 296-1099 (ASPH) info@asph.org (617) 612-2090 (SOPHAS) sophasinfo@sophas.org	(512) 499-4785 tmdsas@utsystem.edu
Opening Date*	July 2	September	May 1
Submission Date**	July 2	August	May 2
Deadlines	Early Decision Program deadline is August 15. Regular program deadlines range from October 2013-May 2014.	Varies according to program.	July 1st for students applying through the JAMP program. Otherwise, August 1st –September 30th, depending on school.
Letters of Recommendation	Send up to 4 references directly to PTCAS using paper or electronic (eLOR) process. PTCAS will disseminate letters to designated programs. Program-specific reference requirements are posted online at www.ptcas.org.	Recommendation letters must be sent directly to SOPHAS electronically.	Recommendation letters accompanied by TMDSAS evaluation forms must be sent to TMDSAS. Applicants are also required to submit one Health Professions Committee Packet OR two individual letters of recommendation from Interfolio or VirtualEvals. One vet letter must be from a veterinarian.
Standardized Test Scores	Send official GRE scores directly to designated PT programs, if institution requires test. Program-specific GRE requirements and codes are posted online at www.ptcas.org.	MCAT, GRE and TOEFL test scores can be sent directly to SOPHAS; other test scores should be sent directly to the program.	All MCAT score(s) MUST be reported directly to TMDSAS by AAMC. All DAT scores must be released to each of the dental schools they are applying with. GRE scores must be submitted directly to Texas A&M University College of Veterinary Medicine using the institution code #6812.
Transcripts	Send official U.S. transcripts directly to PTCAS by program's deadline. Arrange for any updated fall transcripts to arrive at PTCAS as soon as they are available from the registrar's office.	Official transcripts should be sent to SOPHAS.	Send most recent, official transcripts to TMDSAS.

*   Opening refers to the opening date of the application for this cycle
**   Submission refers to the first date that applicants may submit the application for this cycle.

	VMCAS		
Application Service Name	Veterinary Medical College Application Service		
Association	Association of American Veterinary Medical Colleges www.aavmc.org		
Number of Schools	25 of the 28 veterinary medical colleges in the United States, 2 in Canada, and 10 international colleges of vet. medicine participate in VMCAS		
Contact Information	Student Advisor Hotline: (617) 612–2884 vmcasinfo@vmcas.org		
Opening Date*	June 5		
Submission Date**	June 5		
Deadlines	October 2– 1PM EST		
Letters of Recommendation	Electronic evaluations must be sent through eLOR to VMCAS who will disseminate them to colleges. Number required varies by school.		
Standardized Test Scores	Send scores directly to colleges. See college specific requirements.		
Transcripts	Send official transcripts directly to VMCAS by September 1.		

*   Opening refers to the opening date of the application for this cycle
**   Submission refers to the first date that applicants may submit the application for this cycle.

Appendix C
FINANCIAL AID RESOURCES

The most helpful and succinct information on financing a professional education is often published by the relevant associations of schools/colleges, either on their websites or in reference books such as the MSAR and the ADEA Official Guide. Additional standard resources include academic and financial advisors, students' banks, reference librarians, students' undergraduate institutions' financial aid offices, and (once admitted) the professional school/college financial aid office. Be sure to read the information about financial planning in Chapter three of this book as well.

Students should begin researching their financial aid options as early as possible, preferably at least one full year before matriculating. When looking for funding, students should research all levels (national, state, institution, school/college) and should keep in mind the basic sources of funding: family contributions; both need-based and merit-based "free" money (grants, scholarships, fellowships); service pay-back and loan forgiveness programs (such as those by the U.S. military); work (including Federal Work Study); and loans (federally subsidized, unsubsidized, or private).

Students are sometimes reticent about discussing money matters with their prospective institutions; advisors should encourage them to consider financial issues (including whatever financial aid package may have been offered) when deciding which school to accept.

Students are well advised to improve their financial literacy as early as possible USA Funds offers US institutions of higher education free online workshops that guide students through basics such as creating a budget and calculating the total cost of a loan. Students should also discuss financial aid with their prospective institutions and consider financial matters as one variable when deciding which school to attend.

Not listed here are the many loan repayment and consolidation programs, which students will need only after entering their professional programs. Also not listed are the many fee assistance/reduction/waiver programs offered by many application services or admissions offices. Advisors can remind students to look for such programs and to apply early, as many require clearance before the student submits her/his application.

Applying for Aid

FAFSA   Free Application for Federal Student Aid – Federal www.fafsa.ed.gov

GAPSFAS   Graduate and Professional School Financial Aid Service (file form through school to which you are applying)

Federal Aid and Services

DHHS   Department of Health and Human Services (the umbrella organization for HRSA and BHPR) www.hhs.gov
HRSA   Health Resources and Services Administration (part of DHHS; contains BHPR) www.hrsa.gov/loanscholarships/index.html
BHPR   Bureau of Health Professions (part of HRSA)

These three are the main organizations for national financial aid for students in the health professions; their websites include links to numerous grant, scholarship, and loan programs, including the following:

Exceptional Financial Need (EFN)
Financial Assistance to Disadvantaged Health professions Students (FADHPS)
Disadvantaged Students Loans
Health Education Assistance Loans (HEAL)
Health Professions Grants, from the Affordable Care Act
Health Professions Student Loans (HPSL)
Nursing Student Loans
Nursing Scholarships
National Health Service Corps (NHSC)
Primary Care Loans (PCL)
Scholarships for Disadvantaged Students (SDS)

FWS — Federal Work Study

grants.gov — Searchable database of federal funding www.grants.gov

MSTP — Medical Scientist Training Program – NIH; a grant for students in M.D./Ph.D. joint degree programs www.nigms.nih.gov/Training/InstPredoc/PredocOverview-MSTP.htm

NDSL — National Direct Student Loan (now known as the Perkins Loan);

Perkins — Perkins Student Loan (formerly known as NDSL); for post-secondary education www2.ed.gov/programs/fpl/index.html

PLUS — PLUS Loan; non-need based unsubsidized loans for the parents of undergraduate students and to graduate, and professional students studentaid.ed.gov/types/loans/plus

PSEP — Professional Student Exchange Program – WICHE www.wiche.edu/psep

SSL — Stafford Student Loan; subsidized and unsubsidized loans for undergraduate and graduate students www2.ed.gov/programs/ffel/index.html

StudentAid — studentaid.ed.gov

UGSP — Undergraduate Scholarship Program – NIH; offers competitive scholarships to students from disadvantaged backgrounds who are committed to careers in biomedical, behavioral, and social science health-related research. ugsp.nih.gov/programs/ugsp

WICHE — Western Interstate Commission for Higher Education www.wiche.edu

WRGP — Western Regional Graduate Program – WICHE www.wiche.edu/wrgp

U.S. Military

HPSP — Health Professions Scholarship Program – Army, Navy, and Air Force; a service pay-back program www.goarmy.com/amedd/education/hpsp.html (and similar sites for Navy and Air Force)

Other

AAMC   Financing Your Medical Education: www.aamc.org/students/ applying/requirements/msar/tool
                 kit/177064/financing_your_medical_education.html
                 FIRST = Financial Information, Resources, Services, & Tools; includes podcasts and sections for
                 students, residents, financial aid officers, and pre-health advisors.
                 www.aamc.org/services/first/first_for_students

FinAid!   An independent site that provides basic information for students and parents; a nice starting point
                 and introduction, but the focus is on funding undergraduate education. www.finaid.org

NMF   National Medical Fellowships, Inc. (Need-based scholarships for minority students)
                  www.nmfonline.org

Private Loans   Non-government loans offered by banks; these usually make up the difference between whatever
                 aid students are able to obtain and the total cost of their education.

USAFunds   Free online workshops on financial literacy.   www.usafunds.org

Appendix D
Additional Resources

Health Professions Advising Associations

NAAHP, the National Association of Advisors for the Health Professions, is the premier professional association for pre-health advisors: it offers a wealth of materials and is advisors' single most important resource. The following is a summary of its resources and publications, all available through its searchable website, www.naahp.org. The website includes a members-only section.

Publications:

The Advisor. Quarterly Journal for all NAAHP Members. Abstracts of published articles are available and searchable through the "Advisor Abstracts Online" page.

Health Professions Admission Guide: Strategies for Success. Tenth Edition, 2013.

Interviewing for Health Professions Schools. Revised 2010.

NAAHP Directory, available online for members only.

Premedical Advisor's Reference Manual. Tenth Edition, 2012.
    NOTE: Available only to certified pre-health advisors and only through NAAHP.

Write for Success: Preparing a Successful Professional School Application. Third Edition, 2005.

Website:

Advisor Abstracts Online, a searchable database of articles published in NAAHP's The Advisor.

Advisor Resources, which includes an extensive bibliography not duplicated here.

Finding an Advisor, for students or advisors who want to locate a pre-health advisor at another institution or in another state. The site also offers assistance in locating advisors to work with those who are not affiliated with an institution or whose institution does not have a pre-health advisor. www.naahp.org.

NAAHP-NET, a monthly electronic newsletter with regular updates and late-breaking news.

NAAHPSack, a directory of health professions associations, including special phone numbers and email addresses for advisors and free publications. It also houses the annual "Updates" provided by the 19 NAAHP Advisory Council associations. Available to members only.

NACADA, the National Academic Advising Association www.nacada.ksu.edu

General Health Professions Advising

Explore Health Careers, includes extensive information on health professions, summer programs, and articles about the health professions, especially those geared toward minority and disadvantaged students. explorehealthcareers. org/en/home

U.S. Bureau of Labor Statistics Occupational Outlook Handbook, published annually. www.bls.gov/ooh/Healthcare/

Health Care Careers Directory, published annually by the American Medical Association. www.ama-assn.org/ama/ pub/education-careers/careers-health-care/directory.page

Top 100 Health-Care Careers, Dr. Saul & Edith Wischnitzer, 3rd edition (2010).

Postbaccalaureate Programs

NAAHP Postbaccalaureate Information, click on "Postbac Programs"; includes a Frequently Asked Questions page, a glossary, the "A Postbac Primer" article, related articles, and a link to the relevant AAMC webpage. www.naahp.org.

AAMC Postbaccalaureate Premedical Programs, a searchable database. services.aamc.org/postbac/

NIH Programs for College Graduates https://www.training.nih.gov/programs/postbac_irta

Summer Internships, Enrichment, and Undergraduate Research Programs

AAMC www.aamc.org/members/great/61052/great_summerlinks.html

Explore Health Careers explorehealthcareers.org

Special Populations

Diversity Populations (Disabled, Disadvantaged, Minority, Non-traditional, Underrepresented in Medicine)

Also see Chapter 4 in this book as well as Appendix D on Financial Aid and the array of resources for summer opportunities, fee assistance programs, test preparation, and post-baccalaureate options.

AspiringDocs.org, an AAMC site for students underrepresented in medicine; includes a section on "Preparing for Medicine" for pre-med students with frequently asked questions and useful links. https://www.aamc.org/students/ aspiring/

Diversity in the Physician Workforce: Facts and Figures. November 2012. AAMC

Medical Students with Disabilities: A Generation of Practice. June 2005. AAMC

Medical Students with Disabilities: Resources to Enhance Accessibility. December 2010. AAMC

Minority Programs – NIGMS of NIH; includes the MARC and MBRS initiatives, which focus on research opportunities. www.nigms.nih.gov/Training/

Minority Access to Research Careers (MARC), a grant program to increase the number of highly-trained under-represented biomedical and behavioral scientists in leadership positions; provides support for undergraduate research.

Minority Biomedical Research Support (MBRS), a grant program to increase the number of faculty, students and investigators from groups that are under-represented in the biomedical sciences.

MORE Special Initiatives (MORE); a grant program to enhance the research and research training capabilities of institutions with substantial enrollments of individuals from under-represented groups.

Minority Student Opportunities in United States Medical Schools (MSOUSMS) – AAMC, revised biennially. Includes information on recruitment programs, admission policies, academic assistance programs, and financial aid programs for minority students. AAMC. www.aamc.org

National Association of Medical Minority Educators (NAMME), a national organization dedicated to ensuring racial and ethnic diversity in all of the health professions; offers scholarships and information on summer programs. www.nammenational.org

National Institute on Minority Health and Health Disparities (NIMHD), a division of the National Institutes of Health (NIH) that promotes minority health and seeks to eliminate health disparities; includes a number of programs, including the Research Endowment Program that invests in the education and training of under-represented minorities and socio-economically disadvantaged individuals by awarding grants to institutions' endowment funds. www.nimhd.nih.gov

National Society for Nontraditional Premedical and Medical Students, Inc., also known as OldPreMeds.org or OPM, is a professional/pre-professional society to help non-traditional students successfully prepare for, apply to, and succeed in medical school and residency. www.oldpremeds.org

Premed of Color, a website dedicated to providing premedical students of color resources to prepare them for applying to medical school and for excelling as future physicians. premedofcolor.org

Spectrum Unlimited, publishers of medical journals for minority pre-med students, medical students, residents, new physicians, nurses, and allied health professionals. Developed for the National Institute on Minority Health and Health Disparities (NIMHD). www.spectrumunlimited.com/

Summer Medical and Dental Education Program (SMDEP; formerly the Minority Medical Education program, or MMEP); a free six-week summer academic enrichment program that prepares freshmen and sophomores for medical and dental school; funded by the Robert Wood Johnson Foundation and administered by AAMC. www.smdep.org

International Health Programs and Resources

Global Health Education Consortium (GHEC, formerly International Health Medical Education Consortium), an annotated list of websites and related information for those interested in international health. globalhealtheducation.org/SitePages/Home.aspx

International Health Resources,

International Healthcare Opportunities Clearinghouse, a listing of health care volunteer opportunities; provides diverse search criteria and links to programs. library.umassmed.edu/ihoc/index.cfm

International Medical Volunteers Association (IMVA), provides information on how to become an international volunteer and links to hundreds of volunteer opportunities. www.imva.org

World Health Organization, offers internships for graduate students. www.who.int/en

 *Appendix D*

International Students

Many extracurricular activities, internships, research opportunities, financial aid programs, and school admissions are restricted to United States citizens, and advisors can help international students check their eligibility. Before checking, students need to know their visa status. Canadian citizens frequently are under different rules than citizens of other countries. Financial aid is scarce and international students may be required to demonstrate their ability to fund their entire education before being admitted. In addition to those listed below, essential resources include advisors/counselors in international student services offices, financial aid offices, and admissions offices.

Test of English as a Foreign Language (TOEFL) – ETS: required by almost all schools and programs. Language fluency can be a major barrier for international student; students should make a conscious effort to acquire strong language skills. www.ets.org/toefl

Foreign Medical Graduates (FMGs)

Those students who have completed their undergraduate or graduate medical education in foreign countries, and who seek licensing to practice in the United States or to enroll in a U.S. medical school must go through an additional step. The Educational Commission for Foreign Medical Graduates (ECFMG) assesses whether international medical graduates are ready to enter residency or fellowship programs in the United States. The ECFMP Information Booklet, published annually, answers most questions; a link to the current version is on the main website: www.ecfmg.org.

Appendix E
Acronyms and Organizations

AAA   American Academy of Audiology
AAAOM   American Association of Acupuncture and Oriental Medicine
AAC&U   Association of American Colleges & Universities
ABGC   American Board of Genetic Counseling
AACN   American Association of Colleges of Nursing
AACOM   American Association of Colleges of Osteopathic Medicine
AACOMAS   American Association of Colleges of Osteopathic Medicine Application Service
AACP   American Association of Colleges of Pharmacy
AACPM   American Association of Colleges of Podiatric Medicine
AACPMAS   American Association of Colleges of Podiatric Medicine Application Service
AADSAS   American Association of Dental Schools Application Service
AAHE   American Association of Higher Education
AANMC   Association of Accredited Naturopathic Medical Colleges
AANP   American Association of Naturopathic Medicine
AAMC   Association of American Medical Colleges
AAPA   American Academy of Physician Assistants
AAPA-SA   American Academy of Physician Assistants — Student Academy
AARC   American Association for Respiratory Care
AAVMC   Association of American Veterinary Medical Colleges
ACA   American Chiropractic Association
ACC   Association of Chiropractic Colleges
ACHE   American College of Healthcare Executives
ACT   ACT (pronounced as the letters "A-C-T"; formerly known as the American College Testing)
ADA   American Dental Association
ADA   American Dietetic Association
ADEA   American Dental Education Association
AED   Alpha Epsilon Delta, the Premedical Honor Society
ASDA   American Student Dental Association
AHPAT   Allied Health Professions Admission Test
AMA   American Medical Association
AMCAS   American Medical College Application Service
AMIA   American Medical Informatics Association
AMSA   American Medical Student Association
ANA   American Nurses Association
AOA   American Optometric Association
AOA   American Osteopathic Association
AOSA   American Optometric Student Association
AOTA   American Occupational Therapy Association
AP   Advanced Placement

APhA	American Pharmacists Association
AphA-ASP	American Pharmacists Association — Academy of Student Pharmacists (also known as ASP)
APHA	American Public Health Association
APHA-SA	American Public Health Association — Student Assembly
APMA	American Podiatric Medical Association
APMSA	American Podiatric Medical Students' Association
APTA	American Physical Therapy Association
APMA	American Podiatric Medicine Association
ASAHP	Association of Schools of Allied Health Professions
ASCLS	American Society for Clinical Laboratory Science
ASCO	Association of Schools and Colleges of Optometry
ASDA	American Student Dental Association
ASHA	American Speech-Language-Hearing Association
ASN	American Society for Nutrition
ASP	Academy of Student Pharmacists (also known as APhA-ASP)
ASPH	Association of Schools of Public Health
ASR	Additional Score Report — MCAT
ATRA	American Therapeutic Recreation Association
AUPHA	Association of University Programs in Health Administration
AVMA	American Veterinary Medical Association
BCPM	Biology, Chemistry, Physics, Math
BHP or BHPR	Bureau of Health Professions — HRSA, DHHS
BLS	Bureau of Labor Statistics — Federal
CAAHP	Central Association of Advisors for the Health Professions — NAAHP
CAS	Common/Central Application Service
CASPA	Central Application Service for Physician Assistants
CCAOM	Council of Colleges of Acupuncture and Oriental Medicine
CCE	Council on Chiropractic Education
CDC	Centers for Disease Control and Prevention — DHHS
CHE	Chronicle of Higher Education
ChiroCAS	Chiropractic College Application Service — AAC
CLEP	College Level Examination Program
CME	Continuing Medical Education
COA	Committee on Admissions — GSA, AAMC
COSA	Committee on Student Affairs — GSA, AAMC
COSFA	Committee on Student Financial Assistance — GSA, AAMC
COGME	Council on Graduate Medical Education
CumGPA	Cumulative Grade Point Average
DAT	Dental Admission Test
DEAL	Dental Education Assistance Loan
DHHS	Department of Health and Human Services (also known as HHS)
DVA	Department of Veterans Affairs
ECFMG	Educational Commission for Foreign Medical Graduates
EDP	Early Decision Program
EFN	Exceptional Financial Need — DHHS
EICS	International Credentials Service — ECFMG

ETS	Educational Testing Service
FADHPS	Financial Assistance to Disadvantaged Health Professions Students — DHHS
FAFSA	Free Application for Federal Student Aid
FASHP	Federation of Associations of Schools of the Health Professions
FBR	Foundation for Biomedical Research
FDA	Food and Drug Administration — Federal
FERPA	Family Educational Rights and Privacy Act
FMG	Foreign Medical Graduate
FWS	Federal Work Study
GAPSFAS	Graduate and Professional School Financial Aid Service — ETS
GEA	Group of Educational Affairs — AAMC
GHEC	Global Health Education Consortium
GMAT	Graduate Management Admission Test
GME	Graduate Medical Education
GPA	Grade Point Average
GRE	Graduate Record Exam — ETS
GSA	Group on Student Affairs — AAMC
GSL	Guaranteed Student Loan (now known as the Stafford Loan; see SSL)
HEA	Higher Education Act
HEAL	Health Education Assistance Loans — DHHS
HCOP	Health Careers Opportunity Program
HHS	Health and Human Services, Department of (also known as DHHS)
HIPAA	Health Insurance Portability and Accountability Act
HPEA	Health Professions Education Act
HPN	Health Professionals Network
HPSL	Health Professions Student Loans — DHHS
HPSP	Health Professions Scholarship Program (Army, Navy, Air Force)
HRSA	Health Resources and Services Administration — DHHS
IMVA	International Medical Volunteers Association
LCME	Liaison Committee on Medical Education — AAMC and AMA
LOR	Lettters of Recommendation
MARC	Minority Access to Research Careers — NIH
MAS	Minority Affairs Section — GSA, AAMC
MBRS	Minority Biomedical Research Support — NIH
MCAT	Medical College Admission Test
MODVOP	Medicine, Osteopathy, Dentistry, Veterinary Medicine, Optometry, and Podiatry
MR5	5th Comprehensive Review of the MCAT
MSAR	Medical School Admission Requirements
MSOP	Medical School Objectives Project — AAMC
MSOUSMS	Minority Student Opportunities in U.S. Medical Schools — AAMC
MSTP	Medical Scientist Training Program
NAAHP	National Association of Advisors for the Health Professions
NACADA	National Academic Advising Association
NAMME	National Association of Medical Minority Educators
NCCAM	National Center for Complementary and Alternative Medicine — NIH
NDSL	National Direct Student Loan (now known as the Perkins Loan)

NEAAHP	Northeast Association of Advisors for the Health Professions — NAAHP
NET	Nursing Entrance Text
NFME	National Fund for Medical Education
NHSC	National Health Service Corps — DHHS
NIH	National Institutes of Health — Encompasses numerous institutes, including for Allergy and Infectious Diseases (NIAID), Cancer (NCI), Complementary and Alternative Medicine (NCCAM), Dental Research (NIDR), General Medical Sciences (NIGMS), Mental Health (NIMH), etc.
NLM	National Library of Medicine — NIH
NLN	National League for Nursing
NMA	National Medical Association
NMF	National Medical Fellowships
NMSA	Naturopathic Medical Student Association
NRMP	National Residency Matching Program
NRPA	National Recreation and Park Association
NSF	National Science Foundation
NSGC	National Society of Genetic Counselors
NSNA	National Student Nurse's Association
NTRS	National Therapeutic Recreation Society — NRPA
OAT	Optometry Admission Test
OMCIB	Osteopathic Medical College Information Book
OptomCAS	Optometry Centralized Application Service
OSHA	Occupational Safety and Health Administration
OSR	Organization of Student Representatives — AAMC
OTCAS	Occupational Therapist Centralized Application Service
PAEA	Physician Assistant Education Association
PCAT	Pharmacy College Admission Test
PCL	Primary Care Loans — DHHS
PharmCAS	Pharmacy College Application Service
PHS	Public Health Service
PMQ	Pre-Medical [Student] Questionnaire — AAMC
PSAR	Pharmacy School Admission Requirements
PSEP	Professional Student Exchange Program — WICHE
PTCAS	Physical Therapist Centralized Application Service
RIME	Research in Medical Education — AAMC
SAAHP	Southeastern Association of Advisors for the Health Professions — NAAHP
SACA	Student American Chiropractic Association
SAT	SAT (pronounced as the letters "S-A-T"; formerly Scholastic Aptitude Test and Scholastic Assessment Test) — College Board, also known as College Entrance Examination Board
SAVMA	Student American Veterinary Medical Association
SDS	Scholarships for Disadvantaged Students
SLS	Supplemental Loans for Students
SMDEP	Summer Medical and Dental Education Program
SNMA	Student National Medical Association
SOMA	Student Osteopathic Medical Association
SOPHAS	Schools of Public Health Application Service
SSL	Stafford Student Loan

TEAS	Test of Essential Academic Skills
TMDSAS	Texas Medical and Dental School Application Service
TOEFL	Test of English as a Foreign Language — ETS
USFMG	United States [Citizen] Foreign Medical [School] Graduate
USMLE	United States Medical Licensing Examination (Steps I, II, and III)
VE	VirtualEvals
VIN	Veterinary Information Network
VMCAS	Veterinary Medical College Application Service
VMSAR	Veterinary Medical School Admission Requirements
VQE	Visa Qualifying Exam
WAAHP	Western Association of Advisors for the Health Professions — NAAHP
WHO	World Health Organization
WWAMI	Washington, Wyoming, Alaska, Montana, Idaho Medical Education Program
WICHE	Western Interstate Commission on Higher Education
WRGP	Western Regional Graduate Program — WICHE
WUE	Western Undergraduate Exchange — WICHE